INTRODUCTIONS TO SHAKESPEARE

Portrait engraving by Peter Reddick
for *Shakespeare's Sonnets*, 1972

INTRODUCTIONS TO SHAKESPEARE

*being the Introductions to
the individual plays in
the Folio Society edition
1950–76
with a Foreword by*

CHARLES EDE

MICHAEL JOSEPH
London

Designed by The Folio Society, 1977
First published in a trade edition, by arrangement with
The Folio Society
by Michael Joseph Ltd, 52 Bedford Square, London WC1
1978

ISBN 0 7181 1673 9

PRINTED IN GREAT BRITAIN
by W & J Mackay Limited, Chatham
Set in 11 *point Plantin leaded* 1 *point*

Contents

6 CONTENTS

Costume Designs

*These designs have been selected from the many reproduced in the
complete Folio Society Shakespeare, which in itself represents the work
of 35 modern stage designers.*

Foreword

By CHARLES EDE

In October 1976, the Folio Society of London published the thirty-seventh and final volume in its complete edition of Shakespeare's plays, an edition unique in that each play has an Introduction by an eminent figure of the theatre and is illustrated by a distinguished stage designer. The series, as such, represents a remarkable theatrical archive, but not every reader has shelf room for thirty-seven separate plays – many will have a one- or two-volume edition which serves their purpose more than adequately. For this reason, it has seemed worthwhile to issue the Introductions – giving as they do such a valuable insight into the many facets of the Shakespearean scene – as a separate volume. It is also, perhaps, appropriate that the Foreword which follows, should have been written by the founder of the Folio Society and the man responsible for the inception of the series.

When, towards the end of 1971, I finally severed all ties with the Folio Society, of which I could perhaps properly describe myself as the 'onlie begetter', it was with few regrets except for the loss of regular contact with many old friends. After over twenty years in what is necessarily a specialized field, I knew that I was beginning to get stale and that the moment had come for an infusion of new blood, while I had acquired other interests on which I badly wanted to concentrate full time. Among the things that I least regretted, indeed welcomed, was the fact that I no longer had to spend sleepless nights over the Folio Shakespeare, which seemed to have caused us more worries over the years than any other part of our editorial programme. So it was with mixed feelings that I received an invitation to write the Foreword to the present volume. I accepted, firstly because I was touched that I should be asked, and secondly because, like many people, I find it difficult to resist the impulse to reminisce.

The Folio Shakespeare came into being, as indeed did the Society itself, very largely by chance. In this case, I was shown a splendid *édition de luxe*, based on Jean Cocteau's adaptation of *Romeo and Juliet* and illustrated with designs for sets and costumes by Jean Hugo, for the production at the *Soirées de Paris*. These took the form of

woodcuts, the plates showing costumes being coloured by hand, and
they made an immediate impact on me as a fusion of graphic art and
theatre, more remarkably than anything I had seen since Gordon
Craig's extraordinary *Hamlet* (published by Count Kessler in 1928).
In due course it was agreed that we should go ahead with a volume
incorporating Hugo's designs in a somewhat reduced format (the
original edition was to my mind unmanageably large for reading) and
that reproduction should be by drawn lithography as, for technical
and economic reasons, hand-colouring was out of the question. Our
literary adviser, John Hampden, was asked to search out the best text
and recommended that of the New Temple Shakespeare, edited by
M. R. Ridley, which includes variant readings when a Quarto text
exists as well as that of the First Folio. We decided to provide our own
simple 'editorial apparatus' avoiding foot-notes as tending to distract
the eye, while adding a Glossary to cover those few words or phrases
likely to cause difficulty to the reasonably well-informed reader. One
production point is perhaps worthy of comment: characters' names
were printed in a second colour, not for reasons of aesthetics, but so
that the reader's eye could the more easily ignore them, if he or she
wished to concentrate on the poetry alone.

At this stage there was no question of a series and the distinguished
literary scholar, Nevill Coghill, was invited to provide a purely general
introduction. The bastard format was specifically designed to suit the
full-page illustrations, a fact that caused some head-aches in later
years though, by a happy chance, the rather square shape proved
reasonably adaptable to most designers' originals. The book was
published in 1950 at sixteen shillings.

Even before 'Romeo' appeared, it was suggested that we should
follow it with another Shakespeare play, but we had to face the fact
that, once we went beyond a single volume, many members would
expect us to continue until the series was complete. With our limited
resources, one play a year was the maximum we could hope to produce, and all the plays would have to be kept in print, at least inter-
mittently, over a long period, a daunting tie-up of capital for a small
organization. Nevertheless we decided to take the plunge and, happily,
the growth of the Society's membership enabled production to be
increased to four plays a year in the final stages.

Faced as we now were with a series which might continue for four
decades, there was a certain amount of re-thinking to be done. There

had been many illustrated Shakespeares: what was to make ours different was that the plays were to be treated as Theatre rather than 'Eng. Lit.'. We had already used theatre designs rather than 'illustrations' as such, now it was decided that the Introductions should also be of the theatre – by actors, actresses, producers and directors writing from personal experience. But our insistence that the series be treated as theatre, brought in train its own problems.

On the illustration side, our hardest task was to find suitable material, which had been used for an actual production. The first step was to find a production, the result of the search usually producing an *embarras de richesses* for the most popular plays and a complete blank in the case of the more rarely performed pieces. Quickly also, we learnt to our cost that a designer's original drawings are comparatively rarely kept together: once their original purpose has been served, they may well be given as presents to the cast or simply lost. This meant that it was often impossible to go back in time and illustrate past productions, unless these had already been recorded by publication as had the Dali/Visconti *As You Like It*, or been preserved in a public collection like the designs for Beerbohm Tree's 1910 production of *Henry VIII*.

Another hard truth we had to accept was that designs are intended for the wardrobe department or the scene-builders, both trained to interpret the roughest of sketches, which would be quite unsuitable for reproduction. Where these designs had obvious potential, we were often able to get the artist to work them up into more finished drawings, though we always stressed the importance of retaining the spontaneity of the originals.

This is not the place in which to discuss the merits of the designs used for the plays, though I personally still find 'Romeo' the most satisfying. In some cases one artist has been responsible for the costumes and another for the sets, in others two artists have worked together on all the drawings. An odd-man-out is *Macbeth*, second in the series, where the first edition had original lithographs by Michael Ayrton, loosely based on a production in which he had collaborated with John Minton. By mutual agreement, the second edition carried reproductions of the original Ayrton/Minton designs. Only one volume has all the illustrations in monochrome, *Hamlet*, which is also the only play in the series based on a film production. *Timon of Athens* is unique in the series in that it is the only play for which the designs were specially commissioned by the Society. Mention should perhaps also be made of the Noguchi designs for *King Lear*, not only because the originals were collages, but for the extraordinarily complicated symbolism involved in slight changes of costume. A particularly interesting experiment was made with *The Merchant of Venice*, for which the designer also provided the Introduction, in which she discusses the play primarily from her own point of view, and gives a fascinating insight into the techniques of mounting a production.

Indeed it is the Introductions, here printed together for the first time, that are in the end, perhaps the most interesting feature of the series. Their authors read like a roll-call of the major figures in the English theatre over the last three decades, with the addition of a number of distinguished Europeans. There are, of course, gaps; I remember particular disappointment that neither Edith Evans nor Alec Guinness could be represented, in both cases, I believe, from excess of modesty. Apart from the original Coghill Introduction for 'Romeo', all the texts were by people who had been directly involved in a production of the play concerned, apart from two introductions by well-known theatre critics – Ivor Brown writing on *Othello* and Harold Hobson on *Measure for Measure*. The point should also perhaps be made that the Introducer and the Designer used for a volume had not always worked on the same production.

The subject matter of the Introductions varies considerably, though personal interpretation is the underlying theme in most cases. As would be expected, actors and actresses tend to concentrate on the characters and, in particular, the characters they themselves have played, while producers and directors are likely to be more interested in the construction and inner meaning of the plays as a whole. Shakespeare's sources from legend, fable and history, sometimes recent and thinly-disguised, are discussed, as are parallels with life today or the lack of them, which may make interpretation the more difficult. Some writers include surveys of major productions of the past and of Criticism from Pepys and Dr Johnson to the present day, while there are fascinating asides on such diverse subjects as theatrical companies and the architecture of theatres through the centuries.

Not all those who promised their collaboration actually produced the goods and the delivery of copy on time seems, in retrospect, to have been the exception rather than the rule. On at least one occasion, when we were desperate, I dashed off a piece myself and sent it to the author saying that we would reluctantly have to publish it under his name as announced. I am delighted to say that my extremely perishable prose worked like a charm and we got an excellent typescript back almost by return of post. Even when they appeared, some of the texts needed a good deal of editing, the worst having apparently been produced by an author incoherently drunk, and being largely indecipherable. To sum up, the introductions vary a good deal in length and quality, but if read together they make a remarkable sequence. Indeed this is true of the whole series, covering as it does the productions of more than three decades, originating in many cities, including London, Paris, Rome, Berlin, Cracow and New York – and, of course, Stratford-on-Avon. It should be recorded here that much of the success of the series was due to the vision and pertinacity of Brian Rawson, the Director responsible for its general planning and editorship from 1956 until his untimely death in 1975.

Now that the series is complete it seems almost incredible that nearly thirty years ago Folio, with a staff of two men and a girl working in one room, half the time uncertain whether they could pay their own salaries, should have been so foolhardy as to embark on such an enterprise. I am grateful to our successors for carrying it through with such expedition and taste. As Lord Olivier has written, 'It is a very delightful coincidence that the consummation of this series should occur at roughly the same time as the opening of the upper house of the National Theatre.'

King Henry VI Parts 1, 2 and 3

PEGGY ASHCROFT

During my lifetime, and that of probably most of the readers of this introduction, there have been only two outstanding productions of *Henry VI* that I can recall – the first in 1952, directed by Douglas Seale for the Birmingham Repertory Theatre and subsequently played at the Old Vic with great success; and the later production in 1963 and 1964 of Peter Hall by the Royal Shakespeare Company at Stratford on Avon and the Aldwych Theatre, London. The first production I did not see, the latter I took part in. I begin my preface with mention of these two productions because clearly my connexion with one of them is my sole qualification for such a task; and indeed it is only through the experience of working for two years in these plays that I came to know them; having, I admit, only skimmed through them in my early reading of Shakespeare and never having given them much thought. Living for two years in the atmosphere of 'The Wars of the Roses', as our production came to be called, was an experience of a very particular kind.

I would like to discuss why these three plays of *Henry VI* have been so much neglected until recently, and why these two revivals have met with such surprising success. In looking for a reason, Hazlitt's often-quoted criticism comes to mind: 'During the time of the civil wars of York and Lancaster, England was a perfect bear-garden, and Shakespeare has given us a very lively picture of the scene. The three parts of *Henry VI* convey a picture of very little else: and are inferior to the other historical plays.' Granted that they are inferior in literary and poetic quality, in psychological depth, and very often clumsily constructed, with what often seem to be more lords than one can distinguish between, I would dare to cross swords with Hazlitt. Surely they convey several things other than a bear-garden, and of a very profound nature. They are concerned with Shakespeare's detestation of war, his concept of the Divine Right of Kings and of the Curse on all who depose or murder God's anointed; his ambivalent attitude to power – the necessity to wield it and the corruption of absolute power. But Hazlitt's reference to the bear-garden also brings me to what seems a possible answer to the question of why these three plays have so much to say to us now. Perhaps because we are more aware than ever before what a bear-garden the whole world is, we see in these plays a microcosm of so many of the violent and tragic conflicts of our own time. The romantic view of Shakespeare, popular with the Victorians and lasting almost to the first half of this century, has now changed, and we have become more aware of Shakespeare's political absorption and inspired interpretations of man's difficulty in governing both himself and others.

So much has been argued over the centuries as to whether, in fact, Shakespeare wrote the *Henry VI* trilogy, how much he wrote of it, and who else wrote it if he did not – even to parcelling out different scenes to his contemporaries Thomas Nashe, Richard Greene, and George Peele. I could not presume to trespass on this scholar's domain, and only dare to say that – apart from the fact that to a 'mere player' so much of all three plays sounds and feels like Shakespeare – it seems to me inconceivable that even Shakespeare's genius could have reached the mastery of the later histories, the second tetralogy *Richard II*, the two parts of *Henry IV* and *Henry V*, without the 'prentice work' of *Henry VI*. And surely only the writer of *Henry VI* could have achieved the dénouement of the history of the House of Plantagenet in the culminating play *Richard III*, whose authorship has, I believe, been less disputed. With their relationship to that play I would like to deal later.

The production of 'The Wars of the Roses' by Peter Hall at Stratford on Avon in 1963 was an adaptation by John Barton of the three parts of *Henry VI*, condensed into two plays and renamed *Henry VI* and *Edward IV*, and a trilogy was completed by adding *Richard III* – more or less 'in toto'. Inevitably much had to be cut and condensed in the 'Henrys' and the loss of much of the Talbot episodes in Part 1, the touching farewell of Humphrey of Gloucester to his erring wife and the development of the rivalry between her and Margaret, as well as many other scenes and even passages of great beauty, had to be sacrificed with regret; but I think that John Barton's condensation of plot and characters did no disservice to Shakespeare's intention and main theme, but clarified and sharpened the story line of the first three plays. It is a fact not to be overlooked that almost no scholar – or critic – objected to what might have been considered a sacrilege. I think, too, that the adventure – both for the audience and the players – of being able to see and perform all three plays in one day, which we did on seven occasions, provided a unique Shakespearean and theatrical experience. But this is not, I am aware, an introduction to John Barton's adaptation of the four histories, but of Shakespeare's *Henry VI*, Parts 1, 2, and 3.

That they were Shakespeare's first plays seems to me of paramount interest and significance in that it was to history and the problems of kingship and politics that he first applied himself and that in these plays are the seeds of so much of what was to come. There has been discussion among scholars as to whether he (or others) wrote Parts 2 and 3 before he wrote Part 1, but that discussion is outside my sphere – though the early style of Shakespeare seems more apparent in Part 1 than in the other two, which grow in authority and power. One cannot help wondering whether he was already half aware of the huge panorama of history that he was to bring to life. When he invented the scene of the plucking of the roses in the Temple Garden (Part 1, Act II, Scene 4) did he envisage the creation of his *Richard II* (written after *Richard III*), where he would delineate the first deposition and subsequent murder and the beginning of the Curse on the Houses of York and Lancaster ? When he wrote the first scene of Joan La Pucelle he certainly did not dream that another great English dramatist would use the same dramatic device of the Dauphin hiding his identity to test her power of divination. But Shakespeare's scene (Part 1, Act I, Scene 2) provides an interesting comparison to the confrontation of the Maid and the Dauphin in Shaw's *St Joan*. La Pucelle is a very different character from the Shavian saint, but even though the attitude had to conform to the prevalent Elizabethan view that she was a witch, even so Shakespeare's innate perception and humanity would not, or could not, conceal his feeling for her as a heroic and inspired character – whether inspired by God or the Devil, whether saint or harlot, he leaves to conjecture.

In the pathetic and yet noble character of Henry VI himself we see the results of what Shakespeare was yet to create – the guilt that haunted Bolingbroke, his grandfather, after Richard II's deposition and death, the same guilt which Bolingbroke passed on to his son Henry V, who prayed before the Battle of Agincourt –

Not today, O lord

> *O not today, think not upon the fault*
> *My father made in compassing the crown.*

His son, Henry VI, had already said in the earlier play –

> *Was ever king that joy'd an earthly throne*
> *And could command no more content than I ?*
> *No sooner was I crept out of my cradle*
> *Than I was made a king at nine months old*
> *Was ever subject longed to be a king*
> *As I do long and wish to be a subject ?*
>   (*Henry VI*, Part 2, Act IV, Scene 9)

From the moment in Part 1, Act III, Scene 1, when he restores Richard, Duke of York, to his titles to his last moment when he pardons York's son at the moment of his murder, 'O God, forgive my sins and pardon thee' (Part 3, Act V, Scene 6) he is weakened always by the uncertainty of his right to kingship.

These three plays are concerned throughout with war, murder, political intrigue, and ruthless power-politics. But they are also one of the most powerful pieces of anti-war propaganda in our literature. In Part 1 they show us the futility of the war of annexation. The play begins with the funeral of Henry V and the rival factions are immediately disclosed in the bickerings of Gloucester and Winchester, which are interrupted by the Messenger from France, who tells of the English misfortunes there. Bedford, the right arm of Henry V and Regent of France, vows to revive the English victories, but, though the English nobility returned to the battlefields of France and conquered, the victory was an empty one. The most heroic figures, Talbot and his son, die in battle –

> *Thou antic death, which laugh'st us here to scorn,*
> *Anon, from thy insulting tyranny,*
> *Coupled in bonds of perpetuity,*
> *Two Talbots, winged through the lither sky,*
> *In thy despite shall 'scape mortality.*
> *O ! thou, whose wounds become hard-favoured death,*
> *Speak to thy father ere thou yield thy breath;*
> *Brave death by speaking whether he will or no;*
> *Imagine him a Frenchman and thy foe.*

Poor boy ! he smiles, methinks, as who should say,
Had death been French, then death had died today.
(Part 2, Act IV, Scene 7)

They die heroically, but Shakespeare shows the futility of their sacrifice. They are victims of the personal antagonism of York and Somerset, in whom the spirit of chivalry of the Henry V era has been corrupted into political self-seeking.

Though the armies of the Dauphin are brought to defeat and Joan captured and burnt; yet in the affiancing of Henry VI to Margaret of Anjou the seeds of the civil wars in England are already sown. Margaret herself, having made her unholy alliance with Suffolk, was to become one of the main instruments of that war. The scene (Act V, Scene 2) in which Margaret meets Suffolk, and in which, through his sudden infatuation, he conceives the idea of making her Henry's wife and his own mistress, is the only scene in which Margaret appears in Part I. It comes immediately after the brutal capture of Joan and is a marvellous dramatic contrast. It has, I believe, been singled out as one particularly unlikely to be by Shakespeare, but to me the daringly contrived scene, witty, sensual, and comic, could only be his and is a small glimpse of what is in store with Katherine the Shrew and Beatrice; just as, in Part 2 (Act III, Scene 2), in the farewell between Margaret and Suffolk, there is suddenly a spark that will later burn into Antony and Cleopatra.

In Part 2 the theme is of personal vendetta, murder, and revenge, leading on to the wars of York and Lancaster, which occupy the whole of Part 3. Towards the end of Part 2 the sub-plot of the Jack Cade rebellion counterpoints the beginning of the York rebellion. Part 2 opens with the arrival of Margaret, already Henry's Queen; Suffolk having married her by proxy in France. The atmosphere of intrigue is quickly established and the vendetta begins. The first victim is Humphrey of Gloucester, whose murder is carried out by Suffolk's henchmen – the plot inspired by Queen Margaret in her ambition to dominate the king her husband, and, through him, the realm of England. When her lover Suffolk is done to death in revenge her passion for Suffolk is sublimated into her love and ambition for her son Edward, and it is her long-nourished desire for revenge which find its outlet in her murder of York, the usurper of her son's rights. This scene, Part 3, Act I, Scene 4, is one of the most powerful, as

well as the most painful, in the three histories; before it there has been
the killing in battle of the Lancastrian Clifford by the Duke of York
(Part 2, Act V, Scene 2) and the vengeance for his father's death by
the young Clifford on York's youngest son (Part 3, Act I, Scene 4).
Shakespeare's use of this incident is horrific, the horror of Clifford's
killing of the little boy is only surpassed by Margaret's exploitation of
it on the captured York –

> Look York, I stained this napkin with the blood
> That valiant Clifford, with his rapier's point
> Made issue from the bosom of the boy;
> And if thine eyes can water for his death,
> I give thee this to dry thy cheeks withal.
>
> (Part 3, Act I, Scene 4)

It is a full two acts since the murder of Suffolk, but with Margaret's
final cry 'Off with his head and set it on York Gate' one is reminded of
Suffolk's head being sent to the Queen, his mistress, by his assassins.
The consequent murder of Clifford by York's surviving sons con-
tinues the blood-bath which is concluded by the murder of Margaret's
son, Edward, before her eyes at Tewkesbury; and finally Richard of
Gloucester's murder of Henry himself when he is a prisoner in the
Tower.

There are two soliloquies of Gloucester in Part 3: one after his
murder of Henry – 'I, that have neither pity, hate, nor fear' (Part 3,
Act V, Scene 6) – and the magnificent earlier one at the end of Act III,
Scene 4, when he has heard of his brother's intended marriage to
Elizabeth Grey. Both of these present a portrait of what Gloucester
was to become in *Richard III*; the latter soliloquy has sometimes been
incorporated by actors in the later play. This play must surely have
been in embryo, even if *Comedy of Errors*, *Titus Andronicus*, and
Taming of the Shrew intervened. The possibility that the Histories of
Henry VI were undertaken partly as patriotic propaganda for the
House of Tudor would also suggest that *Richard III* was what he was
building towards. One cannot help wondering why – and regretting
that – he never attempted a 'Henry VII'.

Behind the sequence of personal murder and revenge is the whole
bitter background of civil war, and perhaps the most memorable scene
is the one that contains Henry's soliloquy at the Battle of Towton
(Part 3, Act II, Scene 5) –

O God! methinks it were a happy life,
To be no better than a homely swain . . .
Gives not the hawthorn bush a sweeter shade
To shepherds, looking on their silly sheep,
Than doth a rich embroider'd canopy
To kings, that fear their subjects' treachery.

To him enter 'the Son that has killed his Father' and then 'the Father that has killed his son', each enacting their tragic recognition of the deed. Henry's cry 'Woe above woe! grief more than common grief! . . . The red rose and the white are on his face, the fatal colour of our striving houses . . .' and the father's final two lines linger throughout the rest of the play –

I'll bear thee hence; and let them fight that will,
For I have murdered where I should not kill.

The enumeration of murders and the counting of corpses in a Shakespeare play are likely to bring a smile to many as if to say 'What an absurdly melodramatic exaggeration'. Can we afford to ? When we have lived through the Nazi era and witnessed the bloody events in the Congo and other parts of Africa ? Even 'The Mysterious Deaths in the Long Aftermath of Dallas' (*The Times*, 27 February 1967) may one day evoke a play which will rival for wholesale murder Shakespeare's plays of the Wars of the Roses.

When the Hall-Barton production of 'The Wars of the Roses' was revived in 1964 for the quatercentenary a particularly fascinating focus was put on the *Henry VI* plays by their taking place within the whole historical cycle. As I watched the exquisite, poetical character study of the histrionic Richard II, the introvert, artist, and king; and then the sublime comical-historical-historical-pastoral tragi-comedies of the two *Henry IVs* and *Henry V*, it seemed to me that the panorama would become less absorbing when we took the stage with the less-accomplished, more two-dimensional chronicles of *Henry VI*. But perhaps because they had been the starting-point in Shakespeare's mind and because their production had been the original one in Hall's plan of presentation, this did not happen. Although there was no longer such richness of character, such subtleties and brilliance of writing, these early plays held their own and possibly had an advantage in being on the whole a fresh experience for the average Shakespeare theatre-goer.

In their sharper, less subtle way, the characters blaze to life.
Humphrey of Gloucester, the conscientious uncle-adviser; Warwick
the King-maker; the sly fox Winchester; Talbot, pattern of chivalry;
York and his sons, Edward, Clarence, and, finally and shatteringly,
Richard of Gloucester. Who but Shakespeare would have counter-
balanced all these ambitious power-seekers with the pathetic inactive
Henry, a dreamer and a man of no ambition, a devout religious,
developing from a helpless boy-king to a hermit and a mystic? And
who indeed but Shakespeare could have drawn Margaret of Anjou? It
is fascinating that she – a Dark Lady if ever there was one – and proto-
type for Cressida, Cleopatra, Lady Macbeth – was Shakespeare's first
'heroine' – if such she can be called. The portrait he draws is marvellous in its complexity and sureness of touch, from the cunning and
alluring Princess of France, through her intrigue and passion for
Suffolk, her growth into the invincible and ruthless mother of
Edward, 'she-wolf of France'; to her vanquished but stubbornly unyielding agony at Tewkesbury; and, finally, the 'foul, wrinkled witch'
in *Richard III*. How brilliantly the playwright invents this theme –
incorrect historically, for Margaret had been banished by Edward and
had returned to France, where she died. But for us, and, one imagines,
for the probably more informed audience of Shakespeare's time, this
anachronism is acceptable. She becomes for Richard, and the
audience, the embodiment of the Curse on the Houses of York and
Lancaster. It takes four plays to make her one of the great female
characters in Shakespeare – and the full-length portrait has been seen
only in the 'Wars of the Roses' cycle – but she has facets that are not
touched on in any other.

If this introduction is too personal in tone, or too prejudiced in
feeling, you must forgive me. An actor's attitude to a play he has
played in can only be partly objective. But if *Henry VI* has been a
neglected work, it has become, certainly for me, one of the most
absorbing and fascinating of the histories, even if one may not say a
masterpiece.

1967

Titus Andronicus

GERALD FREEDMAN

Titus Andronicus is thought to be one of Shakespeare's earliest plays and his first attempt at tragedy. It is loosely patterned after classic Senecan tragedy, but as usual, Shakespeare has overflowed the bounds of form and written a vividly human, non-classical melange of honour, gore and demonic emotion. Many readers of the play find the seeds of Shakespearean giants like Lear and Othello in Titus, but Titus also exists quite by himself – imperfect and flawed perhaps, but monumental in concept.

Titus Andronicus has been performed rarely in the twentieth century because of the enormous difficulties it presents to actors and audiences. Apparently the Elizabethans were more receptive to blood and gore as theatre staples, just as they were less critical of revenge and sheer evil as motivations for human behaviour. They accepted all the extravagance of emotion and intensity of feeling with a passionate response. How does one create a similar response to horror and violence in a modern audience? It would seem an easy task, living as we do in an era where violence and destruction are presented to us daily in the newspapers and on television. But paradoxically, attempts realistically to recreate physical violence on the stage in the manner of the Grand Guignol now appear ludicrous or stagey. Perhaps real violence has lost its power because it is too familiar. Perhaps our nerve ends have become overstimulated to the point of non-response in the face of what were once unimagined horrors of holocaust and death. Somehow, if one wants to create a fresh emotional response to the violence, blood and multiple mutilations of *Titus Andronicus*, one must shock the imagination and subconscious with visual images that recall the richness and depth of primitive rituals; with the power of poetic conventions drawn from the ancient theatres of Greece and the Orient; with instruments and sounds that nudge our ear without being clearly explicit or melodic; with fragments of myth and ceremony and childhood fantasies that still have the power to set our imaginations racing.

Thus the choice of music, mask and chorus seemed inevitable to me in order to make the violence, gore and horror of this play more meaningful and emotional to a contemporary audience. The solution to a more immediate response seemed to lie in a poetic abstraction of the events existing in an emotional compression of time and space.

In the production for the Delacorte Theater in New York, I took more liberties with the text and form of *Titus* than I ever had with any previous Shakespearean production. I was obsessed with the task of capturing the audience's imagination in a snare of made-up theatre conventions and of playing out the tragedy of Titus within the world of those conventions in an effort to incite the audience to identification, shock and recoil. In other words, I wanted the audience to accept the mutilations and decapitations and multiple deaths with belief instead of humour.

I had recently seen a production where an attempt to deal with the same problems took an opposite tack. The production was set in contemporary times and used modern dress and weapons in an effort to draw positive and obvious parallels between the violence and wholesale murder of our times and the time of Titus Andronicus. It failed by also bringing into play our sense of reality in terms of detail and literal time structure. 'How could Lavinia suffer such loss of blood and still live?' 'Why doesn't Marcus take her to a hospital instead of talking?' 'Titus can't really be cutting off his hand on stage – what a clever trick.' Such questions and concerns are obviously not those of the play or playwright, but they are inevitable if you are invoking a reality embedded in a contemporary parallel.

The solution had to lie in a poetic abstraction of time and in vivid impressionistic images rather than in naturalistic action, and this led me to masks and music and ritual. The abstractions were bold and assertive from the beginning. The setting was non-literal but inspired by the forms and sense of decay and rot seen in the ruins of Roman antiquity. The costumes recreated an unknown people of a non-specific time. The inspiration was Roman-Byzantine and feudal Japanese although again there was no literal use of any specific detail. The materials were leather and wool. The music eschewed electronics, which though non-literal are distinctly of 'our' time. What I needed were those sounds that are part of our inherited primitive consciousness – drums, rattles, rubbed stones, animal horns and stretched strings. The rewards of a non-naturalistic approach become evident in actual production. In one of the play's most difficult moments, the audience audibly gasped when the two heads of Titus' sons were brought on stage. Although they were only empty half-masks on visibly empty wire frames, the audience had accepted the masks as the reality and were properly horrified and disgusted without being led to reflect on mundane and naturalistic detail. The poetic image had successfully substituted for the reality.

I wanted to focus on the main lines of moral conflict; Titus, his family, and the exterior pressures personified by Tamora, Aaron and Saturninus. The production also needed a framework, a strong but flexible device to contain the play and give substance to my invented theatrical conventions. I therefore conceived of a group or chorus that would serve different functions in the play and whose constant presence would both cool and abstract the violence. At the same time this group lent volume and size to my images.

The Roman populace of Act I became a chorus – serving all factions. The 'chorus' next became an 'earth-conscience' for Act II, reflecting in sounds the agonies and strains of the 'natural' moral order in the process of being torn apart. In Act III the group became the interior manifestation of Titus' growing madness and disintegration. In Acts IV and V it took on the functions of a nightmarish fusion of Furies and Fates, a visible personification of the forces let loose by the wrenching apart of the 'natural' order by acts of violence, treachery, and deception.

This sense of 'natural' moral order was substituted for the political order of Shakespeare's play. It was a distortion of the text in order to focus on Titus' tragedy and the play's sense of moral disgust. I felt the political analogies were weak for a contemporary audience and that, in Shakespeare's time, political order and moral order were still conceived and perceived as an entity. The personification of State was often embodied in one person who in turn reflected a part of a cosmic or natural order – and thus the fracture of one created upheaval in all.

There are obviously other solutions to the multiple difficulties of *Titus Andronicus* than those which I chose. It is a challenging play with many hidden rewards in the search for production answers. It seems to me a particularly modern play for today – with its flawed hero, its existence in violence and yet its inevitable compassion. In approaching the play for production, however, I think one must treat the text without condescension or patronization or as a Shakespearean 'failure'. For me, it is unmistakably a successful piece of theatre written by Shakespeare, as is evidenced in its moral concern and in its enormous theatrical trust in performance.

1970

King Richard III

DOUGLAS SEALE

Shakespeare is not only a genius, he is popular; also he is dead. These three simple facts make life difficult for a director, for he knows that, although he is expected to treat any piece of Shakespeare's with respect, he must somehow clear away over three and a half centuries of prejudice, popular misconception, idolatry, and fusty academic quibbling before he gets to what are for him the bare boards of the play. Also in this spring-cleaning the new broom must be wary not to brush aside what is to be learned from the study and achievements of older and wiser brooms who have been over the same ground before. He knows too that he has no author to run to for help over the obscure passages, or advice on how to cut the play down to size. And, for good or bad, the fact remains that Shakespeare's plays with very few exceptions are too long for the present day fashion. *Richard the Third* is not one of the exceptions.

Shakespeare, probably because he was his own director, never gives any clues as to interpretation; none of those cryptic directions in brackets like '(sardonically)' or '(with a half-smile)'. The interpretation of the play, or of a character, even the interpretation of a single line, is the director's responsibility finally. And Shakespeare is not the tidiest of authors. It is not always quite clear what in fact he did mean; his plays are full of misprints, inaccuracies as to plot, characterization; speech-headings are sometimes mis-named; there are lines at whose meaning one can only guess. In *Henry VI, Part 1*, the scene between Talbot and his dying son appears twice, once in blank verse and once in rhymed couplets. But the very untidiness is somehow endearing; one gets a glimpse of the man beneath the mantle of genius. One can picture the hustle and bustle of rehearsals, the arguments, the confusion, and in the middle of it all a man with a part to play, a company to direct, a First Night looming up, and at once one's heart warms to him. Here is a giant, but at least one is in the same line of business.

For all his greatness Shakespeare should never be approached with cap in hand, but with boldness and terrible daring. If you do not, everyone will suffer. The play will seem long-winded and dull, the actors will look foolish or at the best hard-working, the audience will be bored, and the critics will probably blame everybody but the director. If, on the other hand, the play is attacked with vigour and boldness, the worst that can happen to the director is that he will be accused of being disrespectful to the Bard. I have always thought respectfulness a pretty chilly response to make to such a full-blooded writer.

The approach to *Richard the Third* is not without pitfalls. The title itself is misleading. *The Tragedy of Richard the Third* is not a tragedy but a melodrama. But it is a melodrama of gigantic proportions, and written to appeal to the popular taste of an Elizabethan audience. This title is doubly misleading because the play is written in the old classic form of tragedy (in structure it closely resembles *Macbeth*) with one important difference. Unlike Macbeth the character of Richard never develops. He begins a villain and ends a villain, unlike the great tragic heroes who, because of a fatal flaw, fall from a position of power and dignity to their ultimate ruin and destruction. But Shakespeare realized that five acts of unmitigated villainy would become uninteresting; after all, one murder is very much like another. So, he decided to create a murderer with humour. Richard, himself, does not take his skullduggery very seriously – at first. (I will come to the murder of the little princes later.) It is Richard's sense of humour, his wit, and his obvious delight in his own wickedness that has made him a popular, almost likeable, character for over three hundred years. Audiences do not laugh at him as they might at Titus Andronicus making meat pies of his victims, they laugh with him.

Just as Richard contemplates murder with a smile on his lips, so we must approach the play and his character with humour. To take the whole thing deadly seriously is to destroy what Shakespeare wanted most – a vastly amusing, entertaining and exciting play.

The reverential approach to Shakespeare is death. When he wrote *Richard the Third* he was at the beginning of his career, and like any other young playwright he needed a box-office success. He took no chances. The bloody history of Richard III was well known to the public. It had been the subject of many plays, poems, and popular songs. Shakespeare was playing safe. He had a story that was a tried favourite, and a popular actor (Burbage) for the leading part. It was a reasonable gamble and he took the risk. He was not writing a serious study of the man, Richard; he was writing what he thought the public wanted – and what he wanted – a whopping great success. And he got it.

We must, therefore, accept the play for what it is and not try to 'improve' it or raise its moral tone. I remember when I directed the play at the Old Vic I received a very strong letter from a lady brimming with missionary zeal and warning me that I was helping to perpetuate a wicked libel in associating myself with a play the sole purpose of which was to blacken the character of a noble, much maligned gentleman. Enclosed was a tract listing his good and valiant deeds, a quotation from a letter written by a lady after a meeting with Richard in which she vowed he was a very good dancer (so much for that clubfoot!) and well-mannered. My correspondent ended with a touching footnote stating firmly that Richard had always been thought well of in Scarborough!

If anyone feels compelled to justify or rationalize Shakespeare's portrait of Richard III, I suggest he study, not the history books but the three plays of *Henry VI* to which *The Tragedy of Richard the Third* is the natural sequel. Whether or not the details of events in the great trilogy are historically accurate is of no importance. What is important, if one wants really to understand Richard, is that they show us the hell of chaos and violence from which Richard sprang; a chaos brought about by the slow collapse of the feudal system, the undermining of the power of the church by corruption and dissension, the instability of the nation's finances as a result of the protracted French Wars, and the accession of a boy king who was of a monkish disposition and a little weak in the head. The only law was the law of force: the only right, the right of possession. New ideas such as the concept of Nationalism and love of one's country, and the individual man's right to worship his God in his own way were only seeds that were to strike roots later. But as they swelled in the ground, they split the foundations of Feudalism that one day would crash in ruins burying the past as if it had never been. The whole of Shaw's *Saint Joan* is built upon this premise – that if a man is allowed to put himself above the church and think only of God and himself, it will be the end of the authority of the church: similarly, if a man thinks only of his allegiance to the king instead of his allegiance to his feudal lord, it will be the end of the barons; that is, the end of the feudal system. And if their power were ever broken the cardinals and the barons believed (as Cauchon in *Saint Joan* believed) that the world would end in a welter of war. In England, that war was the Wars of the Roses.

If we see Richard (both the play and the man) within that setting we need no psycho-analyst to find motives for what happens. We find ourselves in a nightmare world of blood, fear, superstition and death. A world of perpetual night in which a young girl, waylaid while mourning over the dead body of her murdered king and whose husband, the king's son, has been brutally hacked to pieces by the same pair of hands, can be wooed and seduced by the butcher who did the slaughter. I do not say that amidst all this madness and chaos there are not sound reasons – personal reasons – why Richard is what he is; his deformity, his mother's hatred. But as we are not only the product of our parents but of our grandparents and their parents and grand-parents and of the atmosphere and climate of the times in which they lived, so Richard in the play is what he is because of what has happened not only to himself and to his own kin but to every living soul in the *Henry VI* trilogy.

And yet out of this miasma of bloodshed and treachery Shakespeare has produced a play at which an audience is never quite horrified. Because we can laugh at Richard's wit and audacity, we somehow feel safe. We are carried along, bolstered by this feeling of security, until for reasons political as well as dramatic the playwright decides that the time for fun and games is over. The wheel must be given a hefty turn; curses must be invoked; past sins must reap their deadly harvest. And the moment for this change, of course, is after the killing of the little princes. There is a parallel situation in the death of Arthur in *King John*. In both cases it is the rightful heir to the throne that has been murdered. However, Shakespeare, ruthless man, knows that after so much blood-letting one more murder is after all only one more murder. But a child-murder, a *double*-child-murder, that will really shock! That will take the smile off those silly faces! From that moment on, no more jokes. From that moment on, everything goes badly for Richard; friends desert him, and he, himself, loses that old gaiety and quickness of wit.

> *I have not that alacrity of spirit*
> *Nor cheer of mind that I was wont to have.*

He is troubled with fears of treachery.

Choose trusty sentinels . . .
Under our tents I'll play the eavesdropper,
To hear if any mean to shrink from me.

He reads doubtful omens, he has dreadful nightmares, and his bravery in battle is the bravery of a desperate man.

I have set my life upon a cast,
And I will stand the hazard of the die.

The end of this play is like an avalanche; one stone removed removes another, and we the spectators watch the gathering disaster as from the safety of a warm room. Outside all hell is let loose. We are thrilled – excited, perhaps – but never in doubt that all will be well and that the powers of darkness will be overwhelmed and a new and happier day dawn upon the world with the setting of the sun of York and the union of the White Rose and the Red.

In my production of *Richard the Third* at the Old Vic in 1957, Robert Helpmann played Richard. As one would expect, he brought to the part a very incisive yet highly theatrical quality and great beauty. He was like a glittering spider as he climbed slowly to the back of the stage before turning to attack the audience with 'Now is the winter of our discontent. . . .' in a staccato voice pitched somewhere in the dome of his head. His face was pale and his eyes burned. No man's eyes were ever bigger! He played the early scenes with a wonderfully sardonic humour. And I remember how well he accomplished the transformation that comes over Richard once he is crowned. He no longer had friends, only accomplices. His 'Well, let it strike,' was like an axe falling on Buckingham's neck. I remember, too, how Anne (Barbara Jefford) sat through the whole of that Coronation Scene in terrified silence like a woman hypnotized, unable to make any move to save herself even when Richard says to Catesby, irritably and with no attempt at concealment:

Look how thou dreamst ! I say again, give out
That Anne my queen is sick and like to die.

Her playing of the difficult wooing scene was faultless. And the venom of her denunciation of Richard gave us a hint of what heights she would reach when she came to play Queen Margaret in *Henry VI*.

The old widowed Queen Margaret in *Richard the Third* is perhaps the most difficult part in the play. It is so easy for this Nemesis, this very tangible ghost from the past, to be either a bit of a bore or slightly comic. Fay Compton handled her with such skill and such sureness and authority that it was an example of classic acting at its best.

I have added this Appendix because it is only in memory and in records such as these that an actor's performance can be recalled. And I have been served so well by actors all my life that it would be churlish to pass them by without some sign of recognition. A painter's work is his own record but I myself feel that Leslie Hurry's designs for *Richard the Third* are among the best things he has done.

1961

The Taming of the Shrew

ROBERT ATKINS

After denigrating the female characters in *The Taming of the Shrew* Frank Harris, in his book *The Women of Shakespeare*, goes on to say:

'But the play itself has another and deeper interest for us as throwing light on Shakespeare's life and character. In spite of the enormous success it has had on the stage . . . it is a wretchedly poor farce, and the theme is utterly unworthy of the Master. Some of the play does not read like him; but his hand is quite plainly revealed in the scenes between Katherina and Petruchio; in fact the taming of the shrew is his. One cannot but wonder why Shakespeare ever put hand to such a paltry subject. The answer comes pat to those who believe that he himself had been married unhappily to a jealous, ill-tempered scold. Marriage had been a defeat to him: he could not but see that; in the play he will comfort his pride by showing how even a shrew can be mastered; how violence can be subdued by violence. The moment one looks at the play from this point of view, its sub-conscious purpose becomes clear to one and its faults are all explained. When Katherina obeys her husband, Hortensio asks:

> *. . . I wonder what it bodes ?*

And Petruchio replies:

> *Marry, peace it bodes, and love and quiet life*
> *And awful rule and right supremacy;*

In no other way but as a salve to wounded vanity can one explain Katherina's appalling, foolish lecture to the other wives with which the play reaches its climax in Act V, Scene 2.

> *Fie, fie ! unknit that threatening unkind brow . . .*

Even with the explanation in mind one marvels how Shakespeare could seriously pen such drivel; but he goes on raving for another thirty lines, using the adjectives, froward, peevish, sullen, sour, to give his view of his wife.

'Anyone who knows Shakespeare will find an accent of personal feeling in every line of this silly tirade. The proof that my explanation is the right one may be carried to minute detail. As soon as Shakespeare finished writing this astonishing speech of Katherina he threw down his pen; the last eight lines or so of this play seem to have been written by another hand; the interest had gone out of the thing for him when Katherina was sufficiently humbled and he tossed the play aside.'

Another lover of the Bard, Hesketh Pearson, dismisses the play as follows:

'Shakespeare's final version is a rollicking farce, the subject appealing to him because he must often have pondered on the problem of how to chasten a woman who was making him suffer. Apart from this, the play's only appeal to the biographer is the mention of Stratford people and places in the Induction.'

Among critics past and present opinion on the merits of the play has been much divided, but few have given it unadulterated praise. Pepys thought it had some good pieces in it, but generally was 'a mean play'. On the other hand Dr Samuel Johnson defends it. He says:

'Of this play the two plots are so well united, that they can hardly be called two, without injury to the art with which they are interwoven. The attention is entertained with all the variety of a double plot, yet is not distracted by unconnected incidents . . . The whole play is very popular and diverting.'

Schlegel praises the Induction, as being more remarkable than the play itself, Shakespeare proving himself here 'a great poet: the whole is merely a light sketch, but in elegance and nice propriety it will hardly ever be excelled.'

Hazlitt comments:

'*The Taming of the Shrew* is almost the only one of Shakespeare's comedies that has a regular plot, and downright moral. It is full of bustle, animation, and rapidity of action . . .

'The character of Sly and the remarks with which he accompanies the play are as good as the play itself . . . We have a great predilection for this representative of the family; and what makes us like him the better is, that we take him to be of kin (not many degrees removed) to Sancho Panza.'

The comments of Gervinus are interesting because he disliked the overloading of the play with scenery and unnecessary stage business. He writes:

'The scenes between Petruchio and Katherine might be converted into a mere joke, and that of the commonest order. It is sad to think that a man like Garrick has done this. He contracted the piece, under the title of *Katherine and Petruchio*, into a play of three acts; he expunged the more refined part, the plot for the wooing of Bianca, and he debased the coarse remainder into a clumsy caricature. The acting of the pair was coarsely extravagant, according to the custom which has subsequently maintained its ground; Woodward at the same period acted Petruchio with such fury, that he ran the fork into the finger of his fellow actress (Mrs Clive), and when he carried her off the stage, threw her down. Thus is the piece still performed in London as a concluding farce, with all disgusting overloadings of vulgar buffoonery, even when the genuine play was acted again at the Haymarket in 1844, and was received with applause.'*

James Agate, reporting a performance during 1937, imagined the producer addressing the company before the first rehearsal as follows:

'I say that this tedious and doubtful Shakespearean farce is like a young man devoid of parents, devoid of relations, devoid of flocks and herds, devoid of gold, of silver, and of precious stones, and devoid of the light of truth.'

The long line of commentators are fairly agreed that the play *The Taming of the Shrew* as we know it today was first printed in the Folio of 1623. The problem of the source play, *The Taming of A Shrew*, is, as M. R. Ridley the editor of the present text says, 'one of the most interesting cruxes of Shakespearean criticism'. From the first commentation to the grand work of John Dover Wilson, the research into the relationship of the two plays has been conducted with a devotion worthy of the great tragedies, and the answer is, you pays your money and you takes your choice; no one is any the wiser.

I am inclined to accept the Folio text as an early comedy, the

* This refers to Benjamin Webster's remarkable production: remarkable because of its truth and simplicity at a time when scenery was beginning to overwhelm the plays.

Induction by Shakespeare, the play within a play, part Shakespeare, part anyone, with perhaps a few lines thrown in by the actors.

It was undoubtedly popular during the Elizabethan, Jacobean and Stuart periods, having been presented from 1590 to 1596, though where is not known; at the Globe, Bankside, from 1599 to 1613, and at Court before King Charles in 1633. It is not known to have been acted from the re-opening of the theatres at the Restoration to the year 1844, except as an adaptation by Garrick in 1754, as an after-piece in three acts, entitled *Katherine and Petruchio*, the action being confined to the antics of these two characters. Herbert Beerbohm Tree (later Sir Herbert) revived the Garrick version in the early days of his management. In 1810 J. P. Kemble restored the title of *The Taming of the Shrew* and in the same year the double plot was restored to the stage in the form of an opera written by Frederick Reynolds.

Many people voice the opinion of M. R. Ridley, that of all the plays it is the one that we should least regretfully omit from the canon. As an actor and producer it is my opinion that it would be a pity if, say once every two years, a well-acted performance was not put before the public, for the play is popular, and contains many rewarding roles for the artists.

In production a director should be guided by Shakespeare's text and avoid the modern method of fantastication, movements *à la ballet* and the introduction of vulgar and boisterous stage business, for this peppering-up method, so beloved by many of the modern directors of the Shakespeare plays, hampers the actors in the delivery of the play to an audience.

Shakespearean traditions of performance date only from the time of the Restoration and we do not know how Shakespeare handled his production, but research has given us a good idea of the theatre for which he wrote, and our knowledge of both the possibilities and the limitations of the Shakespearean theatre should provide the yardstick for all revivals of the plays.

On 15th October 1870 *The Athenaeum* attacked the manner in which *The Taming of the Shrew* was performed on the English stage, and from the time of Garrick onwards prompt books for 'The Shrew' contain stage business which defies the text.

For example, the incident of the meat, mutton, in Act IV, Scene I: a most succulent joint should be placed before the starving Katharina, succulent enough to make an audience wish for a mouthful. Petruchio says "Tis burnt', but when Katharina remonstrates, 'The meat was

well, if you were so contented' she is speaking the truth. Later,
Petruchio, solus, tells the audience

> *As with the meat some undeserved fault*
> *I'll find about the making of the bed . . .*

Few productions obey Shakespeare's intention, for a joint, burned
to a cinder is paraded round the stage, smeared with a black substance,
so black, that the cook, after Petruchio has seized him and rubbed his
face in the joint, looks like a blackamoor. This defiance of the text kills
a moment of humanity – a hungry Katharina denied a tasty meal.

When does Katharina capitulate? A favourite moment for most
directors of the play is at the end of Act IV, Scene III, but the text
points to a later moment, Act IV, Scene V, the cue being given by
Hortensio with the line

> *Petruchio, go thy ways; the field is won.*

It was, I think, Sir Frank Benson, who, at the end of Act IV,
Scene III, introduced the business of Katharina picking up a con-
veniently placed knife for the purpose of attacking Petruchio. Then,
under his steady gaze, she plunged the blade into the table, sank
sobbing to her knees, and made an exit with the loving husband
tenderly enfolding her.

From America came the business of the 'Taylor' jumping into his
bandbox and shouting 'What! Strike a man in his own shop . . .', a
line not in the text. From America too, came the business of Grumio,
who, hiding under the table, remains hidden by walking off with the
table on his back.

In 1951 an American *Shakespeare Newsletter* critic reported:

'The almost too obstreperous production made constant use of burlesque and unusual effects. Sly hurls chamber pots about the stage
and doubles as a stage horse with a deer's head; the travelling players
enter wearing Victorian costume; the Lord is a fox-hunting nineteenth
century gentleman; two Kazoos sound entrances; toy hobby horses
are galloped around the stage; a trick fire is lit; a string of frankfurters
is fought over; and a trained pup adds to the general hilarity.'

A few years ago a well-known English producer 'pepped up' the
supper scene by using the 'custard pie' act, a bowl of dough being
substituted for the pie. Petruchio slapped the substance on to the faces

first of the servants and then of poor Katharina, while Grumio skipped through a rope of harlequinade sausages.

A notable revival was staged at the Adelphi Theatre, London, by Mr Oscar Asche and Miss Lily Brayton, in 1904, Mr Asche doubling the roles of Sly and Petruchio. Both parts were magnificently played, but the time necessary for the actor to change caused an act-long wait between the Induction and the play itself. This made nonsense of the close attachment of the one to the other. The play was beautifully but heavily mounted and needed too frequent dropping of the tableau curtain to allow a continuity of action. Sir Barry Jackson is reported to have said 'I had a sensation that the audience spent as much time looking at the tableau curtain as at the comedy itself.'

This revival was very popular, but in 1904 neither the theatrical profession nor the general public had much knowledge of Shakespeare's theatre, and had Mr William Poel, whose Elizabethan revival ideas were beginning to inspire the few, handled this very fine company of players, the story of the impact of the play would have rung down the ages, for the scene would have been a replica of the Globe stage background, with a platform jutting into the auditorium, and Mr Asche would not have been allowed to double.

Recent years have shown a tendency to instil a tongue-in-the-cheek attitude into the delivery of Katharina's 'Whole Duty of Woman' oration. The title of the play should be enough to point the way. It tells us that there will be a shrew and that she will be tamed. It is also of interest to note that the popular oath 'Beshrew me!' links up with the original Shrew (spelt with a capital S) in the old religious drama, where it represented Satan himself, so the taming is the exorcization of a devil.

'The Shrew' may not be one of the best plays, but the parts of the two protagonists are worthy the consideration of the best players, for much of the text shares with the Induction the honour of being from the hand of Shakespeare. In the hands of skilful artists, the lesser roles also demand applause.

The induction does, incidentally, have a bearing on Shakespeare's biography, and that he himself possibly enjoyed many a flagon of Wincot ale is shown in *Small Poems of Divers Sorts* (1658).

Shakespeare your Wincot ale hath much renowned,

> *That fox'd a Beggar so (by chance was found*
> *Sleeping) that there needed not many a word*
> *To make him to believe he was a Lord.*
> *Such ale as Shakespeare fancies*
> *Did put Kit Sly into such lordly trances.*

Present the Shrew that Shakespeare portrayed, add nothing to it that defies the text, and *The Taming of the Shrew* will, for many a year to come, be good entertainment.

May many say with Sly:

> *Well, we'll see't. Come, Madam wife, sit by my side, and let the world slip; we shall ne'er be younger.*

1960

The Comedy of Errors

CLIFFORD WILLIAMS

To discuss *The Comedy of Errors* is a pleasant task, for it means paying tribute to an old friend. There is some additional (immodest) pleasure in that I played some part in distinguishing the light of this particular friend hidden behind the bushel. Before 1962 *The Comedy of Errors* was neglected by both academics and producers alike, despite a production by Komisarjevsky at Stratford in 1938, and another at the Royal Court Theatre in 1952. The latter I saw, but can only recall the Dromios riding about on square-wheeled bicycles and may be confusing this with a ballet by Salvador Dali called *Colloque Sentimentale*! But the Royal Shakespeare Company production at Stratford in 1962 focused attention on the play to such effect that a fairly widespread revaluation followed. The production was taken to London and then on a worldwide tour – Berlin, Prague, Budapest, Belgrade, Bucharest, Warsaw, Helsinki, Leningrad, Moscow, Washington, Philadelphia, Boston, and New York. I will not say that presidents swooned and prime ministers wept, but undoubtedly *Comedy* everywhere ceased to be Cinderella and was allowed to stay on at the ball.

So overwhelming was its reception (I did six revivals for Stratford) that, for me, it became more like Frankenstein's monster than Perrault's fairy tale. The play loped after me tenaciously and unshakeably. Even today I have not escaped it entirely. Conversations with strangers about my latest production (quite possibly a polemical tragedy about a test-tube baby) are likely to end as follows: 'Yes, I did like it, really I did. Not as much, I must say, as *The Comedy of Errors* . . . You did do that, didn't you ? . . . Well, that was nice, wasn't it ? . . . (several sighs) . . . Still, as I say, tonight was quite interesting.'

The Comedy of Errors, written about 1591–2, was one of Shakespeare's early plays. A performance given at Gray's Inn on 28 December 1594 before an excessively rowdy audience provoked a public inquiry into 'great Disorders and Abuses'! These were stated to have been caused by a 'sorcerer or Conjuror' – Dr Pinch must have been indulging in audi-

"THE COMEDY OF ERRORS."

ADRIANA.

Peau de
Soie, or
dull silk
satin.

Miss Diana
Rigg.

ence participation – one of a 'Company of base or common Fellows'. I am glad to say that the company escaped to act another day, while the complainants were apparently committed to the Tower of London!

This inauspicious début seems to offer an early confirmation of the knockabout and *boulevard* nature of the play, and a glance at its pedigree – out of Plautus by Poseidippus, or the other way round – would tend to support this judgement. The play is based on the *Menaechmi* of Plautus, although it is a matter of conjecture whether Shakespeare knew the Latin original or an English crib, possibly *The Historie of Error*, performed at Hampton Court in 1576–7. Plautus, who supplied Molière (*Amphitryon* and *l'Avare*) as well as Shakespeare, himself borrowed freely from the Greek New Comedy, and his *Menaechmi* was probably adopted from Poseidippus.

With twenty plays to his credit, Plautus loved complicated plots, scurrility, gagging, backchat, topical allusion (as libellous as possible) and obscenity. His style was boisterous, his mood pagan, his character-ization – drawn from the Atellan Farce – coarse. But he developed the fabric of comedy first woven in the fifth century B C (he wrote in the third), and he provided a model of earthy realism for those anonymous medieval dramatists who emerged after the Dark Ages – truly dark for the theatre. The sixteenth and seventeenth centuries also turned to Plautus both for the unwritten theatre of the *commedia dell' arte* and for much of Renaissance and Golden Age drama.

Shakespeare was a dramaturgical alchemist. All his life he filched ingredients, prescriptions, and formulae, and never failed to trans-form them. Whoever the supplier – Holinshed, Robert Greene, Plutarch – his chemistry was transcendent. So with Plautus. Shake-speare is never less than honest to the vivacious bawdry of his Roman mentor, but the crude, jolly and essentially pagan *Menaechmi* is tem-pered in the flame of Christian humanism. The result is a delightful piece of theatre, with a firm ballast of poetry and a moral tale to wag the dog! In the Stratford production, the transformation that the Latin original underwent at Shakespeare's hands was beautifully mir-rored in Anthony Powell's costumes – *commedia* in feeling, but subtler in spirit, less boisterous and more witty.

The plot of *The Comedy of Errors* is at once tortuous and naïve. A husband and his wife have been sundered by a storm at sea. Their twin sons (each named Antipholus) have been similarly separated – one with each parent. Twin servants-to-be (the Dromios) have suffered the same fate. Years later Antipholus of Syracuse sets out with his Dromio in search of his brother, and reaches Ephesus. His father, Ægeon, following after him, also arrives in Ephesus – unknown to his son – and is promptly arrested (the merchants of Ephesus and Syracuse are on bad terms) and sentenced to death. The other Antipholus, together with his Dromio, is, in fact, resident in Ephesus, but has, however, mislaid his mother somewhere along the route, though he has gained a wife and an unmarried sister-in-law. The mother, unaware that Ephesus now harbours both her sons and her long-lost husband, is Abbess of the local convent. This situation, complex enough in itself, is further aggravated by a sort of 'seven-year itch' which afflicts the Ephesian Antipholus to the mortification of his wife. It is at this point that the play opens.

More factual than the assorted Illyrias of Shakespeare's later comedies, Ephesus was, in fact, well known in the ancient world, and some of the reasons for this are highly pertinent to the play. Heraclitus said that the Ephesians all deserved to be hanged, and Apollonius tells us why: 'The people are immersed in dissipations and cruel sports, in shows and pantomimes, and Pyrrhic dances; and all places resound with song, and are filled with noise and debauchery.' The principal pursuit was the cult of black magic. Nero hired an Ephesian astrologer, the Emperor Julian was convinced by another that he was the reincarnation of Alexander the Great, and the so-called 'Ephesian Letters' bestowed immunity against death on their possessors. Antipholus of Syracuse is well aware of Ephesus's reputation:

> They say this town is full of cozenage;
> As, nimble jugglers that deceive the eye;
> Dark-working sorcerers that change the mind;
> Soul-killing witches that deform the body;
> Disguised cheaters, prating mountebanks;
> And many such-like liberties of sin:
> If it prove so, I will be gone the sooner.
>
> (Act I, Scene 2)

The climate of black magic is emphasized by Shakespeare not only in his transference of the locale from the Epidamnum of Plautus to Ephesus, but also in the addition of a second pair of twins where Plautus had but one set. For the Elizabethan audience, twinship carried an aura of magic and mystery.

Ephesus was the centre and shrine for the worship of Diana –
'Queen of Witches All'. When Paul the Apostle visited the city, he
found much to deprecate, but he was hardly popular.

'A certain man named Demetrius, a silversmith, which made silver
shrines for Diana . . . called together the workmen of like occupation,
and said, Sirs, ye know that by this craft we have our wealth . . . this
Paul hath persuaded and turned away much people, saying that they
be no gods, which are made with hands; so that not only this our craft
is in danger to be set at nought; but also that the temple of the great
goddess Diana should be despised . . . And when they heard these
sayings, they were full of wrath, and cried out, saying, Great is Diana
of the Ephesians. And the whole city was filled with confusion.'

But Diana was goddess of childbirth as well and, in the light of this
function, her shade may be said to throw a beneficent spell over the
play. Paul, in his famous epistle on marital obedience, thus finds himself temporarily in her court:

'Wives, submit yourselves unto your own husbands, as unto the Lord.
For the husband is the head of the wife, even as Christ is the head of
the church; and he is the saviour of the body.

'Husbands, love your wives, even as Christ also loved the church,
and gave himself for it, that it should be holy and without blemish. So
ought men to love their wives as their own bodies. He that loveth his
wife loveth himself.'

In the play, the same sentiments are presented by Luciana (the sister-
in-law):

> There's nothing situate under heaven's eye
> But hath his bound, in earth, in sea, in sky:
> The beasts, the fishes, and the winged fowls,
> Are their males' subject, and at their controls;
> Man, more divine, the master of all these,
> Lord of the wide world and wild watery seas,
> Indued with intellectual sense and souls,
> Of more pre-eminence than fish and fowls,
> Are masters to their females, and their lords:
> Then let your will attend on their accords.

(Act II, Scene 1)

Luciana, with her Renaissance grasp of the nature of domestic bliss
and cosmic harmony, finds her proper opponent in Pinch, the

conjuror employed by Adriana (wife of the Ephesian Antipholus), in a desperate attempt to 'win back' her husband. Pinch is no more than 'a threadbare juggler, and a fortune-teller . . . A living dead man.' His failure to exorcise the supposed demons infecting Antipholus is set in contrast to the more perceptive and successful analysis offered by the Abbess. Initially, as she surveys the true causes of the friction which exists between Adriana and Antipholus, she shows singular perspicacity. If her remedies – 'wholesome syrups, drugs, and holy prayers' – have their own flavour of quackery, we should remember that she is, in fact, addressing the wrong Antipholus. Possibly – as mother and Abbess – she divines this. Her tongue certainly seems to be somewhat in her cheek. At all events she offers sanctuary – a proposal of Grace in the face of pagan sorcery – and gains time for off-stage explanations that, in turn, permit the play's true function to emerge: the celebrating of the sacrament of marriage.

In the final scenes of the play a core of deep humanism unifies the comedy and the near-tragedy, the foolishness and the sagacity, the paradox and the mistaking. Ægeon is released and reunited with his wife, the Abbess, and both are reunited with their sons. The two sets of twins find each other. One Antipholus takes his wife fondly in his arms again, the other has promise of marriage from the sister-in-law. Confusion is resolved and error prevails no more.

In *The Comedy of Errors*, Shakespeare reveals an early mastery of stagecraft that allows him to juggle elements of varying felicity with cheerful nonchalance. But, more than this, he takes here his first steps along a road that constantly returns to its starting-point – a road for a man in search of his origin and his end, in search of forgiveness and reconciliation, in search of reality and identity. It is a road that Shakespeare travels and retravels from *The Comedy of Errors* through to the last plays – *The Winter's Tale*, *Cymbeline* and *The Tempest*.

> *I to the world am like a drop of water,*
> *That in the ocean seeks another drop,*
> *Who, falling there to find his fellow forth,*
> *Unseen, inquisitive, confounds himself;*
>
> (Act I, Scene 2)

Antipholus of Syracuse speaks with the authentic voice of the Shakespearean traveller, and it is a voice that is heard all through the canon.

1969

Love's Labour's Lost

PAUL ROGERS

Shamelessly, I admit I am in love with *Love's Labour's Lost*. The condition is shared, I will hazard a guess, by most players fortunate enough to have performed it at any time, and certainly by all of us who were in Hugh Hunt's enchanted production at the New Theatre – the Old Vic production of 1949. I chose the word 'enchanted' with due care. Moments of enchantment come rarely – even in the theatre; but when they come, they come to stay – as long as memory survives. For once, Time, Place and Loved Ones were a unity and the moment was as near perfect as I hope to see in an imperfect world. Redgrave, straight out of Hilliard, saying with his white-gold voice 'And bright Apollo's lute, strung with his hair'; or crackling out 'Have at you, then, affection's men at arms.' Mark Dignam, finely pedantic, braying 'Venezia, Venezia, chi non ti vede non ti pretia.' Miles Malleson's perfection of Sir Nathaniel and George Benson the finest Costard: these are the stuff of superlative memories. And the ladies: Angela and Diana; Jane, Yvonne and Rosalind*: their very names ring like bright bells. I love their work in this play for ever, and, in fact, I married one of them.

The designer, Berkeley Sutcliffe, contributed a large share to the magic. According to the fashion for a few shapes and many stairs to speed up the presentation of The Plays, of sackcloth, canvas and painted felt for the actors' dress, he broke every rule. Our settings were marvellously designed and constructed; they would have delighted Tree, and in some circles that statement is the ultimate disparagement. Certainly our audiences were bewitched. Green banks and trees, Armado's thatched lodge and a silken pavilion; a lake and Mercade arriving on a splendid barge; the barge which took the ladies away from their beloved. And drifts of autumn leaves in the dying light. All served to enrich at all times the riches of the play. And the costumes! Such velvet and silk, such padding and quilting, and rich

* Angela Baddeley, Diana Churchill, Jane Wenham, Yvonne Mitchell, Rosalind Boxall.

embroideries and pearls enough to fill a bucket. Quite wonderful! To step for a moment on the earth, I recommend anyone who might question Mr Sutcliffe's method of approaching this play to read the surviving accounts of expenses incurred by Elizabethan players for their wardrobes. These few ragged slips of paper speak volumes of how Shakespeare himself liked his plays dressed.

This cannot be the way to write an introduction – a scholarly introduction, I mean, the kind one expects. *Love's Labour's Lost* is an unexpected kind of play, a young play. It makes me feel young just to think about it; young and somewhat irresponsible. Other, more sober people will write of dates and serious facts. They may discourse on sources and influences. I cannot. I will not. I don't care. The birth date and essential measurements of the Beloved are facts but they are unimportant when the whole adds up to loveliness. Even so . . . one must be specific.

What is the magic? What does the play contain? A theme of charm: the inevitable defeat in the game of love of four delightful young men by four enchanting ladies who are much more than their match. Four young men intent on denying their very youth and nature. Four young women with a different point of view. Possibly Shakespeare's happiest build-up for the comic let-down to come is the blind pomposity of Navarre with his high-flown but idiotic edict, and his two smug friends Longavill and Dumaine. They should have been warned. There were signs and warnings enough. Their more worldly companion, Berowne, questions their wisdom even in the idyllic and untroubled moment at the outset of the play, and Costard, the swain – a clown and a realist – is unable to resist the delights of Jaquenetta within a matter of stage hours after the original publication of Navarre's intention. Everyone is aware of the imminent arrival of the Princess of France and her train, but they seem blissfully unaware of the implicit dangers. At least, Navarre, Longavill and Dumaine are. Berowne is not and, unsure of the putting into practice 'that which each to other hath so strongly sworn', he lays his 'head to any good man's hat, These oaths and laws will prove an idle scorn', and leads off Costard to his rustic gaol with Don Armado for keeper. If dates may be believed Shakespeare uses here, for the first time, a recurring and favourite conceit: the counterpoise of a Court against a company of rustics or 'hard handed men'. He has continually used the abrupt mixture of class to delightful effect in comedies and in other places to heighten the poignancy of a situation, to clarify and sharpen the mood and condition of his more splendid people. The grey little figure of Richard II's Queen doesn't emerge as a person at all until she is brought together with the Gardeners. Hamlet, through the agency of the Grave-digger, is confronted with the stuff of earth and mortality. In the open air, in the company of the Grave-digger and earth and bones, Hamlet is stripped of the mental and physical trappings which until then have been a protection and a suffocation.

This influence of earth and open air as opposed to the safe indoors, is often and fascinatingly employed by Shakespeare. Within the manmade walls of his Court, Lear is able to identify himself with God. The witchcraft of torchlight and the robes of kingship make him look like a god. He behaves in a manner befitting an ancient, selfish, pagan old godhead. To achieve in him a condition of humility and complete self-knowledge, Shakespeare leads him out on to the Heath and into the storm and the destruction of his wits. Eventually, in the company of rejected truth – his daughter Cordelia – his eyes open to the light, 'fair daylight'. His garlands of flowers at the peak of his madness, like those of the unhappy Ophelia, are the poet's symbols of how close to the realities of earth mortals must come before a final release is possible.

In *Love's Labour's Lost* this is expressed in terms of comedy. If the king had kept himself and his fellow scholars safe within the walls of his little Academe, all might have gone more nearly according to plan. But they wander dangerously in the open air from the beginning of the play. The vows which are a denial of Nature's intention are read and confirmed under the quizzical eye of Nature herself. And when the princess and her ladies are come in embassage, the young king might have been less exposed to danger if he had been less churlish and had welcomed his visitors to the cheer and comfort of his palace. Within those walls all would have been on their best behaviour and tied up in tidy parcels of protocol and court procedure. Alas! he makes them camp out in a nearby field. Here they are a prey to heaven knows what Pan-ish mischief and each lady, put completely on her mettle, leads the young man of her choice a great dance, figuratively and actually, before he can succumb charmingly to Nature's reasoning, abandoning his own.

The play is blithely rich in character. Ignore the authorities who write that Berowne is but a sketch for Benedick, that 'Berowne and Boyet, Armado and Holofernes, Costard and Dull, Rosaline and

Maria are each like faint reflections of the other; they run in pairs, as it were, and the power which should have been concentrated on the one is frittered away on both.' This is great nonsense; written by one who has plunged his nose into the printed page without the help of an actor's imagination to breathe life into these people. In fact, the Dramatis Personæ is astonishing in its variety. Anyhow, in this play, by the creation of Holofernes, Shakespeare has his own revenge on all such dull pedants and layers down of academic law. His love of the simpleton makes his portrayal of Sir Nathaniel and Dull the Constable full of sympathy and gentle affection. There was never such a dear, gentle soul as the curate, and one's heart bleeds for him, despite being helpless with laughter, when he 'dries' hopelessly in his role of Alexander. Who, one wonders, was the old courtier gently lampooned in Boyet? For certain he was quickly recognized by the court of Queen Elizabeth I that Christmas evening 1597. He is a splendid, worldly, honey-tongued old sophisticate. His relish for the intricacies of life at Court, for all the intrigues and the delicious ramifications of the game of love played in high places, sets a wicked twinkle in his eye and makes his brain sparkle with courtesies and the most involved innuendo.

Naturally, my main pleasure is centred in the character I have now played twice. Studying Armado, the fantastic Spaniard, it seems almost impossible that the other great Don has had no part in Armado's making. Armado's view of love is very 'de la Mancha'. At the time of writing, the Spaniard, like the Jew in *The Merchant of Venice*, was good for a laugh and a hearty boo; but on each occasion the character ran away with his creator. The stage is set for Armado to be merely a figure of fun, but his goodness and simple honour take hold of our affections and in the end he is wringing our hearts with as simple a line as: 'I have no shirt.' One laughs, but underneath is an awareness of something deep, brave, noble and tragi-comical. We are well aware that the child bragging in Jaquenetta's belly is certainly Costard's. The Don is more fortunate: most readily and nobly he embraces paternity. The flame of his fantastic imagination begat this child and he will love devotedly the red snub-faced creature – when he remembers who, what and why the child is. It is this flavour in the part which makes me favour wholeheartedly the disputed allotting of the final lines of the play not to the princess but to Armado. The great ones and the lesser folk melt away and the bemused touchstone of the play is left

alone (or, as Hugh Hunt envisaged it, with a sheltering arm about his lady's shoulders) to bid you all the gentlest of good nights. Armado and Moth are the only two people about whom there can be any question as to how they came to be in the park of the King of Navarre. The king and his companions and the country-folk live there. The princess and her train come visiting with a most practical mission. But Armado and Moth . . . ? In Hugh Hunt's production we had been out on the lake in a punt and came ashore for our first scene. This whim gave actors and audience alike a curious sense of the difference of the strange couple from the rest of the people in the story. Armado is 'a refined traveller of Spain'. His veracity is questioned by his host Navarre, but never his nobility. How came he here? And how did he come by Moth? Moth could be anything. Clearly, he is very small in contrast with the rangy old Spaniard. Is he a by-blow of some court through which Armado passed at some time, the settlement of a bad debt or a tiny waif the traveller found abandoned on a roadside? Whatever his origin, Moth has grown into a sharp-witted, alert and nimble-tongued imp whose zest for life is most agreeable and whose devotion to his master is very touching. I have long nursed a fantasy that in addition to being a foreigner in a foreign land, Armado, in the manner of his great contemporary, is somewhat deranged – gently and harmlessly, except . . . I suspect he is an incendiary! Why else, when planning a diversion for the nobility, does he suggest the king would have him 'present the princess, sweet chuck, with some delightful ostentation, or show, or pageant, or antic, or *firework*'. 'Firework' is the key and Holofernes is either in the know, or suspects the suggestion; for the idea is quashed by simply ignoring it and plumping solidly for the presentation of the Nine Worthies, highly suitable, educational and (since Holofernes could not foresee the duel) an entertainment without hazards. I admit to *knowing* how Armado came to Navarre.

Like Quixote, Armado had been reading too much. But not only of tales of Romance and High Adventure, there was also inflammatory stuff about disaster and the properties of those elements of earth, water, air and *Fire*. One day, in a moment of extreme inspiration, his brain spinning with the beauty of Fire, Armado put a torch to the hangings in his closet. Gradually, the Fire drove him through the rooms and passages of his castle until, at last, he was standing at the far side of the forecourt, or perhaps he went to the top of a small hill, the better to view this unique spectacle of his own contrivance. And there he stood until nothing but a smoking shell remained. Then, with a strange sense of fulfilment, he put his sword upon his shoulder, turned his back on all which had gone before and walked off into the world.

In this play, the young poet's craftsmanship is a supreme pleasure. If I force myself to make choice of the scene which, for me, most vividly displays the craftsman and the poet at work in almost celestial double harness, I must plump for Act IV, Scene 3. Here is a brilliant mixture of prose soliloquy, the close-knit verse-forms of the lovers' individual poems to their ladies, and the rhymed couplet interchanges between the aware and the unaware. Such a pitch of versifying is reached that, when Costard and Jaquenetta come into the scene, their rustic rudeness cannot break the spell. Unlike their kind anywhere else in the Plays, they subscribe to the mood of the scene, speak verse and, where they have the line ends, they rhyme as nimbly as the rest. But their presence seems to affect the scene in more than mere content because, when they go, the verse gradually opens out in a turmoil of young love, agitation, boasting and vying one with another, to the wide freedom of the great speech, whose form, excitement and ravishing beauty beggar description and move me to tears. Shakespeare was wickedly aware of the effect he had achieved for the next sound after Berowne's

> *Allons ! Allons ! Sow'd cockle reaped no corn;*
> *And justice always whirls in equal measure:*
> *Light wenches may prove plagues to men forsworn;*
> *If so, our copper buys no better treasure*

is a belch from Holofernes, who has just taken an excellent dinner with the Curate.

Love's Labour's Lost has everything; high, low, and fantastic comedy; a troupe of young lovers, a king, a princess, witty ladies and light-hearted gentlemen; a company of charming other people; a masque of Russians, a hunt for the deer, and an entertainment every bit as funny as the Mechanicals' play in 'The Dream'. And there is something more. This is the wonderful key change towards the end of the play at the height of the fun. Mercade makes his entrance. Mercade, one of the shortest and most effective parts ever written, is an Angel of Death. He brings into the rustic scene of light hearts and high spirits the sense of responsibility to those born great, and the inescapable knowledge of mortality to all who crowd the stage. Cupid and Death stand side by side. The action ends in a sadness which conceals, nevertheless, a promise of warmth. All will be well when the duties of the world have been completed; when the old King of France has been suitably mourned and the truth of love has been tested by time. Although 'Our wooing doth not end like an old play', Jack *shall* have Jill. But nothing can ever again be quite the same. Spring gives place to winter. '. . . greasy Joan doth keel the pot'. And 'The words of Mercury are harsh after the songs of Apollo'.

1959

The Two Gentlemen of Verona

DENIS CAREY

It used to be said – and, for all I know, still is – that the only way to present Shakespeare is to 'play him straight'. What nonsense! If Shakespeare were played straight, as indeed it sometimes is at boys' schools, women would be banished entirely and Cleopatra played by some squeaking boy dressed up to look like Queen Elizabeth and wearing a breastplate for the battle scenes. There are those who say that this would be no bad thing. We have not, as far as I know, any record of the author's opinion on the subject of actresses, but in the comedies especially the ever-present allegory of Man's pilgrimage in search of eternal love and perfect beauty, can be somewhat lost at the sight of a live young woman, venal and vulnerable, wayward and radiantly sexual in the role of the heroine. No. No one would now seriously suggest that Shakespeare should be habitually played by an all-male cast. That would relegate his work to the brooding of scholars and the tedium of the classrooms. Perhaps, in fact, we have to thank women for unwittingly rescuing Shakespeare from obscurity! Certainly I have never seen a Rosalind that did not woo me, win me, enchant me and reduce me to tears. I had forgotten – there was one exception, a misconceived and epicene production at the Old Vic. But then there were no women in it – Rosalind was played by a man.

I am afraid that I can offer no apology for making this introduction a personal one. My association with Shakespeare's plays has always been practical and I must invite the reader to turn to the scholars for an exposition of the mystery that lies within them.

This introduction, then, is a brief account of the production of *The Two Gentlemen of Verona* at the Bristol Old Vic in 1951, contrasted with a somewhat more famous production twenty years later – Peter Brook's *Midsummer Night's Dream*, first presented at Stratford-upon-Avon in 1970, which toured the world from August 1972 to August 1973.

I remember very clearly travelling down by train from London to Bristol in the company of Hugh Hunt in the autumn of 1951. Mr Hunt was then Director of the Old Vic and it had been suggested that the

Bristol Old Vic should present *The Two Gentlemen of Verona*, a virtually unknown Shakespeare, which would be seen first in Bristol and
afterwards at the Old Vic in London. Characteristically I had only just
read the play and was badly shaken. Could the author really be grateful
to anyone for preserving this youthful, unfinished, minor exercise?
The inconsistencies, the lacunae, the chasms in the text, blur the eye
and numb the brain. Had we been able then to enlist the services of
John Barton, whose garnering of the production of *The Wars of the
Roses* shines as one of the most precious jewels in the diadem of the
Royal Shakespeare Company, it would have been an easy matter. It
has been said of Mr Barton, whether it be true I know not, that he was
so able to emulate the great man himself when adding the occasional
speech or odd lines to his recension of the Histories, that after a time
not even he could tell which was Barton and which was Bard. But this
was twenty years ago and the blessed union between the back-room
scholars of Cambridge and the company of players at Stratford had
not yet taken place.

I asked Mr Hunt if it were not possible to change the play. Mr Hunt
replied, happily, that it was too late and so we went ahead.

I was, of course, blind like Proteus and, like Proteus I changed.
Slowly, with an invisible and subtle stealth, the play's very imperfec-
tions creep inside the heart, its faults become virtues, its youthfulness
intoxicating, its innocence its triumph. To the jaded palate Julia has
more vulnerability than Portia, Launce can evoke more tears than
Launcelot, Lucetta has more character than Nerissa and the Duke is
more darkly fun than either of his counterparts in *As You Like It*.
Consider the lovelorn Valentine –

> *What light is light, if Silvia be not seen?*
> *What joy is joy, if Silvia be not by?*
> *Unless it be to think that she is by,*
> *And feed upon the shadow of perfection.*
> *Except I be by Silvia in the night,*
> *There is no music in the nightingale;*
> *Unless I look on Silvia in the day,*
> *There is no day for me to look upon:*
> *She is my essence, and I leave to be,*
> *If I be not by her fair influence*
> *Foster'd, illumin'd, cherish'd, kept alive.*

III.I. 174–184

Why this is the very ecstasy of love!

Slowly the characters take shape and breathe life, inhabiting a world of their own. Verona is as insubstantial as Illyria.

(There is a game, by the way, to be played on a summer's afternoon in a deckchair, spotting the seeds or young shoots of later plays. One can satisfy one's self-conceit for hours.)

The focal character in the play is undoubtedly Proteus – a dark, introverted young man, an only child and motherless. Like so many young people in Shakespeare, he is gnawed by self-guilt and envy, much given to soliloquy. How many changes of form was Proteus to assume as play followed play before Prospero finally broke his staff? Had Shakespeare so wished, Proteus could have brought his world crashing down round him. But this is a comedy, and the power of forgiving love is triumphant – as shown by Valentine's lines to Proteus after his treachery has been revealed –

> *And, that my love may appear plain and free,*
> *All that was mine in Silvia I give thee.*
>
> v.4.82–83

Much has been written of this passage, but is there any need to look further than Valentine's desire to share his discovery of love with his friend? The young Flower Power people of the sixties would have understood perfectly. Incidentally the Proteus in the production at Bristol did indeed marry his Julia.

And what of those two wisecracking lads, the irrepressible Speed and the doleful Launce, with what care the young playwright had constructed their scenes. The parts were no doubt created for the two boys who created the Dromios in *Comedy of Errors* and they must have invented much of their patter for themselves. Surely Launce has the best first entrance of any comic in the whole canon. What a wealth of exaggerated despair lies in the words –

> '*Why, man, if the river were dry, I am able to fill it with my tears;*
> *if the wind were down, I could drive the boat with my sighs.*
>
> II.3.52

Michael Aldridge gave a stunning performance as Launce, a gangling youth in shirt and breeches of maybe sixteen years, plucked from the bosom of his family to be lost in the foolish world outside.

No mention has yet been made of a character whose casting is of paramount importance and should not be undertaken lightly. I refer, of course, to Crab. He is, after all, a reflection of his master who was closer to the heavenly light than *his* master, Proteus, until he was transformed in the wood by the revelation of self-knowledge. But it is not only Launce that Crab follows. He dogs – if I may be pardoned the expression – his master's master. Crab's ingratitude is a mirror of Proteus' infidelity. How many times when Proteus has betrayed himself do we find that egregious hound shuffling on, a silent reproach to perfidy?

Long before we started rehearsals on the play, I visited the Lost Dogs Home in Bath with Mr Aldridge, where every uncouth mongrel cried out to be taken on in the role. Mr Aldridge became so fond of the tyke eventually chosen, that it was in doubt for a time whether he had become more attached to his dog than to his wife. Well, it happens. I wonder, by the way, whether the original Crab had a tendency to walk backwards?

With the Fourth Act we plunge deep into the wood of make-believe. Outlaws, knights, innkeepers appear at the stroke of a pen, the heroine taken prisoner, the treacherous lover unmasked, till the scales fall from his blinded eyes and he emerges whole, cured by the power of love. There is everything here from Brokers' Men to Principal Boy. Here are the Babes in the Wood, together with Robin Hood and his Merry Men and the sure knowledge that, in the end, as in Aeschylus, the good will prevail!

What is remarkable is that in this early work, the pattern is firmly set for the later comedies; the moment of choice, the departure, the pilgrimage, the wandering in the wood, the attainment of self-knowledge through the power of love; the Duke, representing order and the comics, commenting on their masters and all things under the sun, round off their tiny universe.

The production of a play by Shakespeare is a tease for any director. We have become obsessed with the idea that Shakespeare is a 'modern' dramatist, that his plays are as pertinent today as they were in his own time. There are directors who, to ride their own hobby horses, will do him violence with impunity, any period in time for costumes, any mutilation of the text to serve their ends. The truth of the matter is that our society is as far removed from that of Shakespeare as it is from the ancient Greeks. We live in an age of disorder, corruption and unbelief. The business of a modern director ultimately is to offer in

our dark ages some glimpse of the poetic visions of heavenly harmony
that is the root of the Shakespearean ethic. We might do well to
remember the dramatist's own words – however hackneyed they may
be –

> *The man that has not music himself,*
> *Nor is not moved with concord of sweet sounds,*
> *Is fit for treasons, stratagems and spoils;*
> *The motions of his spirit are as dull as night,*
> *And his affections dark as Erebus;*
> *Let no such man be trusted.*

On the purely practical level, then, the set and costumes should
reflect the poetry of the play to be presented – the period is immaterial
– and the costumes should *be easy to wear*. I remember asking the
designer who had created a highly elaborate costume for Olivia for a
production of *Twelfth Night* at the Old Vic, whether the actress would
be able to sit down. He replied, 'Does she have to?' It was at the same
dress rehearsal that Richard Burton, who was playing Sir Toby, tore
off his ruff which was stifling him saying, 'Well, that's going for a
start!'

The production of *The Two Gentlemen of Verona* at Bristol was
simple enough. The costumes were romantic Italianate, the set warm
columns cunningly arranged in perspective. Masked minstrels came
on in the opening dawn, who were later to serenade before Silvia's
house. There were games of chess and blind man's buff and much
poring over maps by Julia and Lucetta. At the end, when the other
actors had departed, Launce was left alone on the stage in the fading
light, looking lost. Suddenly he remembered and whistled. Crab flew
on to the stage and the two of them walked off together.

To our surprise the production was a vast and heartwarming success. As success does not come easily in the theatre, I make bold to set
down the main ingredients as they appear to me.

A play by Shakespeare that was virtually unknown, the critics
therefore had no opportunity to make comparisons!

A seasoned production unit, namely – J. Hutchinson Scott, even
then the most experienced theatrical designer in the business; Julian
Slade, the composer, whose first real professional assignment this was
and who has the exceptional gift of bringing happiness with his music
wherever he works; the director; and, in Nat Brenner, an experienced

and *wise* production manager. (How rare wisdom is in the theatre! So many disasters could be avoided with the help of a production manager who knows when money can be spent and who really advises.)

The absence of any lighting expert!

A *young* company who had already tasted the sweet smell of success in the first half of the season.

Good parts for all!

The simple fact that all the actors could be *heard*.

Hard work, luck and – ignorance!

So here I am in my declining years – why declining? In my advancing years – having just completed a world tour as an actor in Peter Brook's production of *A Midsummer Night's Dream*. Twenty years later and a vastly different experience. In retrospect how settled and secure the early fifties now appear. Osborne was unknown, Beckett unheard of outside the intellectual circles of Paris, Anouilh was the darling of every repertory company, the musicals were *The Boy Friend* and *Salad Days*. Yet, even then, Peter Brook was a power in the theatre. Now, two decades later, he stands unmistakably as a genius, a guru, a magician, a smiling mischievous Puck, a visionary with a soft quiet voice that can pierce your soul, a man of steel who will bend but never yield.

On his rare visits to the company in Washington, in Paris or in Munich, we would sit on the floor of the stage after the performance in what Gemma Jones called a 'grave circle' and he would ask questions – what was the performance like that night, what did we feel about such and such a scene, how did we find the audience. Rarely did he offer much comment. The company had to explore for themselves.

Rehearsals for this tour were held in Paris in a vast bare room which savoured of a Cistercian monastery. There were no chairs and when people were not performing they lay on mattresses. There were no outside distractions, no domestic ties, only the play which we inhaled and lived. Twenty years ago a director plotted the play once, scene by scene, and if the moves did not work they were sometimes changed. But with Mr Brook rehearsals are a period of disciplined anarchy in which the actor is compelled to strip – not literally, this was not nude Shakespeare – to search his subconscious, to endure the pains of communion, to overcome the travail of communication, but above all to 'do his own thing'. Rehearsals were a process of analysis, of improvisation, of exercises, of playing games. The aim was release and self-awareness. Anyone's suggestion would be explored and worked on, props would be tried out and rejected. The result was that the production was never finished! Performance was merely a part of the continuing process of exploration of life itself.

Here we have two productions separated by only twenty years of two plays written close together – yet how wide the gulf. They have much in common. There are the four lovers, there is the pilgrimage, the test, the journeying through the wood and the redemption through love. But though *The Two Gentlemen of Verona* and the lovers' part of *A Midsummer Night's Dream* were probably written about the same time, the four young people are vastly different. In *The Dream*, though Hermia's revolt against her father brings her to brief prominence and is the mainspring of the mortals' part of the play, yet the quartet are equally balanced in mood – four healthy youngsters in love. In *The Two Gentlemen of Verona* the allegory is precise. Proteus and Valentine, the changeable and the constant, the dark and the light, are two facets of the same person – as are Julia and Sylvia, with Sylvia as man's idea of womanhood, an ideal, a goddess, the symbol of perfection. Yet Julia and Proteus are more sharply defined characters than are the lovers in *The Dream*.

But in both plays Shakespeare's moral force and his message of love shine even more brightly today in contrast to this very naughty world. *The Two Gentlemen of Verona* is a play for the young.

1974

King Richard II

JOHN GIELGUD

Richard the Second is a ceremonial play. In spite of its long cast-list only a small group of characters are of the first importance, and most of these are very broadly stated, especially in the early scenes. The young king himself, though his personal beauty and the subservient manner in which he is treated (as he sits idly on his throne) must draw all eyes to him immediately, is only lightly sketched at first in a few enigmatic strokes. It is not until after his return from Ireland, almost half way through the play, that his inner character begins to be developed by the dramatist in a series of exquisite cadenzas and variations. In these later scenes the subtleties of his speeches are capable of endless shades and nuances, but, as is nearly always the case in Shakespeare, the actor's vocal efforts must be contrived within the framework of the verse, and not outside it. Too many pauses and striking variations of tempo will tend to hold up the action disastrously and so ruin the pattern and symmetry of the text.

King Richard and the Actor

The actor of Richard cannot hope at any time during the action to be wholly sympathetic to the audience. Indeed he must use the early scenes to create an impression of slyness, petty vanity, and callous indifference. But he must also show himself to be innately well-bred, sensitive to beauty (as *he* understands it, though he cannot see the beauty of the dying Gaunt), lonely in his aloof position of kingship, young, headstrong, frivolous, and entirely out of sympathy with the older men who try so vainly to advise him and control his whims.

In the later scenes, however, the lovely lines he has to speak can hardly fail to win a certain sympathy for him, and he gradually becomes more understandable, and so more pitiable. But owing to his utter lack of humour and his constant flood of egotism and self-posturing, he can still risk becoming tedious and irritating, unless the finer shades of his character are very subtly conveyed.

It is essential for an actor playing Richard to find the exact line of progression and disintegration, first by grading the successive scenes as they follow one another (with their shifting changes of mood in a continually minor key) and then by developing the detail and constructive pattern of the speeches. These must flow at a melodious but varying pace, at the same time avoiding any pauses or business which might tend to drag them out intolerably.

Richard is one of the rare parts in which the actor may enjoy himself, luxuriating in the language he has to speak, moving in consciously graceful lines. Yet he must seem, physically, to be ever on his guard, shielding himself, both in words and movements, from the dreaded impact of the overwhelming outside circumstances which lie in wait to strike him down. He is torn between the intrinsic weakness and fearfulness of his nature and the pride and fastidiousness of his position and breeding. He strives continually to retain his kingly dignity, to gain time by holding it up to the light before his enemies (as he will actually hold the mirror up, later on, in the Deposition scene) while he prepares inwardly to face the shock of the next unknown humiliation that may fall upon him; until, cast out finally into the empty darkness of the prison, he is forced to realize at last that neither his personal beauty nor his kingly station can save him any longer from the inevitable dismay of contemplating his private doom.

Thus the actor has a dual responsibility. He must present the action of the king suffering his factual defeats – the news of his favourites' deaths, the surrender at Flint, the insults of the Deposition scene, and the farewell to his queen. Yet he must somehow contrive at the same time to execute the poetic intricacies of the text with the full beauty of its musical intention by using a completely lucid (and possibly stylized) method of vocal and plastic interpretation. For good verse-speaking, even at its best, can only be projected, so as to hold an audience, by the artificial technical means of tone, emphasis, and modulation. The task may seem an impossibly difficult one – to play, as it were, in two different styles at once. But this is actually a question of technique. A good actor experiences emotion – or imagines the experience of it vividly, which is not quite the same thing. Finally he selects, through trial and error at rehearsals, what he wishes to convey at each given moment of his performance. He has the double task of both living in his role and of judging his own effects in relation to his fellow players and the audience, so as to present an apparently spontaneous, living, pattern, carefully devised beforehand, but capable of infinite shades of colour and tempo, and bound to vary slightly at every performance. The actor is, after all, a kind of conjuror, and, in a part like Richard, he will find infinite possibilities to put his skill into practice, playing, as Richard himself plays, on the feelings of an audience until they are at one with the complicated nature of the character, so that, even when they cannot approve his actions or sympathize with his misfortunes, they come to understand his problems, and can leave the theatre at the end of the play with the satisfaction of having shared in his unique experience.

The Text and Principal Characters

Whether the scenes of the Aumerle conspiracy in the fourth act should be omitted or retained is a difficult question to decide. Many people think that they are not by Shakespeare, and that they may have been cobbled together by another hand to pad out the necessary playing time when the Deposition scene, owing to its controversial political implications, was omitted in Elizabeth's day. Certainly these scenes have a strong flavour of fustian melodrama, and many of the lines can seem ridiculous unless they are delivered with consummate power and tact. Also they prolong the play considerably. On the other hand they are of considerable value to carry the somewhat monotonous tone and style of the main part of the text, and they serve to make a complete break between two of the great scenes of Richard's grief (the Deposition scene and the Farewell to the Queen), and the final soliloquy and the fight in the prison, which gain considerably in their effect if Richard has been absent from the stage for two scenes beforehand. Also of course they contain the famous description of Richard's entry into London in the power of the triumphant Bolingbroke, and the first references to the wildness of the young Prince Hal.

The opening of the play, though dramatically effective in reading, presents considerable difficulties on the stage. The implications of the king's complicity in the murder of Gloucester (which has taken place before the action begins) are hard to convey to a modern audience less familiar with history than the Elizabethans, who seem to have had a curiously detailed knowledge of (and interest in) the intricate topical events of the times chronicled by Holinshed and so faithfully related in the Histories of Shakespeare. The quarrel between Mowbray and Bolingbroke, which begins the first scene in such a dramatic and effective way, is repeated (only with more formality) in the tournament scene, with only the short duologue between the Duchess of Gloucester and Gaunt to separate them. This intermediate scene is equally difficult, since it refers almost exclusively to the murder of Gloucester; the duchess appears without any introduction and has no further part in the action. Yet we must remember her when her death is announced several scenes later. In all three scenes the action is formal and static, and it is difficult to sustain the necessary progression. The king cannot be more than an enigmatic protagonist. His motives seem to be deliberately understated by Shakespeare, while the sub- sidiary characters of his queen and favourites are barely indicated, except in their flattering, subservient, attitude towards him. Ceremony and fine speaking must combine to hold the interest of the audience here. Mowbray's fine tenor speeches, Bolingbroke's strong blustering ones, and the deep bass warning tones of Gaunt; these contrasted voices must hold the early scenes together by using all the musical variety of which the actors are capable.

Unfortunately, throughout the play, the verse seems to be too evenly distributed, and often with more music than sense of character. Everyone, whether gardeners, exquisites, or tough realistic nobles, speaks in images, parentheses, and elaborate similes, and though this Elizabethan richness of metaphor gives, in reading, a beautiful, tapes- tried, and somewhat Gothic effect (like an illuminated missal or a Book of Hours), the artificial style tends to become somewhat in- digestible on the stage, and stands between an audience and their desire to get on more intimate terms with the characters and their situations. It is therefore especially important to have actors for the chief parts who are strongly contrasted individual types as well as being skilled speakers of verse.

The more simply the characters are played, on broad, conventional (but not too melodramatic) lines, the scenes appearing to flow smoothly and swiftly with the correct stress and phrasing (but without too much elaboration, either of action, grouping or pausing), the better will the beauty of the general pattern emerge and the interest of the audience be sustained. Then, and not before, the actor of Richard may be allowed, like the solo violin in an orchestra, to take certain liberties with his cadenzas, developing their intricacies with legitimate effect in an almost unlimited variety of pace and detail, in contrast to the plodding ground bass of Bolingbroke, Northumberland, and the nobles.

Many of the shorter scenes in the play can produce an exquisite effect, especially the little duologue between the Welsh captain and Salisbury (which foreshadows the delicate yet sinister effect of the murderers waiting for Banquo on the lonely heath in *Macbeth*) and the famous episode of the queen and the gardeners at Langley. These passages should have a romantic, simple charm in contrast to the formality of the great scenes which precede and follow them.

There are several difficult links, such as the scene of Ross, Willoughby and Northumberland after Gaunt's death, and the dialogue of the three favourites after they hear of Bolingbroke's return, which seem almost like choral exercises for three voices. These scenes should, perhaps, be directed expressly from this point of view rather than as dramatic scenes of character. The quarrel of the peers, too, before the entrance of Richard in the Deposition scene, is difficult to stage without a dangerous risk of becoming ridiculous (the throwing down and picking up of gloves and so on), and it is advisable to make some discreet cuts to avoid bathos both here and in the Aumerle conspiracy scenes, if it is decided to include them. The character of York, used by Shakespeare as a kind of wavering chorus throughout the play, touching yet sometimes ridiculous, can be of great value to the scenes in which he appears, if the actor and director can contrive between them a tactful compromise between comedy and tragedy. To make him a purely farcical character (as has sometimes been attempted) is bad for the play and quite opposed, it seems to me, to the intention of the dramatist. The women in the cast are very shadowily drawn, and they are difficult parts for actresses to clothe with flesh and blood, though vocally and pictorially they can make a considerable effect – the two duchesses old and proud, the little queen so young and helpless – in the somewhat conventional episodes allotted to them.

Most of the characters, except Gaunt, York, Carlisle and the two duchesses, seem to be young and full of life, and there should be something of the same impetuous brilliance that is so wonderfully vivid in *Romeo and Juliet* in the way they glitter and struggle and hurl themselves towards their fates.

This is a play, above all, which must in performance be melodious, well orchestrated, youthful, headlong, violent, and vivid. It must not be heavy or dragging, and the actors must know where they are going in their long speeches. Every advantage must be taken of the contrast of scene with scene, and all must be done with a poignant appreciation of detail and variety both as regards lyric and tragic values. At first we must see the lightness of Richard's character, his fatal, obstinate frivolity, unchecked by the baleful warnings and implacable nobility of Gaunt. Then, as we reach the heart of the play, the king's own heart and soul are gradually revealed to us by Shakespeare, as he is forced, by the realization of his favourites' death and the desertion of his countrymen, to abandon his contemplative poetic fantasies, and turns to face the brutal reality of Northumberland's hostility and the grim determination of the ruthless Bolingbroke; though, with the later plays in mind, Shakespeare allows the usurper a certain fairness and sense of guilt in his triumph, making him show hesitation and some apparent distaste in his own achievement and the final calamity of Richard's murder.

The great problem, it seems to me, is to achieve a straightforward musical rendering of the verse, and yet to combine this with a sense of exciting actuality in the action. The events in the play must really seem to happen, and yet, as in an opera, the music of the lines must be neither slurred, dragged nor unduly hurried. In short, the technical brilliance of the poetic writing must be correctly orchestrated and executed, with the added colour of character and personality, while at the same time the shock of the actual events presented must appear to be spontaneous and realistically convincing. The poetry must be welded imperceptibly to the dramatic action to a point when the audience will accept the two together – and, if successfully managed, the two styles of comment should support one another to create a complete harmony of effect.

My own Acquaintance with the Play

I first played *Richard the Second* in a production at the Old Vic in 1929 with scenery by Paul Smythe, directed by Harcourt Williams; Donald Wolfit played Mowbray and the Bishop of Carlisle, Gyles Isham Bolingbroke, Martita Hunt the queen.

I directed the play for the first time for the O.U.D.S. at Oxford in 1936, in collaboration with Glen Byam Shaw. On this occasion David King Wood played Richard, and Vivien Leigh the queen. The Duchess of Gloucester was played by Florence Kahn (Mrs Max Beerbohm), Bolingbroke by John Witty, and Mowbray by Peter Watling, who has since written several successful plays. Michael Denison played Scroop.

This production was, to my mind, more satisfactory than either of

Eric Porter
as Bolingbroke.

Richard II 1952

the other two I have attempted since. Motley designed for me a permanent setting, a Gothic structure consisting of a skeleton screen flanked by two stairways, with a gallery above, on the Elizabethan principle of an upper and lower stage. The balcony was used formally, for the walls of Flint Castle and one or two other scenes, to vary the pictorial action. The grouping was foursquare and symmetrical, and the throne, placed dead centre under the back wall, was used by Richard in the Opening scene, and later by Bolingbroke, in the Deposition scene, with no variation. The prison was indicated merely by a ring of light surrounded by darkness, and the king fought his way out, ran up the steps at the side to escape his assailants, and was finally killed by Exton, who stood, barring his flight, at the top of the staircase. He fell down headlong to the lower stage, where the knights covered his body with a cloak, and Bolingbroke and his court were then discovered on the balcony above to speak the closing speeches of the play. The exterior scenes of country and garden required some imagination on the part of the audience, but the swift passing of the action, without scenic changes, save for the lighting, seemed to suit the flow of the verse and the contrasting effects of the action far better than in my two later productions, when I inadvisedly elaborated my ideas to attempt more complex changes of settings, and only succeeded in slowing down the tempo of the play and so destroying much of its continuity and formal splendours.

In 1937 I directed the play again at the Queen's Theatre, London. I played Richard, Michael Redgrave was Bolingbroke, Peggy Ashcroft the queen, Leon Quartermaine John of Gaunt. Motley again designed the decor.

In 1953 I directed the play at the Lyric Hammersmith. On this occasion Paul Scofield played Richard, Eric Porter was Bolingbroke, Herbert Lomas Gaunt, Joy Parker the queen. Later in the same year I took the same production to South Africa, playing Richard myself, with Noel Willman as Bolingbroke and Paul Daneman as Mowbray and Carlisle. We acted the play at the Rhodes Centenary Festival at Bulawayo, Rhodesia.

1958

Romeo and Juliet

NEVILL COGHILL

Whoever can take pleasure in a poetry as strong as it is sweet, or be touched to pity by the romantic story of a fatal love, will long since have made the discovery of *Romeo and Juliet* and will think all introduction a superfluity, if not an impertinence.

It is indeed a play that conceals no difficult problems in philosophy or interpretation. Every character is unmistakable, not one conceals an enigma, and the plot is of a perfect simplicity. The moods and intuitions it evokes, the values it assumes in spiritual things are as manifest as they are acceptable to every uncorrupted nature; for the play celebrates the holiness of the heart's affections and the magic of being young and leagued in love against the world, against the stars in their courses.

As for its poetry of language, it is dangerous and perhaps useless to speak of anything so immediately apparent to every reader, especially since in writing of it a critic is beset by lyrical impulses that flow from the play itself, induced currents infinitely feeble in comparison with their source. Many writers have fallen back upon direct quotation from their favourite passages, unable to commend or expound it better than by itself, as if a rain-maker were forced to wait for real rain before he could begin on his sympathetic magic. The best among them can only coin a phrase or two; even Coleridge, himself a great poet and a great critic, can say little more of it than

'It is a spring day, gusty and beautiful in the morn, and closing like an April evening with the song of the nightingale.'

This is indeed an evocative phrase, but how does it help our understanding? The play instantly and of itself creates all the moods necessary to its comprehension, and children no older than Juliet was can be fully moved by it and can act it movingly.

If it is easy to experience as a poem, it is also easy to see how it should be presented as a play. There never can be any doubt how a scene should be taken, and it can only fail in beauty by some gross and wilful perversity in production, crass vulgarity or mere incompetence.

For those that play the lovers and other persons of rank in the play it is true that an unaffected aristocracy of voice and bearing are needed, and that noble simplicity is not always easy to find, nor are nurses common that have a genius equal to that of the part of the Nurse, but if it be difficult sometimes to cast the play it easy to think how it should be cast. A producer is likely to find more to puzzle him in purely technical problems such as the building of a balcony, the contrivance of a duel, the design of a tomb or the harmonies of a lighting-plot.

Even if there may have been at some time a doubt how to present the play or some part of it, all such doubts have been for ever laid in the masterly exposition made by the late Harley Granville Barker in the second series of his *Prefaces to Shakespeare*, published in 1930. There is nothing more that need be said on that aspect of the play.

The problems it has offered to scholarship have also been solved with some finality, and it may be thought in place to repeat here the chief results of long researches in connection with the sources of the story and the circumstances of its first appearance as a published play. I have taken the account which follows on these matters from the work of Edward Dowden and Sir Edmund Chambers who are in main agreement as they are of first authority.*

The story came from Italy. One element in it, that of avoiding an unwished marriage by taking a death-counterfeiting drug, has been traced even farther afield to a work called *Ephesiaca* by one Xenophon of Ephesus in the fourth century AD. But it was in the fifteenth century that the tale began to assume the form we know and to master the imagination of Europe. At least five Italian authors handled it between 1476, when it appeared in *Il Novellino* of Masuccio of Salerno, and 1554 when Matteo Bandello included it in his *Novelle*. A Frenchman, Pierre Boaistuau, then turned the Bandello version into French in his *Histoires Tragiques* of 1559, and this in turn was translated into English by William Painter and published in his *Palace of Pleasure* in 1565–7. Then, also from Boaistuau, another Englishman, Arthur Brooke, took the tale and rendered it into some three thousand lines of rather rumbustious, clog-footed verse in 1562; this poem was Shakespeare's immediate source, from which I quote a few lines as specimens of the raw materials of his first unquestioned masterpiece:

* *The Tragedy of Romeo and Juliet* edited by Edward Dowden. Arden Edition, 1900. *William Shakespeare* by E. K. Chambers, 1930.

And tell me who is he with vysor in his hand
That younder dooth in masking weede besyde the window stand.
His name is Romeus (said she) a Montegewe.

The style is reminiscent of John Gilpin, though 'more condoling' as Bottom the Weaver would have said.

And even at this day the tombe is to be seene;
So that among the monumentes that in Verona been,
There is no monument more worthy of the sight
Then is the tombe of Juliet and Romeus her knight.

Out of this rattle-trap romance, and perhaps out of the *Palace of Pleasure*, Shakespeare made his play.

The date at which he did so is not absolutely certain, but Dowden conjectures that it was in 1595 and Chambers concurs, though he is willing to extend it to the first half of 1596. There are more than stylistic or subjective reasons for this unanimity, for instance a ballad on the theme of Romeo and Juliet, evidently inspired by the play, was entered in Stationers' Register in August 1596.

Not long after its first production the pirates descended upon the play. There seems to have been a not uncommon practice of play-theft in the late sixteenth and early seventeenth centuries, effected by two principal means, namely the bribing of an actor to betray his part and as much as he could remember of other parts, and the use of a system of shorthand stenography during a performance. Thomas Heywood, actor and playwright, complained in 1608 of the treachery of actors who 'have used a double sale of their labours, first to the Stage, and after to the presse' and he adds that 'some of my plaies have (unknown to me, and without any of my direction) accidentally come into the Printers handes and therefore so corrupt and mangled (copied onely by the eare) that I have bene as unable to knowe them, as ashamde to challenge them'. Elsewhere he wrote:

Some by stenography drew
The plot: put it in print: (scarce one word trew:)

Within two years of its composition *Romeo and Juliet* was stolen by 'stenography' or actor's betrayal, or both, and published in mangled form. This was the First Quarto of 1597. Two years later a more authoritative text appeared and supplied some 775 lines missed by the stenographer. This, the Second Quarto of 1599, is the substantial basis of modern texts. The play was reprinted at least once and perhaps twice before it was issued in the First Folio of 1623. It was a popular piece.

In the preface to his edition of Shakespeare, Dr Johnson wrote of him:

'By what gradations of improvement he proceeded, is not easily known; for the chronology of his works is yet unsettled.'

Today, although no absolutely final settlement has been reached or seems possible for every play, there is a large measure of agreement as to the order in which Shakespeare wrote his works and in this essay I shall follow that established by Sir Edmund Chambers in my attempt to trace the 'gradations of improvement' in Shakespeare's art as a tragic writer, in which *Romeo and Juliet* marks a definable phase. It is the phase in which medieval and particularly Chaucerian traditions show themselves more strongly than any other, and when these are appreciated the special kind of art that gives form and quality to *Romeo and Juliet* lends a sharper pleasure to all that seems natural and spontaneous in it. And it is a joy to see a kinship between our first and our greatest poet.

Romeo and Juliet was Shakespeare's tenth play and third tragedy. So far as we may believe he had written the three parts of *Henry VI*, *The Comedy of Errors*, *Richard III*, *The Taming of the Shrew*, *Titus Andronicus*, *Two Gentlemen of Verona* and *Love's Labour's Lost*, if we follow the scholarship of Sir Edmund Chambers.

This zig-zag back and forth between comedy, history and tragedy was to continue throughout Shakespeare's life as a writer. It was not until the year 1595–6 that he produced an unchallenged masterpiece in each of these fields; it was the year of *Romeo and Juliet*, *Richard II* and *A Midsummer Night's Dream*. He had topped the first high crest of his career.

All these three plays owe something to the art of Chaucer, especially *Romeo and Juliet* in which a shaping medieval tradition is fundamental; whatever he may thereafter have added of his own or of the Renaissance he was then turning to an older civilization, not so much native as nationalized, which in other minds, such as that of Jonson, was already yielding to a new view of life, something more classical, more godless, more loveless, a view of life later to be crystallized in the philosophy of Hobbes.

That this is no guess about Shakespeare's affinities at that time may easily be seen from *A Midsummer Night's Dream*. The names in this play of Theseus, Hippolita and Philostrate are all taken from *The Knight's Tale* and, which is more important, the character of Theseus himself. It is one of a godlike nobleness and consideration for others, expressing itself in a wise and philosophic eloquence, with monuments of kindly humour. It is the embodiment in a play of all that Chaucer gave to his Knight and to Duke Theseus, the presiding hero of the Knight's story. It is also Shakespeare's first full study of the magnanimous man, the 'gentleman' of the English ideal which was forged for us by Chaucer, Malory, Spenser and Shakespeare out of feudal and chivalric notions, and securely based in Christianity.

Another telling touch, though less important, is the famous image of buckets in a well used by Chaucer to describe the moodiness of one of the lovers in the *Knight's Tale* and by Shakespeare for the sorrows of Richard II. It may also be that the burlesque treatment of Pyramus and Thisbe, *à la* Peter Quince, was suggested by Chaucer's more serious account of them in *The Legend of Good Women*, though Shakespeare may have got the notion from Ovid, as Chaucer did.

But it is in *Romeo and Juliet* that particular touches and pervasive influences are most strongly seen. One such seems to stem directly from *The Parliament of Fowls*. It is Mercutio who borrows it for his theory of dreams. These arise, says Chaucer, from our habitual occupations and desires:

> *The wery huntere, slepynge in his bed,*
> *To wode ayeyn his mynde goth anon;*
> *The juge dremeth how his plees been sped;*
> *The cartere dremeth how his cartes gon;*
> *The riche, of gold; the knyght fyght with his fon;*
> *The syke met he drynketh of the tonne;*
> *The lovere met he hath his lady wonne.**

Mercutio has the same notions, and uses like instances though he expresses them with more verve; oddly enough this famous speech appears in Folio as if it were in prose:

* The weary hunter sleeping in his bed, his mind turns again to the woods; the judge dreams how his pleas have prospered, the carter how his carts are going; the rich man dreams of gold, the knight of fighting with his foes; the sick man of drinking from the cask; the lover dreams that he has won his lady.

'& in this state she gallops night by night, through Louers braines: and then they dreame of Loue On Courtiers knees, that dreame on Cursies strait: ore Lawyers fingers, who strait dreamt on Fees, ore Ladies lips, who strait on kisses dreame ... Sometime she driueth ore a Souldiers necke, & then dreames he of cutting Forraine throats, of Breaches, Ambuscados, Spanish Blades ...'

The most pervasive influence however, one which gave Shakespeare the definable form of tragedy that we see in *Romeo and Juliet*, came from *Troilus and Criseyde*, a poem that later with help from Lydgate was to offer material for Shakespeare's *Troilus and Cressida*. As this influence is that of an artistic form, a shape partly discerned in and partly imposed on a given story by craftsmanship in obedience to a theory of composition, it is helpful first to assess the forms of tragedy used by Shakespeare before he turned to the Chaucerian model writing in *Romeo and Juliet*.

As I have said, he had already written two, *The Tragedy of King Richard III* (so it is headed in Folio) and *Titus Andronicus*. Considered as a tragedy *Richard III* may be thought somewhat amorphous. History does not lend itself readily to doctrines of form. In so far as it can be said to have an abstract shape it is the rise, triumph and dejection of a villain. It is in fact a tragedy to no one except Richard himself. Seen from this point of view it can be roughly fitted into the theory of tragedy outlined and illustrated by Chaucer's Monk, a theory taken from Boethius whom Chaucer had translated:

'Tragedye is to seyn a dite of a prosperite for a tyme, that endeth in wrecchidnesse.'

But *Richard III* is best appreciated not as an isolated play but as a last and most dreadful episode in the great expiation paid for the sin of Bolingbroke's usurpation and all that followed from it. It is in fact like an episode from a great miracle cycle, the episode of Anti-Christ before the Second Coming. Oddly enough, fortuitously no doubt, Richard's last speeches of defiance and despair echo the sentiments put in the mouth of Anti-Christ in the fourteenth-century Chester play of that name.

Richard III, if it be a tragedy, is a tragedy of terror not of pity and his defeat is, to an audience, a happy and holy issue out of all affliction and to be received with a kind of gloating joy from which compassion is expunged.

Titus Andronicus is also entirely concerned with horror. Indeed the horrors are so monstrous that I have often heard it said that it would be 'great fun' to produce, though I have never seen a production. The play has a better shape than history allowed to *Richard III*. It is the 'Revenge shape', ultimately to be that of *Hamlet* also; a succession of unnatural injuries inflicted, a tortuous plan formed to revenge them, an accomplishment of that revenge in the unrelenting spirit of an eye for an eye, and two if possible. Hideous as this may seem it embodies a kind of 'wild justice' as Bacon would have said and the play ends on a note of hope, somewhat cursory perhaps, at least in the Folio version. But Quarto gives no quarter:

> *Her life was beastlie and deuoide of pittie*
> *And being dead let birds on her take pittie.*

Folio alters these last lines and adds four more:

> *Her life was Beast-like, and deuoid of pitty,*
> *And being so, shall haue like want of pitty.*
> *See Iustice done on* Aaron *that damn'd Moore,*
> *From whom, our heauy happes had their beginning:*
> *Then afterwards, to Order well the State,*
> *That like Euents, may ne're it Ruinate.*

It is a long way from such stuff as this to *Romeo and Juliet*, and an even longer way to *Hamlet*. The pities are present in *Hamlet*, but they first appeared in *Romeo and Juliet* and it was from Chaucer that they came.

Troilus and Criseyde is a formal tragedy on the Boethian plan. The essence of this is the form already quoted, a fall into wretchedness after a transient happiness. The reason given as proper to tragedy for this fall is the operation of Fortune. She turns her wheel and we rise upon it to a fickle joy; she turns it still and we fall into some awaiting Hellmouth. Our fall has nothing to do with our deserts, for though Fortune may laugh to see pride humbled she is no less delighted to turn her wheel against the innocent. This was the shape of tragedy as Chaucer understood it when he came to write *Troilus and Criseyde*. He passed no judgement on his faithless heroine; it was the pity of it that struck him:

> Iwis, I wolde excuse hire yet for routhe.

Fortune, not Criseyde, is the villainess of Chaucer's poem. A fatal
destiny had marked the lovers out for separation and sorrow from the
start. There was nothing either of them could have done to escape it,
unless they had made their love known to the world, which by the rules
of love they were obeying was unthinkable. By the same rules it was
right that Criseyde should be of a shrinkingly feminine disposition,
and so when parted from her lover and protector Troilus, and sent
among the violent Greeks, her yielding to Diomedes was no less
inevitable than her separation from Troy. Hers was a predestinate
fall, and her character co-operated with her destiny. Such a nature in
such a situation can only submit to it, can only be pitied.

Juliet is a stronger character than Criseyde and her strength is
partly drawn from her conception of the holiness of the bond of love;
she is to take and takes the sacrament of marriage. Thus her love is
one with her will as well as with her wishes. Not she but her lover is
banished and it is then that she might have shown Criseyde's weakness
and yielded to the County Paris but for the deep sanctions that
support her love. The Nurse, that garrulous go-between and maker
of comedy, so loving, meaning so well and such a worldling, is the
female counterpart of Pandarus; and she tempts Juliet to the easy
solution of her troubles in much the same style of consolation as that
in which Pandarus tries to calm Troilus in a like predicament.
Criseyde is to leave Troy, but what of that? There are many other
girls to choose from:

> *And over al this, as thou wel woost thiselve,*
> *This town is ful of ladys al aboute;*
> *And, to my doom, fairer than swiche twelve*
> *As evere she was, shal I fynde in som route,*
> *Yee, on or two, withouten any doute.*
> *Forthi be glad, myn owen deere brother!*
> *If she be lost, we shal recovere an other.**

These arguments are no less repudiated by Troilus than are those
of the Nurse by Juliet:

---

* And besides all this as you know quite well, this town is full of ladies all
around, and in my opinion I shall find any number of them prettier than any
twelve such as she, certainly. One or two anyhow. And so be glad, my dear
brother! If she is lost we shall recover another.

JULIET *What saist thou? hast thou not a word of joy?*
        Some comfort Nurse.
NURSE   *Faith here it is,*
        Romeo is banished, and all the world to nothing,
        That he dares nere come backe to challenge you:
        Or if he do, it needs must be by stealth.
        Then since the case so stands as now it doth,
        I think it best you married with the Countie.
        O hee's a Louely Gentleman:
        Romeo's a dish-clout to him . . .
JULIET *Speakest thou from thy heart?*
NURSE   *And from my soule too,*
        Or else beshrew them both.
JULIET *Amen . . .*
        Auncient damnation, O most wicked fiend!
        Is it more sin to wish me thus forsworne,
        Or to dispraise my Lord . . .

Certainly Criseyde is the weaker of the two; one blow of fortune is
enough to bring her ruin about. But Romeo and Juliet are battered by
successive blows. It chances that her only love is sprung from her only
hate, it chances that Mercutio is killed by Tybalt when Romeo, with
the best intentions, comes between them, and Mercutio is hurt under
his arm, it chances that the Friar's letters to Romeo are not delivered,
it chances Romeo reaches the tomb a moment before Juliet awakens
from her drug, and takes his own life thinking her dead, it chances
that Juliet is left alone with her lover, his lips still warm, and there is
no one to stay her from stabbing herself.

Such seemingly predestinate calamities bring the catastrophe as
surely as the turn of Fortune's wheel. Rather than make a central
figure of a fabled Goddess as the authoress of all these woes, Shakespeare chose another image to embody the idea of a supernal will at
work in the destruction of his lovers. Instead of Fortune he made the
stars responsible, and this notion too he may have taken from Chaucer.

There is a stanza in the tale of the Man of Law, striking in itself and
still more so in this context:

Paraventure in thilke large book
Which that man clepe the hevene ywriten was
With sterres, whan that he his birthe took,

That he for love sholde han his deeth, allas !
For in the sterres, clerer than is glas,
Is writen, God woot, whoso koude it rede,
The deeth of every man, withouten drede. *

The stars are their enemy and there are moments when they seem to read a little of their fates in that large book. Romeo, for all Mercutio's jesting on their way to the Capulet festivities, has some premonition of doom:

> *for my mind misgiues,*
> *Some consequence yet hanging in the starres,*
> *Shall bitterly begin his fearefull date*
> *With this night's reuels, and expire the tearme*
> *Of a despised life clos'd in my brest:*
> *By some vile forfeit of vntimely death.*

The Chorus had told us at the beginning that they were star-crossed lovers, and the stars are used as a *leit-motif* of the inauspicious through the play, with Fortune as a synonym. Many are the phrases of foreboding used by the lovers and even by other speakers less conscious of fatality.

> *I would the foole were married to her graue*

says Lady Capulet when Juliet refuses the County Paris, little knowing how soon her wish was to be granted; and Juliet with a fuller intuition, as she sees Romeo descend the rope ladder from their wedding-chamber window, cries

> *O God ! I haue an ill Diuining soule,*
> *Me thinkes I see thee now, thou art so lowe,*
> *As one dead in the bottome of a Tombe.*

And when Romeo is told of her supposed death, he recognizes his true enemies:

> *Is it euen so ?*
> *Then I defie you Starres.*

* Peradventure in that large book which people call the heavens it was written in stars at the time of his birth that he, alas, should have his death for love. For in the stars, more clearly than glass, it is written, God knows, could one but read it, the death of every man, never fear.

It is by an art such as this that the play is given its shapeliness. A thought-form governs the play, all that seems most natural is willed in harmony with what the middle ages thought the true nature of tragedy.

Troilus and Criseyde and *Romeo and Juliet* are the two perfect examples of this form. It is a form peculiarly suited to a story of unfortunate love, for love, of all our passions, seems to us the most manifestly predestined, the most pitiful in its crosses.

Shakespeare never used this form in its full simplicity again. Fate, Fortune and the stars were insufficient to account for every human suffering. Suffering is the theme of all tragedy and poets give it form according to their vision of its causes, of how it is to be endured, and of what if anything may be salved from the wreck. The cause imagined may be Destiny or the Gods, or it may be the wars of good and evil that surround a man or enter into him; or it may be a concatenation of these. Shakespeare always shows us them at work upon noble natures, so that we see the suffering deeply and richly endured. Death and waste are shown us at the end and yet our experience is not one of waste, hardly even of death, but of strengthening and hope. A Fortinbras or a Malcolm will set all to rights, will start with a clean slate. Lear dies a man redeemed, Othello kills himself to redress the balance of justice that his folly and passion have upset; the deaths of Romeo and Juliet heal a feud for ever. Hope and strength come to us with pity, and it is pity above all that is contained by the special tragic form in which *Romeo and Juliet* is cast; there is much pity in the many other forms of tragedy he was later to write; but it is here seen for the first time flowing from the fresh fountain of medieval vision;

Lo, pitee renneth soone in gentil herte.

1950

A Midsummer Night's Dream

RALPH RICHARDSON

The stage history of *A Midsummer Night's Dream* has been, in miniature, much the same as those of its more popular fellows in the Shakespeare canon – it has reflected the passing pageant of theatrical fancy. The text has been decimated to provide at least one opera, Oberon has been played by a succession of women, and the fairies have appeared in gold, in green, in red, as Romantic ballet dancers and as street urchins. But the play's inherent qualities have kept it consistently before the public. There are, of course, innumerable opportunities for scenic extravagance and ingenuity, opportunities of which every age has taken full advantage. Although it contains no great role, it does have a well balanced cast of characters excellently chosen for their variety, all of them amusing to watch and exciting to perform. But above all there runs through the play an atmosphere of enchantment and gaiety which unifies the diverse elements, the boisterous 'mechanicals', the comedy of mistaken identities, the touches of malevolence and the poetry, into one, timeless whole.

It is generally accepted that 'The Dream' was not originally written for the public, but as a masque for a private celebration, and, to judge from the events in the play itself, almost certainly for a wedding. It was then recast into its present form for public performance at the Globe, between 1598 and 1600. A most imaginative reconstruction of an early performance is the theme of *Moonlight at the Globe* by Ronald Watkins. As he shows, the actual scenic resources would have been slight but extremely well adapted to the quick pace of the action and to the broad daylight in which the play was given. Both these factors have been completely lacking in the playhouses which have existed since the Restoration, where scenery has tended to slow down the action and swamp the poetry.

Undoubtedly at its first, private, performance, *A Midsummer Night's Dream* would have had that lavish decoration that the Elizabethans were wont to give their masques, and the provision for this did not disappear from the text when the play was translated to the public stage. It is not surprising, then, that although the actual play did not please at the Restoration, it did provide a quarry for the anonymous librettist of *The Fairy Queen*, an opera-spectacle by Purcell. The pedestrian level of the adaptation and its complete negation of the original poetry is saved by Purcell's vividly pictorial music. Although no longer Shakespeare, *The Fairy Queen* is still enjoyable entertainment, as those who saw its revival at Covent Garden in 1946 can testify.

During the eighteenth century *A Midsummer Night's Dream* appeared irregularly, but with the middle of the nineteenth it entered a new phase in its history. An early female Oberon, Madame Vestris, an actress of considerable personality, at Covent Garden, and Samuel Phelps at Sadlers Wells, re-established 'The Dream' in public favour. From then on, for some sixty years, most of the actors and actresses of note appeared in it. Ellen Terry played Puck in 1856; Phelps, George Weir, Arthur Bourchier, Oscar Asche, Nigel Playfair, Beerbohm Tree, all played Bottom; Lysander was played by such matinée idols as Lewis Waller, Basil Gill, Forbes Robertson; and Hermia and Helena by Ada Rehan, Lilah Macarthy, Laura Cowie, Mrs Benson and Julia Nielson.

The productions in which they all appeared were models of historical accuracy and realism, for this was the order of the day. The British Museum was ransacked for designs to deck Theseus' palace, and A Wood near Athens became the butt of all those who disliked their stage forests full of real rabbits, real bracken and real waterfalls. A revolution was due. It came in 1914, a year that saw the disintegration of so much that had been accepted for so long. Harley Granville Barker, whose productions, in the words of a contemporary critic, 'had already swept the stage of some of its close clinging cobwebs of convention', turned his attention to 'The Dream'. *The Daily Telegraph* describes 'the apron stage, the decorative curtains for a background and only two set scenes . . . The Palace of Theseus is a place of massive white columns with black decorations and a background of star-spangled black yielding to reddish-purple.' The Wood seems also to have been of a striking simplicity and to have set the pattern for most of the subsequent revivals.

My own first meeting with 'The Dream' was when I studied it with my schoolmaster in the manner prescribed for the examination.

Everything about the play was anatomized – the internal and external evidence, the strong and weak endings, the sources of the plot – a dry-as-bones examination with never one word to let in the idea that the work had been written first and foremost as a work of entertainment, of delight and of laughter. All that was a strict taboo, something quite unheard of, but as far as I was concerned, this attempted desecration was completely unsuccessful.

It has always seemed to me that from every point of view *A Midsummer Night's Dream* is a perfect play, and I feel that Pepys' dislike of it is one of the oddest curiosities of literature.

It is certainly perfect from the actor's point of view. Every single part in it is a joy to play, and an actor, in his desire to play all of them, might well echo the similar sentiments of Bully Bottom.

There are no difficulties with any of them, no awkwardness to overcome, no unaccounted links missing, no shady corners of obscurity – the only difficulty lies in drawing them to perfection.

But even though I have never seen a bad production of the play, I have equally never seen a perfect one. The demand for a flawless string of matched pearls is all but impossible to realize.

When I myself study a part in Shakespeare, I try to find out all I can about it, reading the text in as many forms as possible, including a photostat that I possess of the first *Folio*. But I am always conscious of the fact that Shakespeare – in the printed page or acted on the stage – must always come to us at second hand, and that the real naked body of the play will never be embraced by man in this world; the incarnation existed only once in time – in the mind of the author William.

I have had the happiness of essaying many parts in this play, and I have played Bottom in many productions. Once, to my shame, when I was nineteen, I fell asleep in the part, while waiting out of sight behind the fairy bank after the ass's head had been taken off. I also played the part in Tyrone Guthrie's production at the Old Vic in 1937. The whole production was a deliberate harking back to the Victorians, with Mendelssohn's music, Taglioni fairies, and the spirit of 'tuppence coloured' pervading everywhere. It was produced at Christmas-time in that pantomime atmosphere of magic and high spirits which has made this one of the best loved of all Shakespeare's plays.

1957

The Merchant of Venice

JULIA TREVELYAN OMAN

I would like to describe how a designer, a practitioner in the theatre, approaches the task of creating the visual aspects of a production. I hope that this outline will both help to introduce a well-loved comedy and also preserve a record of the designer's share in a successful production. It is seldom realized that a designer will start work on a production almost simultaneously with the director accepting a commitment. The gestation period of the visual side is ignited by the first mention of the play, the period, the participants and the resources, which may be casually given by 'phone, on passing in the street or at a formal summoned meeting in a production office. The designer's past experience and mental visual store of images cascade forth spontaneously with the director's request for co-operation and creation during the following months and must immediately be controlled in order to accommodate the immediate requirements of the direction; rarely does the first impact relate to the final production. Too often a designer is stimulated only to be crushed by a director's unconsolidated ideas, which prove to be without chance of backing; by experience the designer learns to assess the sincerity and security of the approach, recognizing it from the mere whim of a director requiring a designer's sincere flow of ideas which he can use as a thinking base to stimulate his own imagination from which a scheme is presented to a management.

13 May 1969 brought a telephone call from Jonathan Miller with the announcement that he had been asked to direct *The Merchant of Venice* for the National Theatre and he wished that I should design the sets and costumes, a request that ended with a consolidating of the offer by saying that my agent could contact the Administration and discuss terms for the contract. Having three years before spent an extraordinary and stimulating five months working with Jonathan Miller on the film for BBC Television of *Alice in Wonderland* I had no compunctions as to our work compatibility and accepted, as the

"THE MERCHANT OF VENICE"
SHYLOCK

Julia Trevelyan Oman
1970

dates for drawings and production rehearsals worked in satisfactorily with my other commitments.

Simultaneously, with the first mention of the play, the director stated that he wished the scene set during the 1890s and to place particular emphasis on the Jewish banking scene at that period. I commented that I would be far happier if the setting was in the 1880s; only the previous year I had designed *The Enigma Variations* for the Royal Ballet which was set in the 1890s and I prefer to research a new decade for each production. Fortunately either period suited the scene so the 1880s gave their style to the production.

My immediate impulse when commencing work is the study of the original play or opera and to obtain the discs or tapes of past productions, when I listen and relisten till my subconscious accepts the rhythm and timing, and the sense becomes stronger and stronger. Study with the spoken word from an early stage production is an enormous aid for a designer; the recognition of the duration of a sentence or speech will enable an imagined timing of movement by the director, or a conceived action by an actor within an area, which will not make inordinate demands upon him. Often I will pace an area while playing a tape to ascertain the actor's ability to move within the designed space on the stage. Certainly the book will be to hand from the start. My elegant gold-edged India paper complete edition of Shakespeare only surfaces till I can make an immediate purchase of a cheap paperback to work on. The most satisfactory editions of Shakespeare to work with, from a designer's point of view, are the red covered Cambridge University Press volumes, with their clear print and with ample margins at the top and sides of the page for the inevitable notes on sets, properties and costumes which pepper a designer's constantly pocket-carried copy.

Recalling my design progress on this or any other production is greatly facilitated by the copious notes of appointments I make in my diaries and the daily aide-memoire, and trivia relating to the work on hand made in my 'black books': hard backed notebooks which travel everywhere in my handbag and now run to a dozen or so volumes each with dated entries for work or telephone conversations or budgets – most essential records for smooth running work.

During the last week of July 1969 my film commitment finished, my next few months' work could be reviewed and time would now permit research for *The Merchant of Venice*. I drove to north London to spend an hour talking to Jonathan Miller to discover any particular brief he held for the designer; this was our second conversation and first meeting on the production. On the setting his only concern was for swift movement from locale to locale with no heavy scene changes and no dropping of the front of house tabs; the use of the same backgrounds redressed during the action with different properties to identify the change of time and location. Strangely enough we both simultaneously suggested the same book of photographs as an atmosphere bible and period look for the costumes, *Un Fotografo Fin de Siècle* by Primoli, an Italian book which had been obtainable in London only during the last year; photographs of Venice and Rome during the last two decades of the nineteenth century arresting for their domestic composition during a period of rigidly formal behaviour in the face of the recording camera; the eighteen-eighties equivalent of the 'snap', remarkably honest with flat unatmospheric lighting.

The designer's brief held acquaintance with the staff of the National Theatre, and knowledge of the available resources for the production had to be considered. This was the first invitation I had received to work at the Old Vic and though I had known the front of house from Gallery to Stalls since a shilling-seated, queue-standing schoolchild, I had never stood upon the stage and considered the practicalities of a production for that house. Knowledge of the Royal Opera House and the cramped conditions backstage prevented my instant collapse when taken by the General Manager to meet the production management of the theatre and view the scene for my future labours. Only too apparent was the truth that my scenery must be simple and any setting must be permanent with only property embellishments to indicate the change of time or locale. The lack of passage in the wings, of storage behind the stage and complications of running a new production smoothly into a repertory were only too apparent and chorused by all from the General Manager to lowest scenehand.

The National Theatre did not consider it necessary for a designer to have first-hand knowledge of a location being used in a realistic production, as they considered books on Venice could be used from libraries in London to provide adequate information. This opinion I felt impossible to agree with. Mid-August 1969 took me, flight paid, to Milan for meetings with an Italian director to discuss a proposed production.

While in Italy I extended my visit, taking the train from Milan to Venice. The National Theatre, however, generously gave me a cheque to cover the train journey, though the expenses came not grudgingly from my own pocket as I realized one must support one's own procedure of idea development wherever one fails to find adequate support from a management. On this occasion, having sixteen years previously visited Venice, I personally knew the power of the architecture and atmosphere, the light and living conditions, which would relate to my design work: knowing a little 'is a dangerous thing' and sixteen years gap gave me intense uneasiness, a personal reacquaintance was essential; physically no book can give such an original conception as direct contact with an environment.

While in Milan, en route for Venice, I browsed in bookshops and combed the cards for reproductions or photographs of paintings of the late nineteenth century in Italy. The chance find of cards led to the acquaintance with little-known painters whose work, such as that of de Nittis or Signorini, reflected atmosphere and style of the period far more strongly than the work of greatly more recognized painters. The look of photographs, pulled from a pile of ill-assorted titles, subsequently proved as much a bible as Primoli for the production. Negri, totally unknown in England, photographed the country scene, the Gobo family at home, during the eighteen seventies; charm, with a total lack of sophistication, are respectfully recorded in a book of red sepia printed photographs. Without personal prowling such stimulating information never is uncovered.

With my camera constantly clicking I spent five days in Venice. Inevitably the Jewish ghetto and museum had to be studied. Situated off the Grand Canal in the area of the main railway terminus on the opposite bank, the heart of the ghetto is centred on an irregular cobbled square unusually bare and open to the sea and winds. The architecture is flat, lacking the excrescences so characteristic of Venice, the light is solid, not shafted or dappled, too, too undramatic to be utilized when the powers of selection are there to be used.

The assembly of ideas arrives through the continued recording of detail, at first somewhat indiscriminately; only through perseverance does the general concept arrive; the statement is seen through the repetition or uniqueness of an architectural comment. The camera must overshoot in order to record and return information when months later the production detail is being finally put onto paper and exact information must then be to hand, no time then to have lost or neglected to record at an early stage.

The backs of rough sheets of foolscap paper take the first vague flow of the architectural plan. The Venice of the National Theatre must relate to the dimensions of the stage and with tracing sheet upon tracing sheet layered together with sellotape and fixed over the scaled stage plan the metamorphosis develops, an appearance of structure to relate to the action. The early fluid thoughts on paper are totally unselfconscious, they are personal for the designer's eye alone, only after endless editing will they be shared with the director; by then though still plastic and subject to grand or minor change, the chrysalis is produced for comment.

With the *The Merchant of Venice* the two locations of Venice and Belmont had to be permanently set with only minor moves of properties or revolving of doors between scenes. Short scenes with casual conversation must mask preparations for serious deliberations and adequate acting area on the forestage to be constantly paraded must remain free of incumbrance. Action for the next scene must flow from a direction different from the former, a progress from prompt to off prompt, from up stage to down stage, a balanced and constantly well used arena.

Venice to the off prompt, left of the stage, Belmont to the prompt side, right of stage, definite locations, but action to flow upstage and across each during each scene – only the commencement and culmination to be in the specified setting. The central back of the stage must be common to both.

The pink brick Gothic element of Venice seemed alien to the 1880s scene, the grey stone and Renaissance detail with circular arch and swag decoration presented an atmosphere more congenially commercial, complementary to the costumes and credible with the text. More preferable the corrupted concept of Victorian Renaissance architectural detail, coarser and more florid in treatment, certainly more suitable for the scene. Now printed and always to hand, the innumerable photographs taken in Venice to confirm or reject a search for authentic atmosphere, texture, structure or scale.

Within the scaled model of the stage and proscenium, supplied by the National Theatre production department, rough elevated shapes of scrap card started consciously to show the major blocks from the thought on the scaled ground plan, working to a scale 1:24 metric.

Weight based card figures appear in the model prior to any architecture, if the scene is not correctly related to the human all sense of
conviction and credibility is impossible; without logical scale the
ultimate will never be achieved, where text and human action must
relate to their environment.

On prompt and off prompt two structural towered blocks develop
arched at ground level and with a fixed upstage wing angle, the central
downstage joint left free, with the arched flats to rotate and reveal the
scene within. The loggia to prompt located Belmont and to off prompt
Venice, closed as exterior opens as an interior setting. A ground level
on stage and over the loggia a balcony, a fully practical doorway to be
utilized for the arrival of Portia during the trial scene; a neutral background common to both scenes of action.

A peculiarity of the National Theatre's stage at this period was the
false proscenium constructed to remain in situ for all a season's
productions; this fixture held exits into the wings. As one wished the
audience's whole vision to be held in Venice, necessary masking in a
suitable architectural character had to be evolved; this took the form
of two openings framed as doors which would have led on the off
prompt to the Borsa and on the prompt to a church.

By mid-November the rough model having been approved by the
director, scaled architectural drawings were now started. The final
mounts of architectural reference were prepared and logically mounted
alongside a dyeline print of each piece of scenery. By giving the
construction workshops and scenic artists adequate reference to
enable them to produce a designer's requirements, a vast number of
drawings, photographs and colour samples must be assembled and
cross-referenced in order to make the statement on paper self-
explanatory when the designer is not available to be consulted. The
photographs show texture on surfaces, the style of stone work envisaged, rough greyed and unpainted wood, bleached by sun and rain;
porous brickwork with strange irregularities interlaced with crumbling
mortar; crazed and cracked stucco hanging skin-like from the walls;
these visual comments immediately speak to a sensitive and creative
craftsman who is endeavouring to interpret into paint and canvas
matter of a more substantial nature.

By early December the final model was completed. Dyeline
prints from the architectural drawings were mounted on stiff card
and assembled into model form. Working correctly to scale most

structural problems can be ironed out in model stage prior to expensive construction and time-consuming alterations at a date closer to the production. The model and set of architectural elevations and plans were then presented to the production office of the Theatre for them to check and correct any technical mistakes which they could find.

By running through the script and moving the action with card figures across the model, the flow of scene into scene developed from Venice to Belmont and back again. Each scene setting was marked on a separate plan and suggested properties were marked. With a simple permanent setting properties play a vital part for atmosphere and action and it is essential to consider them from the outset of set draughting as their scale relates to the space available on the set and larger requirements must be budgeted for cost and workshop labour.

By giving the period of 1880 to the production props had to be selected which were suitable for action and behaviour at this period. Giving an interesting location to the first scene was important; a café suggested itself, from reference and knowledge of atmosphere, one similar to Florians in the Piazza San Marco in Venice was evolved; elaborately painted wall panels were set into the loggia and white-clothed tables set to the foreground and interior. Waiters opened and closed the hinged arches of the loggia or raised the pigeon-shitted sunfaded blinds over each opening. Photographs of café scenes at this period were consulted for the correct shaped coffee pots, cups and the most characteristic carafe and glass of water always produced when coffee is served in Italy.

Inevitably Portia's loggia must for the casket and other scenes at Belmont have the style of a Victorian Drawing Room. The small area could only accommodate the minimum of props and these had to be selected with utmost consideration. A lace covered dressing table with necessary toilet accessories for the first scene to be replaced by a small sofa during the casket scene, a chair and the inevitable casket stand. The casket stand had to be firm, light and easily transportable; this important scene must be enacted in close proximity to the audience, and as no pre-setting would be possible the casket stand must be carried by Portia's servants to the acting area. The inspiration for the design came from a tall Victorian jardinière, where the flowerpots would have rested the caskets were placed. The stand, about six foot high overall, had a turned central stem of wood stained and polished as mahogany; the embellishment and decoration came from small brass roses fixed as ormolu under the trays and as a decorative finial at the summit of the stand; these were made with great skill in the property department of the theatre. The caskets were designed as Victorian imitations of Renaissance reliquaries suitably decorated for each different metal.

A vast list of small personal props were listed as the costume designs developed the characters and at a later period when rehearsals started. As one's knowledge grew of each individual their attributes became apparent and had to be catered for accordingly. Salerio and Solano, with their smart walking canes, Old Gobbo with his basket and chicken from the country, briefcases, documents and endless letters, all to look convincing and accurate for the period.

The trial scene, set as though in camera, required a vast table and ten chairs. The careful planning and the dividing of the table into sections for setting permitted this important and imposing prop to work within the script without diverting the audience's attention from the action; chairs were set swiftly by court officials and a menacing gas mantle hung overhead. Every movement in the script and every line had to be analysed and thought through as to its relation to the 1880s. When a pen was produced the correct steel nib and wooden holder were essential; the document must be blotted with a roller blotter and ruled with a circular baton. Endless research at the Victoria & Albert Museum and in the London Library produced the answers from which drawings and notes were made; the results were satisfying to the eye as the knowledge of their accuracy stood forth.

Once the scenery workshops have sufficient drawings to start construction of the set the attention is concentrated on the costume designs, research and selection of fabrics. While the designs for the set were in progress on the drawingboard thoughts began to develop to simplify the tenuous start of colour drawings of the characters. Prior to starting drawing, whenever possible I try to see the actors and photograph them; the print is then kept constantly in front of me while drawing and then mounted alongside the final design as an aid for the wardrobe. Working in this way enables the final drawing to resemble the artist and the designer does not conceive a creation totally unrelated to the physical appearance of the actor. This short meeting of designer and actor is enormously valuable as it gives an opportunity for peculiarities to be discussed, which might have been neglected and caused grievances at a more difficult period.

The vast pile of reference material which had accumulated during the past months was sorted through and placed in a file marked with the character's name. A huge heap of books with pages marked were taken to be xeroxed and relevant sheets were mounted for each design. Alongside each costume was placed a separate sheet showing picture references for any item of clothing which might help the cutter in the wardrobe.

The appearance of a cultivated and wealthy Jew during the late nineteenth century had been recorded by photographs of well known international banking families. Study of the clothes, features, watches and tiepins of the Sassoons and Rothschilds set in mind the ambience in which Shylock would have moved, for his associates in business would certainly have worn clothes similar to those well documented gentlemen. In order to get the cut correct of the standard frockcoat to be worn by Shylock a pattern had to be found in *The Tailor & Cutter* trade journal of 1880; the length of coat, the width of lapels and placing of buttons always denote a decade. The height of the silk top hat and the width of the brim were checked in a hatter's catalogue and the illustration xeroxed and given to the milliner to make the hat. A stiff high wing collar, a 'Bedford', the style's name learnt from an illustrated department store's catalogue, had a height of 2″ at the front and $1\frac{7}{8}$″ at the back; a compromise had to be made as the actor required a freer movement of the neck than this would have permitted. Lists were made of all the subsidiary parts of the costume which it was possible and cheaper to purchase; grey gloves, black socks, white shirt and gold cufflinks. The cravat was made of a black silk with grey stripe and the trousers cut from legal type black and white striped cloth. The costume for Tubal was treated in similar manner to Shylock's but cloth of a lesser quality was found and aged to show his standing, and a plain black cravat worn round the neck. To particularly notify Shylock's Jewish belief, he wore a Keepeh, the small skull cap; for the scene before his house a Tzitzit, the long cloth worn to go to the Synagogue, adapted in shape and doubled in length to give the freedom of movement required for the actor's action; the cloth was constantly returning to the wardrobe during rehearsals for minor adjustments as the production was developed.

The black frockcoat was also adopted for Antonio and Bassanio with trousers of different variants of black stripes. Solanio and Salerio wore, to contrast with the sombre business black, more casual suits seeming close to so many of the young Venetians photographed by Primoli and Negri. Salerio in a dark chestnut brown check tweed, seeming doubtless to an Italian to be in the style *al Inglese*, a look much admired at the turn of the century and considered most dashing. Solanio's costume was of herringboned black cloth with a slight surface texture, the jacket was high buttoned at the neck with a small collar and braided on the edges. The wardrobe of the National Theatre combed the London cloth merchants to produce endless sample pieces of tweed, facecloth, drill and twill for inspection; great care was taken to see the fabrics resembled those available during the 1880s. Hideous problems arrived in mid-January when no merchant in London could provide a light white wool with small grey stripe as required for the young lover Lorenzo: by chance I had to go to the Hamburg State Opera for talks and the wardrobe there were able to trace the desired cloth from a German supplier who obviously was well in advance that season of the English market.

Bassanio, apart from his formal frockcoat worn at the Trial, required two extra changes. The bold check used for his jacket worn at his first appearance was in keeping with the other young gentlemen, though far more attention was paid to the flattering cut stressing his elegance. By small details in cut, or maybe ageing of a fabric, so many small comments on a character can be pointed; a button missing, a worn elbow, a torn hem or frayed collar: with Bassanio all was immaculate, not a braid worn or shoe unpolished. The casual calculated look of the young Venetian was emphasized by his long scarf and tilt of his chestnut coloured bowler hat. At Belmont and for the casket scene Bassanio and Portia appeared as having recently returned from riding, he in immaculate light cream breeches and black jacket, she with a riding habit looking as an Impressionist painted Amazon; the sense of country reflected through the dress.

The aping of his master or of a hero could at a glance be detected in the dress of Launcelot Gobbo. Misunderstood and ill-fitting imitation of Bassanio's style, the jacket of a lesser tweed and visibly too tight, the trousers of the same colour but displaying too much sock – detail which aided the actor's interpretation. Old Gobbo, with failing eyesight, ragged rough hair and grizzled moustache, wore a sunbleached twill coat and well-aged trousers; in aspect a characteristic peasant from the background of a Negri photograph.

Portia's suitors, the Princes of Aragon and Morocco, required a considerable amount of research before the designs could be produced. The Prince of Aragon was presented as an Ambassador with a formal diplomatic dress with the sash of the order of Calatrava. Morocco, with full Negro features, wore a black frockcoat with gold embroidered front and scarlet sash as a Sultan.

Portia required more complex changes of costume and more elaborate detailing than Nerissa and Jessica. A wealthy lady with style and taste in dress. Most important of all was the foundation, the period silhouette; the correct corset and bustle worn with sufficient petti-coats, even the fractional differences within a decade are detectable in the development of the deportment dictated by lacing and boning. From corset and bustle patterns of the 1880s the wardrobe department made the foundations. These the actresses at a first fitting became familiar with and discovered their restrictions and the requirement of special movement and method of sitting. These garments were then worn constantly through rehearsal. Portia's first scene was played in a peignoir of pale coffee lace, light in weight and quick to change from into the formal silk for the first two suitors. This elaborate dress was of pale orange silk with a central panel of coffee-coloured lace over pleated satin; certainly the eye was drawn to Portia through colour and distinction of dress contrasting with Nerissa's modest fawns and less exaggerated cut of corset, and Jessica's simple modest muslin and demure flowered straw hat. As well as Portia's Amazon Habit which has previously been referred to, she wore a legal gown and cap for the Trial Scene with small gold rim spectacles.

The citizens of Venice were developed in a style reflected in the paintings of Fauretto, Signorini, Inganni and Serra, shawl shrouded peasant women with sun-bleached clothes, waiters, servants and carabinieri who peopled the set and moved props, drew a drape or pushed an arch into position.

Finally fittings finished, scenery constructed and painted, Venice and Belmont arrived on the stage. The first 'fit-up' is always on a Sunday afternoon and evening. Now the director physically feels the space created and can solve particular problems which have occurred during rehearsal. The speed with which it is essential scene must follow scene; the possibility of faster flowing action can now be practically timed. Having shown the Lighting Designer the model and described the effect of light required from scene to scene, now the first sight of Venice's atmosphere materializes. Light as natural as possible is required, when the quality of the scene painting is of a high standing, light off the flattage and onto the actors.

From lighting and scenic rehearsal to rehearsals with actors and an endless search to perfect the details of set, props and costume. Wigs are adjusted, make-up corrected and redeveloped until the final preview evenings and then to the First Night when the designer can no longer strive to perfect the production of so many months through research, drawing and direction.

1974

King John

STUART BURGE

Rarely, I suppose, in dramatic history have international politics been regarded with such an assured sense of the ridiculous as in Shakespeare's *King John*.

The lunatic carryings-on during the first half of the play – the extravagant claims on either side between France and England on the question of the succession – the arrogance and bullying leading to the discomfiture of each in turn before the walls of Angiers as France, Austria and England insult one another, fight a bloody and inconclusive battle with one another, and finally join forces in order to give Angiers the doubtful privilege of their occupation – the irony of Hubert's position as umpire in these schoolboy war games, followed by his sagacious and politic suggestion for an alliance by marriage – the mind-bending double talk of Pandulph, the Pope's envoy, as he blackmails the French king into once more disjoining the hands so recently and religiously conjoined with England – all are executed with a sense of farce which, when related to the tragedy of the human situation, can transcend all other dramatic forms, and provide rich and rewarding material for satire.

The satirical comment in the early part of the play is largely in the mouth of the Bastard, and a lesser poet, having created this brilliant character, might well have been content to have him remain a commentator, aloof from the action throughout. But, by having him embrace with such cynical enthusiasm the corrupt 'commodity, the bias of the world' against which he had railed with such devastating effect, the play is moved into a quite new dimension.

> *And why rail I on this Commodity ?*
> *But for because he hath not woo'd me yet;*
> *... Well, whiles I am a beggar, I will rail*
> *And say there is no sin but to be rich;*
> *And being rich, my virtue then shall be*
> *To say there is no vice but beggary.*

Since kings break faith upon commodity,
Gain, be my lord, for I will worship thee.
(II.1.587–98)

In the end, such cataclysmic unconcern for human life and happiness
as this 'commodity' implies must lead to tragedy, and Shakespeare's
attempt to mingle so many ingredients – satire, farce, tragedy and an
incomparable psychological observation – has rarely been so successful.
In our own time, writers like Wedekind or Brecht (in *The Caucasian
Chalk Circle*) have attempted it, but never with Shakespeare's unique
understanding of tragedy.

His apparent relish for the anarchy and outrageousness in the early
part of the play must, in the end, be sublimated to the requirements of
his humanity and sense of order; the satire is gradually transmuted by
the agony of Constance, the unbearable poignancy of Arthur's terror
and Hubert's remorse, the extraordinary death-scene of John the
anti-hero, and the Bastard's final appeal for order – an appeal which
has echoed down the centuries.

Shakespeare's Olympian view of politics in *King John*, combined
with a deep investigation into the complex character of the name part
and an apparent leap in style as the tragedy overtakes the satirical
opening, seems to confuse a number of critics. They feel obliged to
excuse the play's unusual structure on the grounds that it is based on
another historical play, *The Troublesome Reign of King John*, which is
twice its length and full of strangely Shakespearean echoes. But whatever the evidence as to that play's origins, and what there is seems to
be conflicting, it is dangerous to lean too heavily on it when attempting
a performance. Too often an audience, under the impression that it is
watching a straightforward history play told as it were from the point
of view of the establishment, finds it ill-structured and even boring.

The truth of the matter is that *King John* is a work of imagination
based on some traditions of history likely to be acceptable to protestant
Elizabethans, but written in a markedly different style to the three
parts of *Henry VI* or even to the later histories.

It calls for a highly theatrical presentation to match the emphatic
style of writing. A strong expressionistic design is needed to reinforce
and demonstrate the concept, for instance, that figures of the establishment may be objects of ridicule imprisoned within their own jingoistic
traditions or capable of the most macabre and criminal cynicism. Such

a designing style can be of immense help, too, in promoting the mood and clarifying the author's standpoint to a modern audience who, if faced with even the token trappings of authentic period costumes and set, may be misled into thinking in conventional historical terms of reference.

It needs bold effects on stage to match the mood of the first scene in Act II. Lines like Philip's

> *We'll lay before this town our royal bones,*
> *Wade to the market-place in Frenchmen's blood,*
> *But we will make it subject to this boy.*
>
> (II. 1. 41–3)

or John's

> *Then God forgive the sin of all those souls*
> *That to their everlasting residence,*
> *Before the dew of evening fall, shall fleet,*
> *In dreadful trial of our kingdom's king!*
>
> (II. 1. 283–6)

suggest the hint of megalomania that moved Lewis Carroll to such inspired extravagance in *Alice in Wonderland*.

In the production for which the designs in this edition were conceived, the rulers were presented as a royal flush of playing cards clearly defined in their own colours, with the Bastard in free and easy leather. By presenting them in this way the spirit of these early scenes was more easily caught and by reason of a convention so far removed from naturalism, all necessity for the realism of arms and armour was happily avoided. Moreover these trappings of autocratic power provided for the actors a feeling of rigid and blinkered tradition from which they emerged as their façades were eroded and their humanity revealed.

The turning point in the humanizing process comes with the sensational first scene of Act III, in which Pandulph, with his blistering attack on the French king, mercilessly destroys all hopes of a peaceful alliance. Constance, by supporting the Pope's envoy with such enthusiasm, out of ambition for her son, adds an edge of irony to the tragedy of her mind's derangement at the news of Arthur's loss in the next scene; but for the moment she is triumphant as the vacillating French king is finally forced to let go the hand of England –

CONSTANCE *O fair return of banish'd majesty !*
ELINOR *O foul revolt of French inconstancy !*
KING JOHN *France, thou shalt rue this hour within this hour.*
BASTARD *Old Time, the clock-setter, that bald sexton Time,*
  Is it as he will ? Well, then, France shall rue.

(III. 1. 321–5)

But the simplicity of Blanche's assessment of the situation speaks for all the victims of oligarchic ambition –

Whoever wins, on that side shall I lose;
Assured loss, before the match be play'd.

(III. 1. 335–6)

From here on it is a tragedy of victims, as not only the innocent, but also the arrogant originators of such damaging folly and devious mischief, are one by one divested of all that outward show of finery which for so long has been their protection – first Constance, then Arthur, and finally John, the account of whose fatal career remains, however, constantly laced with the most interesting and perceptive threads of irony and comedy.

This is dazzlingly shown in the scene of his second coronation before his clearly discontented barons, which begins –

Here once again we sit, once again crown'd,
And look'd upon, I hope, with cheerful eyes.

(IV. 2. 1–2)

and goes on first to observe the dizzy trajectory of his psychopathic behaviour as he reels under the news of each disaster – the barons' revolt, the invasion of the French, the death of Elinor, the forebodings of the mad prophet of Pomfret – then to display his terror that the barons should discover him to be the author of Arthur's supposed death, a terror which provokes his deranged attempt to shift the blame on to Hubert for the black deed which he himself had so specifically ordered – and ends with the paroxysms of delight and relief he exhibits when Hubert confesses to having failed to carry out his orders.

This is followed by the touching scene of Arthur's actual death, which provides a stimulating contrast of moods and creates a splendid foundation for the final act.

. . . vast confusion waits,

As doth a raven on a sick-fall'n beast,
The imminent decay of wrested pomp.
(IV. 3. 152–4)

But Act V must always present problems in performance. It is hard to
escape the impression that the author has felt obliged to include too
much historical incident and gratuitous information. Nevertheless,
Shakespeare's satirical sense never fails him and the act starts off with
John clutching at straws with yet another recoronation (for the third
time), this time at the hands of Pandulph, who takes charge of the
performance as 'holding of the Pope' his 'sovereign greatness and
authority', only to be told peremptorily by John in the next breath –

Now keep your holy word, go meet the French,
(V. 1. 4)

Within the next scene the power of the Pope is seen to be held in
complete contempt by both sides. The last we hear of Pandulph is an
impotent complaint,

The Dauphin is too wilful-opposite,
And will not temporize with my entreaties;
He flatly says, he'll not lay down his arms.
(V. 2. 124–6)

An economical but effective way of demolishing Popish pretensions in
the eyes of an Elizabethan audience, an audience which in the earlier
play, *The Troublesome Reign,* was subjected to many a troublesome
scene extolling the virtues of a Reformation in embryo and attacking
the evils of Popery.

But it is in the last scene of *King John* that the legend of history
provides the author once more with the kind of material that enables
him to capture the remarkable style of the first four acts. Although his
main preoccupation is the re-establishment of order, the scene is
realized in an extraordinary and haunting atmosphere. The bizarre
death by poisoning of a man responsible in his time for so much
villainy takes on overtones of tragedy when our anti-hero, with his
mind deranged in the last agony of mortality, sings himself to death.
His apprehensive son wonders at it –

. . .'Tis strange that death should sing.
I am the cygnet to this pale faint swan,

Who chants a doleful hymn to his own death,
And from the organ-pipe of frailty sings
His soul and body to their lasting rest.

(V. 7. 20–4)

But John finds his son's tears too bitter to provide the cooling comfort he begs to reprieve the hell within.

And none of you will bid the winter come
To thrust his icy fingers in my maw;
Nor let my kingdom's rivers take their course
Through my burn'd bosom; nor entreat the north
To make his bleak winds kiss my parched lips,
And comfort me with cold. I do not ask you much,
I beg cold comfort ...

(V. 7. 36–42)

Theatrical sensibility of this order, if it is truly interpreted, will transcend all possibility of melodrama or easy sensationalism at the end of a play in which the author has never spared his derision for all those who abuse the responsibility of power. Power and its misuse may be the theme of the play, just as the necessity for established order is its conclusion, but it is the examination of the human qualities of those he derides which inspires the poetic and theatrical imagination in a text which remains infinitely subtle and rewarding for interpretation today.

1973

King Henry IV Part 1

ROGER PLANCHON

I recommend you to skip the preface, leap (poetically) on to a horse, and set off in pursuit of those great feudal figures as they slaver with fury in a last fling before tipping over.

The Renaissance knew how to convince us that individuals were men formed on a grand scale, that the popes of Rome were top people and that the smallest petty king would swallow a murder or an incest for his breakfast. But in *Henry IV* there are no monsters, there is no Incarnate Evil; even the angels have withdrawn. The characters are men who are at once simpler and more complicated; Hotspur, for instance, in his dealings with Lady Percy, might lead us to think that they were complete misogynists. The ladies come off very badly. Nobody pays any attention to one of them; the gallic unintelligibilities of the other are not understood. The huge knights are well depicted. It is an extensive gallery; look at the old sorcerer in armour, Glendower. Time has not flaked the paintings. Read the play.

This is an historical chronicle where every detail lives. The stage gets breathing space; we move from the waxed paving stones of a throne room to the smears of stale vomit in the backyard of a brothel. That is no inconsiderable matter. The bourgeois drawing-rooms of our modern plays, with their psychological interior decorations, smell stuffy by comparison with this mad gallop from one castle to another across whole provinces in order to rush to the slaughter-house: the frantic and ceremonious duel of the final act.

Less stuffy than *Richard III* or *King John*, *Henry IV* is an enormous pleasure. Each of its characters juggles his words, gets drunk on them and is caught up in the action just as in the other histories; a kingdom is sold at auction, but with enjoyment and in a more undisciplined and, in fact, much more intelligent form of construction.

Today the French are making the novel undergo a starvation cure, and they disapprove of this play for its variety of episodes. In the seventeenth century they stuffed the theatre into a corset. This unfortunate precedent prevents them from appreciating the pleasures of

a symphonic, baroque method of construction. I have been convinced
by certain English commentators that the French spirit has done great
damage here.

An ordinary play lasts three or four hours; here you have twice as
much. The action is sketched out upon a stage whose boards measure
ten metres by ten, and then deployed across the vastest imaginary
space. The whole span, as one can feel it with its rallentandos and its
dramatic accelerations, is confined in this trivial handful of hours of
clock-time. It is like those peasant banquets where you have to swallow two immense soups one after the other. Bad luck on the sensitive.
The outstanding pleasure of *Henry IV* lies in this joy, in this man-
handling of time and space, in this lack of restraint.

Theatrical dialogue is a *matière* in the sense in which the term is
used in modern painting. Squeezed out of the tube, it does not serve
to define the problem, but hardens to fix the nature and contours of
human beings caught up in a particular action. Conflict of ideas
abstracts the character; the course of the action and the *matière* of the
dialogue give him a solid base. Shakespeare makes use of all the verbal
ironmongery of the tournaments, of courtly love and of knightly
jousting. He turns it into honey by distilling the poetry from it. Clad
in the armour of this rhetoric the Falstaffs, Henrys and Hotspurs come
forward for a tournament in which words are pointed and break off
like lances. In order to enjoy the story you must like paddling in this
verbal compost, where part of our childhood comes back to us . . .
You must enjoy those long speeches which Shakespeare constructed
in poetic form in order to achieve greater opacity. The average speech
in the theatre develops an argument, but these long speeches of
Shakespeare's are arguments whose words radiate outwards and ex-
plode. I find myself appreciating the substantial difference between
unreeling and radiation, between the linear and the circular expression
of ideas.

The fact that my English is rudimentary will explain this naïve
approach, but I believe in it.

This immense rhetoric, this perfection of expression became actual
reality; this poetic flowering, the history of a nation. Historians may
produce precise details and corrections in order to discredit the version
of history given here, but they will never be able to convince us; they
would need to write with the freshness and fire of the young Percy.

So there is *Henry IV*, a poet's splendid meditation on history. Civil war has turned a kingdom into a pigsty where the pigs battle for provinces because they wish to know where legitimacy resides. Within his deepest self, inside his palace, Henry IV tries to hunt it down; it is parodied in the taverns; it is chased along the roads; on the battlefields armies, those splendid hounds of morality, clash noisily to establish by force of arms that power is in the hands of the usurper or that legitimacy will be able to beat down any rival.

From our evening papers we learn that in Berlin, in Formosa, in Saigon and so forth it is still a question of the legitimacy of power . . . Commentators have established the pattern from the chronicles: the usurper goes from treachery to treachery, seizes power and is then crushed so that morality can triumph. In *Henry IV* the usurper triumphs and this reversal of things makes morality seem somewhat ambiguous. It is well known how much commentators have written in order to reassert the play's morality, but the ambiguity of it is all the more striking for that.

Bolingbroke dreams of a crusade to a distant Jerusalem and, when he has to die in his bed, chooses a dim room of his palace which is named 'Jerusalem'. Is that divine will? Or an esoteric symbol? Or a final ironic point? . . . Your personal philosophy will not give you the key here, but it will allow you to write a thesis on the divine character of royal functions in Shakespeare's works or on the way in which his figures exploit this divinity in order to justify royalty. Henry IV, for instance, cannot undertake this crusade, since he is a usurper, or else he only dreamt of it in order to 'busy giddy minds with foreign quarrels'. His regrets, his doubts, his repentance in that case are only the psychological justifications of a workable policy, and accordingly without interest: his sincerity is only a measure of his degree of mystification. According to which thesis you write you can say either that it is important for the symbolism of this monarcho-religious morality that Henry should kill Hotspur, or else that Shakespeare has here condensed the historical transition from feudalism to monarchy, showing that the establishment of a centralizing monarchy depended on the disappearance of the great feudal figures. Don't we, in fact, see that the second revolt (the Archbishop of York's) is a parody of the first – I suggest that a quotation from Hegel should be introduced supporting the thesis that historical events happen twice, once as tragedy and the second time as farce – and don't we learn when the revolt has been crushed that the national war against the French is

about to follow ? (This is the place for various quotations about history
and its tricks: see how we have moved from a mystical crusade for
the 'liberation of Jerusalem' to a common-or-garden war.)

It has been said that Shakespeare was providing a moral solution to
a basically political problem, but in this case the traditional plot
(triumph of the usurper followed by his downfall) takes an unexpected
turning, so that it might be truer to say that Shakespeare solved the
moral problem by political means. This twist casts a debatable light on
a certain morality. Shakespeare stages its trial in such a way that we
needn't be bored by the speeches for and against, and are not asked to
condemn anybody. The monarchy is victorious and feudalism chokes
itself in its outdated attempts at revolt. The spectators are the jury;
they have nothing to judge but only to understand; they are spectators
because they must learn that they are also actors.

At this point I would like to introduce a parenthesis. The Théâtre
de la Cité production of the play has got a bad name. This is because
it made Henry kill Hotspur surrounded by his myrmidons like Achilles.

Undoubtedly we went farther than Shakespeare's stage directions
allowed, and we were wrong to do so. If we had to show the same thing
today we would produce it differently and try to be less clumsy. But it
is surprising that those who held this against us – spokesmen of
monarcho-religious morality – did not realize that in a sense this
scandal brought out the fact that the divine star placed upon Henry's
brow shone all the more brilliantly because he was not bothered by
sentiments such as honour or loyalty, and that this is a profound
expression of the theological principle which puts the divine on a
special plane and demands that it should be judged by special standards, and that this in turn is something which we for our part have
found scandalous. True, the papers said that our concern was naïvely
to show that the side which was best equipped morally and militarily
must win the war. But enough of this parenthesis, since it is a bit late
in the day to point out that the historical and ideological transition
from feudalism to monarchy was all the more interesting to us as not
only opening the way to both explanations but actually demanding
them.

This is where we should bring on the obese Falstaff, or rather
allow him to sprawl across the page. When accused he is his own
counsel and his plea is so brilliant as to turn him into the prosecutor-
general who finally overcomes the spirit of solemnity. But isn't he, too,

marvellously ambiguous? 'As an individual he is negativity itself; it is as a representative of the people that he is a source of liberation.' An amusing contradiction which should be followed down all its twists and turns.

When we held a public discussion on the play a Villeurbanne worker who was visiting the theatre for the first time in his life summed up the plot on the following lines: the boss's son has broken with his family, knocks about the night-clubs a bit, then joins the army to go and fight in Indo-China; he comes back and takes over the factory where, his dad having died, he proves a rather stricter master, not scrupling to have his own friends put in prison.

This is a good summary and quite as eloquent as the fifth act's monologue on honour. It is a shocking summary, just the kind Falstaff himself might have made. It expresses a refreshing popular sanity. Falstaff must rise again; our own sanity demands it. Those who take him off to the Fleet once more must be seen as a menace.

This epic also contains a secret inner meaning which ought to please the archaeologists of the psyche. Does it not show the long-drawn-out return of a son to his father? The old 'struggle' of which Kafka spoke? Another version of the old legend of the frustrated father? The father dreams of having a good son; what he sees is a debauched wreck and his double, a rebel whom he would like to have as a son. Here we have the son cut in two, divided as always into Good and Evil. Then the roles are reversed: the pseudo-evil (Henry) kills the pseudo-good (Hotspur) for the sake of the kingdom. Or, to put it another way, the King-Father finds an agent to kill the good son who has proved to be just as false as the real one; hence the brutality of this baptism of blood, the pivot of the play on which the plot balances.

> *Be bold to tell you that I am your son,*
> *When I will wear a garment all of blood,*
> *And stain my favours in a bloody mask,*
> *Which washed away shall scour my shame with it . . .*

But the father's murder is no less obvious. Does not the prince kill his father's double, Falstaff, by means of a prison sentence? This, surely, is the deeper meaning of the magnificent parody in Act II, scene 4.

These scenes, heavy as wagons in a Western rumbling into the sunset, contain no lesson. The play takes us by the hand and leads us along the paths of distraction, dream or meditation. Nor do these paths diverge. It remains for you to plot your journey and for me to put on my armour and justify this preface by a confidence: this is the play which gave me my first great pleasure in the theatre (it was only much later that it was included in the repertoire of the Théâtre de la Cité). In a sense it is true to say that it decided the course of my life.

My relations with it are not really clear-headed enough for an analytical foreword, so you must press on, turn two or three pages. I wish you the same first love.

1965

King Henry IV Part 2

BREWSTER MASON

Being asked to play Falstaff is a fascinating and exciting task and at the same time somewhat daunting.

So much has been written about him. Endless speculations about his cowardice, his 'ill-angel' relationship with Hal, 'Shakespeare's supreme comic genius', 'Lord of Misrule' and so on. Much of this writing is stimulating to the reader and often useful to the actor. But it is only by one's personal voyage of discovery in studying the play, working in the cut and thrust of rehearsals and finally in performance, that these academic opinions and speculations as to Shakespeare's intention can be tested.

I have had the great good fortune to perform Falstaff many times in a wide range of auditoriums and in various countries. This experience has proved to me the 'universality' of the man. But I jump ahead.

Before I first began to rehearse the part, I read a good cross-section of criticism and studied the text. All this gave me a sniff at the bone. Reminding myself that comedy is a serious business and that good comedy only emerges from a firm basis of character, I tried to find some basic traits in Sir John's character, some strong pegs on which to hang the comic hats. Obviously he eats and drinks hugely. But is he a coward? The apparently obvious proof of this is in the early scene on Gadshill in Part 1, but it is proof which does not really stand up when considered in the light of later scenes. Is he a liar? Again, apparently so. Witness the stream of untruths in the first Tavern scene. But I quickly came to see that there was danger here too, because the process of interpreting an earlier scene in the light of a later one to some extent short circuits Shakespeare's mastery in unfolding his plot and characters to the audience.

In striving for the reality of Sir John's character I was left with a mere catalogue of his actions. The more I tried, the more I seemed to be walking on quicksand. That Sir John never does! So it seemed a good idea to concentrate initially on the one huge reality. Falstaff's *bulk*. References to this occur throughout the plays, though always in

SIR JOHN FALSTAFF

PART 2.

ACT 3 Sc 2.

ACT 5 SC 1
SC 3

suede cloth.

silk (sateen?)

gilded one lap
fasten at
back with
straps &
buckles.

Padded + studded under sleeve
of hessian attached to leather
tunic.

Robert Haffenden 1970
Joan Bridge.

different form. 'Huge bombard of sack', 'hogshead', 'tun of man', 'huge hill of flesh', 'roasted Manning Tree ox with a pudding in his belly'.

I spied on fat men for weeks, observing their behaviour. Like all mankind, they were sometimes sad, sometimes funny; they all had their separate 'quirks and quiddities', but they did have certain traits in common. Most of them were graceful and splendidly balanced, excellent dancers; often witty, they loved to talk and, surprisingly, nearly all had an abundance of energy. Good humour and an air of contentment accompanied their enjoyments of the flesh-pots. In short, they were companionable creatures. If these characteristics were true of these men who were but ordinarily fat, how much more would they be so of a man of Sir John's immensity? For, even more than most of Shakespeare's inventions, *he* is most certainly larger than life!

The padding was ordered. It was a start.

From the moment I began rehearsing 'in the flesh', as it were, and started to feel the size of the man, the most curious thing happened. An important Falstaff characteristic began to emerge – his self-awareness; and from this the obvious corollary – his self-possession. 'Thou see'st I have more flesh than another man, and therefore more frailty.' *Part One III 1*. And, when walking before his page, 'I do here walk before thee like a sow that hath o'erwhelmed all her litter but one!' *Part Two I 2*. It was one thing to say the lines, imagining the fat; it was quite another to say them with feeling! This self-awareness in Sir John contains, or so it seems to me, a certain astonishment at his own bulk, and it is one of the endearing things about him, and certainly the most enduring. The earliest example of this occurs in Part One, in the scene on Gadshill. The prince bids him: 'Peace ye fat-guts! lie down; lay thine ear close to the ground, and list if thou cans't hear the tread of travellers.' To which Falstaff replies: 'Have you any levers to lift me up again, being down?'

It is a funny line, however one says it; but I discovered that if it is delivered with a sort of wide-eyed incredulity it is funnier. Later, following through the idea of Falstaff's surprise at his own bulk, I modified it further, adding an accusing note that Hal didn't realize the gravity of his suggestion. But by then it was not a conscious modification, it was a natural one that emerged in performance. A good laugh became a rich one. It is a small proof, if any be needed, of Shakespeare's genius in creating true depths of character. But the depths have to be plumbed.

As the rehearsals continued I began to realize the need to 'control' the part. Although I felt secure at base one of his character, he is so mercurial that I had to watch him all the time.

Cheap laughs are usually easy to get but often diminish character. Good laughter from truthful playing lingers in the air and increases the pleasure of the whole play as an 'after taste'. This was early brought home to me when tackling the Gadshill scene, which is difficult to control because the incidents there can come perilously near to farce. And they come nearest to it when Falstaff runs away:

> PRINCE   ... *Falstaff sweats to death,*
> *And lards the lean earth as he walks along:*
> *Were't not for laughing, I should pity him.*
> POINS   *How the rogue roar'd!*
> *Part One II 2 (119–122)*

Academic theories as to Falstaff's cowardice (although interesting) become idle speculation when it comes to performance. Yes, he runs away. But he is the *last* to run away and he does offer a blow or two. He is deserted. But the most helpful clue to me was to remember my banker – his self-possession. Running away underlines the point. Good generals and 'old soldiers' know when to retire. Now, as in a later scene, I found his 'discretion to be the better part of valour'. And I reminded myself that in Falstaff's time robbers were hung! So I tried a very fast retirement with honour, aiming a blow here and there and bellowing the while. Just how this is controlled has its importance when in the first Tavern scene, that follows hard upon, the audience is surprised by the beaming, wicked sincerity of 'By the Lord, I knew ye as well as he that made ye!'

Half way through rehearsals I felt that I had at least come to terms with Falstaff's bulk, but it was quickly obvious that *performing* that bulk was going to be a considerable physical strain. Shakespeare, as always considerate of his actors, has allowed for this and there are recovery scenes in which Falstaff does not appear. Even so, I often heaved like a stranded whale in the wings.

And I had to keep alert mentally because the antics of the old rogue are so bold and fast, and his changes of mood so mercurial. Sir John has the kinetic energy of a bear, one by turns slumberous, quick-witted, fast-moving yet suddenly immovable. These quick changes of mood are all aspects of his self-possession.

It is an interesting private point that during my acquaintance with Falstaff I was able to read faster, talk with more assurance and, although not a witty person by nature, on occasions could find a *bon mot*.

The much discussed father-son relationship between Falstaff and Hal is an absorbing one, although I found little to support it in the text. On the contrary, although they 'horse about' together, Falstaff always pays Hal the respect due to him as a prince and it seems a friendship based on that uncommon but not rare relationship that can exist between an old man and a young, that flourishes the more because they are not related by family. It is not stated explicitly, but in the sinews of the text it is clear, that Falstaff admires Hal. Of course he seeks preferment and protection from him, but there is a real affection behind the oft-reiterated 'sweet nag' and the fulsome 'comparative rascalist sweet young Prince'. Hal clearly enjoys Falstaff's company, admires his adroitness, his subtlety of language (which they both enjoy), his banter and zest for life. The first Tavern scene expresses this. Much of the high quality of the comedy stems from this special relationship between the two men. But the one thing that underlines and enriches all this is the tenuous thread by which Shakespeare leads the audience to accept the rejection of Falstaff by Hal. It starts early, at the end of *Part One I 2*, where Hal, musing alone, reveals:

> *I know you all, and will a while uphold*
> *The unyok'd humour of your idleness;*
> *Yet herein will I imitate the sun,*
> *Who doth permit the base contagious clouds*
> *To smother up his beauty from the world,*
> *That, when he please again to be himself,*
> *Being wanted, he may be more wonder'd at,*
> *By breaking through the foul and ugly mists*
> *Of vapours that did seem to strangle him.*
>
> *(217–225)*

and end in *Part Two V 5*:

FALSTAFF   *My king, my Jove! I speak to thee, my heart!*
PRINCE   *I know thee not, old man, fall to thy prayers;*
   How ill white hairs become a fool and jester!

> *(51–53)*

There are links along the way – all significant. Thus, towards the end of the first Tavern scene (*Part One II 4*) the hilarious mood changes:

FALSTAFF ... *whom means your grace ?*

PRINCE *That villanous abominable misleader of youth, Falstaff, that old white-bearded Satan.*

FALSTAFF *My lord, the man I know.*

PRINCE *I know thou dost.*

FALSTAFF *But to say I know more harm in him than in myself, were to say more than I know: that he is old (the more the pity) his white hairs do witness it, but that he is, saving your reverence, a whore-master, that I utterly deny: if sack and sugar be a fault, God help the wicked ! if to be old and merry be a sin, then many an old host that I know is damn'd: if to be fat be to be hated, then Pharaoh's lean kine are to be loved. No, my good lord; banish Peto, banish Bardolph, banish Poins; but for sweet Jack Falstaff, kind Jack Falstaff, true Jack Falstaff, valiant Jack Falstaff, and therefore more valiant, being, as he is, old Jack Falstaff, banish not him thy Harry's company, banish not him thy Harry's company, banish plump Jack, and banish all the world.*

PRINCE *I do, I will.*

And later in *Part Two II 4:*

PRINCE *By heaven, Poins, I feel me much to blame,*
So idly to profane the precious time;
When tempest of commotion, like the south,
Borne with black vapour, doth begin to melt,
And drop upon our bare unarmed heads;
Give me my sword and cloak: Falstaff, good night.

Time was he would have stayed. Delicate gear changes in playing are required here because both moments come on either side of high and noisy comedy.

The other major discovery was how essential it was almost to alienate the audience's sympathy with Falstaff in certain scenes in Part One and later in Part Two in order that they should more readily accept the justice of the rejection. The subtly sardonic, sometimes bitter, humour of Falstaff in his decline, of a melancholy yet defiantly optimistic, philosophical old man, also served to raise the comedy to a different level.

This deliberate alienation of the audience I found to be necessary, and I think it was Shakespeare's intention. It starts with the battle scenes at the end of Part One, and it is difficult to do because Falstaff is by then established as such a lovable old rogue that audiences have difficulty in accepting his baser qualities.

But it cannot be denied that his action in misusing the king's press (although he treats it with droll humour) is despicable. Equally, 'there's not three of my hundred and fifty left alive' is due to incompetence – and he knows it. In Part Two his defaming of Doll is foul and his treatment of Mistress Quickly unpleasant. I felt it important to stress the pettiness of his nature as displayed in the scene with the Lord Chief Justice. Here is a man he can't influence and with whom he is at a disadvantage and his wit is not so sharp.

If the many facets of his personality are presented clearly, as I tried to do, and one is able to control the man, then he emerges as the 'engine' of the play. He exercises this function not only by the things he does and says in the main action, nor even by his confidential asides in the soliloquies to the audience (when he so often comments on human behaviour, adding richness to our understanding of the other characters), but supremely as the catalyst who aids Hal to emerge as 'the mirror of all Christian Kings'. It may be a romantic idea, but perhaps Shakespeare had in mind that Hal's contact with the humanity of Falstaff helped him to an understanding of the people over whom he was to reign – that Falstaff 'mirrored mankind' to that end. But ultimately, perhaps, Hal had to reject him because he held that same opinion later to be expressed by Dr Johnson, 'It is certain that either wise bearing or ignorant carriage is caught, as men take diseases one of another; therefore let men take heed of their company'.

1975

King Henry V

MICHAEL CROFT

There is little in *Henry V* to comfort those serious students who look in their Shakespeare for some gritty layer of contemporary significance. Its subject is kingship, not in any constitutional sense but in the strong-arm terms of its time; its background is war and the glory of war, not the pity and horror of it. It takes for granted that patriotism is aggressive and nationalism militant and that on any day of the week one Englishman is worth several Frenchmen. What have these outworn attitudes to do with the depressed state of England today, the fallen giant, reeling from one domestic crisis to another, the poor relation of the European community, compelled to grovel to the French for entry to the Common Market, and latterly to beg on its knees to the once-despised Arabs for oil to keep the blood flowing through its industrial arteries?

Yet it is absurd to regard the play merely as a poetic piece of mediaeval jingoism. Shakespeare is never merely a piece of anything. Equally wrong to derogate Henry, as Hazlitt did, because he bears little resemblance to the ruthless real-life conqueror on whom Shakespeare based him. Wrong also, as some modern directors have done, to try to interpret the play in the light of their own radical or pacifist convictions, though Shakespeare dropped a strong hint in the night scene with Williams and Bates that he was well aware what the ordinary soldier thought about the honour of dying for king and country. His real concern is not with the ordinary soldier, except to show the mettle of which the English yeoman was made. His purpose is to praise the king, not to bury him. He sees Henry, as his contemporaries did, as the Star of England, and the play can be fairly appraised in dramatic terms only if one accepts Shakespeare's standpoint.

But the play is about other matters too, none the less real because of its murky politics and glorification of English conquest. It is about the English character (or, in the soldiering scenes, the British character), idealized, perhaps, but not to a point where it eludes recognition. It is about a concept of honour and chivalry, qualities which, however rare and futile they may seem in conditions of modern scientific warfare, are still held dear by many of those pitched helplessly into the battle-fronts, as the fighter pilots of the last war and the men who fought in the desert campaigns would testify. It is about the mystique of courage (English courage, it is true – the French come off pretty badly in this respect), the fighting courage which draws men together in an exultation of spirit till they are prepared to take on impossible odds; and there is an immediate analogy here between Henry's defiant 'Bid them achieve me and then sell my bones' and Churchill's brave assurance to the beleaguered British in 1940, 'We shall never surrender'.

Above all, the play abounds in passages of marvellous poetry, from the ringing rhetoric of the campaign speeches to the profundity of the monologue on ceremony, from the descriptive richness of the first four Choruses to Burgundy's sombre lament for a once fertile land laid waste by war and Exeter's moving elegy on the deaths of York and Suffolk.

I have not space in these pages to comment upon the play in detail but will merely offer some personal views about it and in particular about Henry himself, based upon three productions I have directed and many others I have seen over a period of twenty-five years.

It has become a critical fashion to write Henry off as a dull dog, something of a hypocrite, good for soldiering but not much else or, at the other extreme, a hero too good to be true. I suspect that some of this hostility springs from the fact that our dramatic critics, however sharp of intellect, do not themselves, by and large, possess the stuff of which heroism is made. It is difficult to envisage the members of the Critics' Circle even following Henry into the breach, still less leading the attack upon it.

There is also an historical and literary antipathy to Henry, dating back, I think, to Dr Johnson, who could not forgive him for his treatment of Falstaff, or for the calculating basis on which he chose to consort with the Falstaff crew. Johnson's charge of 'priggishness', on the strength of 'I know you all' early in *Henry IV*, *Part 1*, has clung to Henry through the ages, and despite the efforts of the great Shakespearean scholar, Dover Wilson, to obtain a broader view, the label still sticks.

For all that (and I think the case not proven), when we come to

Henry V we are dealing with the king resolute, not the prince way-ward. If he lacks something in human dimension, he still cuts a colour-ful figure; through the fire of the heroics, it is still possible to see the clouds of human doubt; behind the solemn robes of office, there is a jesting spirit waiting to break out; so that it is difficult to reconcile the Henry who exists on the printed page with the lifeless character which some critics have seen in him and, indeed, which some actors have made of him in performance.

True, he is introduced by the prelates in the first scene as some-thing between a spiritual saint and an intellectual superman but by the end of the scene it is impossible to take the clerics seriously. Indeed, I wonder if they are meant to be taken seriously at all. Henry's abrupt interruption, 'May I with right and conscience make this claim', while the Archbishop is meandering his way through the mysteries of the Salic Law, suggests that Henry did not take them seriously himself; and when the worthy prelates, 'We of the spirituality', urge him to seek his rights 'with bloods and sword and fire', it seems reasonable to assume that Shakespeare's intention towards them was partly satiric.

With the advent of the tennis balls, however, the regal mask is off. The newly reformed king, who can 'reason in divinity', whose purified body seems to contain 'celestial spirits', shows himself distinctly human. Like any other sensitive being, he is cut to the quick by a public insult. If his reasons for making war (for which one must go back to his father's dying words in *Henry IV, Part 2*) were dubious in the extreme, on a personal level the icy and angry sarcasm of his response to the Dauphin's message is as lively as one could wish.

The next serious criticism comes with his treatment of the three traitors at Southampton, where first he plays cat and mouse with them, lures them into a false sense of security and then, to their infinite surprise, presents them with their own death warrants. His conduct here can be justified, I suppose, in the sense that he wished to emphasize the price of treachery to his assembled lords, and in any case, the traitors deserved what was coming to them; but one cannot defend the relish with which the game was played. This method of delivering justice does not accord well with the conduct of an ideal king, though in fact it is of a piece with the games we have seen Henry play before. This is the vicious side of the practical joker who once played callous, if harmless, tricks upon poor Francis, the Drawer, who turned the tables on Falstaff at Gadshill, and who will later play a crude if soldierly game of bluff with Fluellen and Williams. Nevertheless, in these moments our hero falls some way short of the expected standard.

There is a lot to be said, however, for his bitter requiem on false friendship to Thomas Scroop:

> *O, how hast thou with jealousy infected*
> *The sweetness of affiance.*

This is a speech of great beauty. It suggests an emotional capacity in Henry and a trust in intimate friendship which is nowhere else evident in the play. Unfortunately it loses effect in performance because we have never been shown or even told that this close friendship existed.

Scroop is merely a shadowy stereotype who passes from Southampton to eternal oblivion as suddenly as he came. Perhaps Shakespeare placed the conspiracy there because he wanted to show this susceptible and emotional side of the king's nature. Whatever the reason, the scene holds up the action when the Chorus has already told us we are on the way to France, and for this reason directors today tend to cut it heavily.

Henry next comes under critical fire for his murderous threats to the governor of Harfleur. Unless the town surrenders, he will raze it to ashes and unleash his soldiers in an orgy of destruction. It is a bloodthirsty and appalling speech (and a burden for the actor who has to deliver it while he is still drawing breath from 'Once more into the breach') but it seems to me defensible in relation to the purpose, which it achieves, of persuading the town to surrender without bloodshed. If one wishes to find fault with Henry's methods of warfare, this is the wrong place to do it; and I suggest that an age which has condoned Hiroshima and the fire-bombing of defenceless cities on the desperate assumption that the end justifies the most terrible means, is not best fitted to sit in judgement on the less 'sophisticated' methods of persuasion used by an English leader long ago.

Time and again in writing these notes, I come back to the central issue, how to assess the conduct of this warrior king in modern terms and each time I come back to the same answer, that one cannot. His conduct must be viewed in the context of its time. He made war when war seemed a natural condition of life. He was a conqueror when conquest was proof of a nation's strength. He took England to war with France because it was a national assumption that England *would* war with France:

When did you refrain from us, or we refrain from you . . .

'Ask the wave that has not watched war between us two', wrote Kipling some five hundred years later. Unless one accepts these major premises one had best leave *Henry V* alone and hurry on to *Troilus and Cressida*, for instance, where Shakespeare portrays war and the warrior heroes in a very different light.

Nevertheless, after Harfleur, there is little in our hero's conduct that needs to be justified. Throughout the long marches and against the intimidating odds, he moves from strength to strength. He rejects Montjoy's first demand for his ransom with the taunt that, though his numbers are few and sick, they are equal to the larger army of the fully-fit French. More than that, when they are in health, one Englishman can take on three Frenchmen. Then, having chided himself for boasting thus, he mockingly attributes the fault to 'the air of France' which has 'blown' that vice in him. This is the Henry the soldiers love to hear, talking a soldier's language. It is also the inspirational leader, who could pull them back from retreat at Harfleur by hurling doubts upon their manhood, questioning their parentage, reminding them of their yeoman pedigree and urging them back to teach the inferior French what fighting was really about. The inspiration persists through all the following scenes until it reaches a blazing peak at the moment of 'the happy few' on Crispin's Day.

This great speech, like so many of the Shakespearean 'gems', has been so often treated as a set piece that its original force and intention are easily obscured. It needs to be seen, dramatically, both in its immediate context and in relation to the night scene before it. The Chorus has already described the pathetic state of 'the poor, condemnèd English', while 'the confident and overlusty French' play dice over the number of prisoners they will take. We have seen, too, for the first time, Henry alone, with his own inner doubts on the outcome of battle, and still plagued by conscience by the crime his father committed in order to gain the crown.

He has been mocked, too, by his own rank and file, has heard their doubts and fears, and been reminded by them of the heavy responsibility that will lie on his head for the soldiers slain in the battle. Henry's mood, by any reckoning could hardly be thought optimistic.

When the army assembles for battle, looking, as a French lord says, 'like island carrions', the mood of the leaders is deeply despondent. The talk is all of the superior strength of the French and their relative freshness for battle. There is a fatalism in the air. Salisbury goes to his post with doleful words of next meeting his comrades in heaven. Westmorland sows the seeds of dejection further by wishing that the army was another ten thousand strong. It is on this note that Henry joins his captains. He has sensed their mood and at once sets out to counteract it, making capital of the greater glory they will gain by being so few in number. In combating their doubts, his full genius as a leader finally comes out; he lifts their spirits by the strength of his own and then, as his speech gathers force, his imagination takes wing; he foresees the historic nature of the day and seizes upon the name of Crispin as upon a badge of honour that can be worn for all time. In blazoning his own vision before his men, the vision itself takes fire; his army is 'a band of brothers', 'a happy few' with every soldier, however 'vile' his condition, on equal terms beside him. It is a marvellous moment, irresistible surely, even to those sitting in the theatre not overfond of the soldiering life, and it has an explosive effect on Westmorland, whose morale is uplifted to the point where he now wishes that he and Henry could take on the French army alone. In this mood, the oncoming Montjoy, with his second demand for ransom, has no chance. Henry rejects him with a speech pitched on the same level of mystic intensity, yet salted throughout with a rough jocularity that must lift still higher the morale of his poor soldiers.

Leadership: this also is what the play is about, and I submit that, as leaders go, Shakespeare makes his Henry as exciting a figure to follow as any. In a fashionable phrase, he has *charisma*.

There are a few more points I would like to offer, suppositions only, which I hope might provide some stimulus to those tackling the play for the first time. From a director's point of view I consider the scene in the Dauphin's tent on the night before Agincourt the most fascinating in the play; that, apart from the Dauphin, the French lords in this scene are anything but confident and overlusty, though they may give that appearance; that they are, in fact, as nervous and apprehensive as most fighting men are in the long night before battle, and that there are as many hidden tensions below the surface of the dialogue as in any short scene in Chekhov. In any case, the French lords should never be played as elegant nonentities but as the proud fighting men they were, and the French king is not the senile idiot which so many directors make him, but a desperate realist trying to goad his divided nobles into unified action and bitterly aware of the military liability he has acquired in the person of his own son. I consider the fourth Chorus in this play to be one of Shakespeare's greatest pieces of atmospheric description, and the long scene which follows it, fluctuating between tense, soldierly talk, broad comedy, and kingly introspection, is one of the best dramatic scenes in all Shakespeare; and in this scene, the character of Williams, like that of Eros in *Antony and Cleopatra*, has a quality that cuts through all critical defences and goes straight to the heart.

Finally, a word on some of the productions I have seen, which include most of those in London and Stratford since 1950.

The best Henry of all, to my mind, the most rounded, believable and honest in performance was Richard Burton whom I was fortunate to see at the Old Vic in the mid-fifties when he looked like becoming a great actor, not merely a household name. I had seen him earlier (1951) in the same role in the Stratford history cycle, the whole of which was a wonderful theatrical experience.

I don't think the play had been performed in 'cycle' before and at that time I myself and, no doubt, the Stratford directors, were much under the influence of Dover Wilson, who taught us to look afresh at *Henry V* in its organic relationship to the preceding history plays, and there was immense excitement in the discovery.

Amongst many other unusual productions it is worth mentioning John Neville's honourable but misplaced attempt at a Brechtian treatment of the play at the Old Vic in 1960, with Donald Houston as the king, and one production, even more misplaced, *in modern dress*, at the Mermaid in 1960. Perhaps only a director with Bernard Miles' buccaneering and indomitable spirit would have elected to give an essentially mediaeval subject a modern dress treatment, to stage the battle of Agincourt against back projections with a barrage of sound effects of last war artillery attacks, and allow Henry to play the first scene, with its tennis balls speech, attired in *cricket* flannels, having just come in from the nets.

The most brilliant production to my mind, however, was not in the theatre but in the cinema. This was Olivier's film, though the comic scenes and indeed his own performance, suffered from some theatricality. It was also far and away the most successful film treatment of

Shakespeare I have seen, the only film, in fact, where the imaginative use of cinematic techniques enhanced what Shakespeare actually wrote, where the camera faithfully served the poetic image without eliminating the poetry. In this sense, it must rank higher even than the magnificent Russian film of *Hamlet* where, for all the cinematic brilliance, so much of the play was sacrificed that it almost ceased to be Shakespeare's *Hamlet* at all. Olivier's film is a masterpiece, and thankfully it remains intact to provide a marvellous introduction to this play for those who have not yet discovered it.

1976

Much Ado About Nothing

DENISE COFFEY

Europalia, the E.E.C. Festival of the Arts, was held in Belgium in October 1973, with the special theme that year of welcoming Britain into the Community. Exhibitions, concerts and theatrical events, with British theatre represented by the Young Vic, went to the celebrations in Brussels. We performed a play written by a thirty-four-year-old actor who, like us, was part of a London theatre company. The play was *Much Ado About Nothing*, the writer William Shakespeare.

This introduction is my account of Frank Dunlop's production of *Much Ado*, which I hope will illuminate the play for you as much as it did for us. Frank Dunlop has great insight into Shakespeare's work and reveals the text better than any director I know today.

Let me tell you something quickly about the Young Vic Theatre itself. It opened in 1970 and was named the Young Vic by its founder, Frank Dunlop, in homage to George Devine and the previous Young Vic Company (1946–51). The new theatre would continue their tradition of productions which are adventurous, simple, imaginative. The seats to be cheap, so that young people can try a first taste of Shakespeare or Beckett, Pinter, Osborne, Goldsmith and others, without spending too much of their hard-earned money. A fresh look at the classics without encrusted tradition, a direct look at the author's work. It's very exciting (and demanding) to play as we do at the Young Vic, to an audience which doesn't know how the play ends, and are shocked and thrilled by Shakespeare as a new discovery.

The aim is to have a popular theatre that's as accessible as a public library, with classical plays (not necessarily old) presented in simple and informal surroundings, unlike the plush, posh, expensive, un-welcoming (for young people) atmosphere of most theatres when the Young Vic began. Of course, since 1970, fringe theatre has become very much a part of London life, but when we began there was no real alternative theatre for people to visit.

The building itself (architect Bill Howell) cost sixty thousand pounds and is a mixture of a true Elizabethan theatre, a Greek theatre and a circus. The octagonal auditorium can seat about 450 people, sitting on red-painted wooden benches on three sides of the versatile thrust stage area. Actors can appear from anywhere . . . through the audience, up on the balcony, from a tunnel under the stage. Milton Shulman, the theatre critic of the London *Evening Standard*, described *Scapino*, the opening production, as '. . . an explosion of electric eels'. A hallmark of Young Vic productions is the energy and vitality, physical and mental, of the actors. Nothing less will do in that exposed arena.

Back to *Much Ado*. Carl Toms created Sicily for us with a silver ramp sticking its glittery tongue out into the audience, a red and silver house with a shady balcony, a black iron-railed staircase, a palm tree beneath which Beatrice would weep from shock, having heard what her cousin really thinks of her, and a red-beaded curtained bower for Benedick to conceal himself to listen to what his friends have to say about *him*. This simple set served (as in Shakespeare's theatre) for all the locations in the play.

Shakespeare's Sicily. An Island. With a cruel and rigid social code. The household of the Governor of Messina which contains himself, his brother, his daughter, and an orphan in his care – Beatrice, whose shafts of wit and flights of fancy make her free from insular thought and a mocker of the social code. A dangerous young (or maybe not so young) woman!

This is a story of Sicily and, as such, dictates the social attitudes in the play. Apparently some people feel incredulous that Claudio should be so violent in his reaction to the apparent promiscuity of his betrothed and that Leonato is so harsh towards his beloved daughter and only child. It's the same attitude that people have towards Isabella in *Measure for Measure*. Why won't she sleep with Angelo? After all, her brother's life is at stake; how selfish of her to prize her virginity above that. Shakespeare sets his characters in dilemmas which at this remove of time seem impossible for us to understand. But is that really true? When we were rehearsing *Much Ado*, there was a report in the paper that a father and his new son-in-law had been charged jointly with the murder of his daughter because she wasn't a virgin on her wedding night. The defence was that the family had been shamed and disgraced and that the young husband had the right to kill his offending bride. Sicily 1973.

Shakespeare's source for the Hero-Claudio part of the play was taken from Ariosto's *Orlando Furioso*, and another ingredient from Bandello's *Novelle*, together with Beatrice and Benedick from his own remarkable invention, and with his usual magic alchemy he turned the elements into gold. Sorry about the flowery adjectives, but I'm with Ben Jonson... I admire Shakespeare 'this side idolatry'.

Our production was set in nineteenth century Italy, during the Risorgimento, when small local wars, very much like Don John's uprising, were raging. This period also yielded an opportunity for dazzling uniforms for Don Pedro and his followers, and, for Don John and his men, the remnants of their banditti-style uniforms, all insignia torn from them in capture. Dogberry was dressed in the traditional Italian police uniform with tricorn hat and white gloves. His volunteers were muffled in long overcoats, bowler hats and umbrellas against the rainy night. (Shakespeare is specific about the weather of what crime reporters call 'the night in question'. Borachio says 'It drizzles rain'. Act III, Scene 3.) The town band (trumpet, trombone, flute/piccolo) wore respectable dark suits with bandsmen's peaked caps. The civilians in the nineteenth century setting looked properly prosperous, as befits their comfortable bourgeois circumstances.

Imagine then a Sicilian domestic palace, washing hanging on the line, being disrupted by having to host Don Pedro and his followers (who had stayed there on their way to the campaign against Don John), not to mention the defeated and forgiven Don John and *his* followers. 'My dear friend Leonato hath invited you all – I tell him we shall stay here at the least a month, and he heartily prays some occasion may detain us longer,' says Don Pedro in Act I, Scene 2. A huge expense for Leonato. Was his invitation quite freely given, I wonder? And did the Elizabethan audience laugh at this moment, recognizing the queen's habit of moving in with her vast entourage and staying for weeks at a time, eating her hosts out of their larder? Queen Elizabeth slept here. And here. And here. And very often, apparently, bankruptcy followed. However, Leonato sees some hope of recouping his expenses, for he believes that the prince (Don Pedro) wants to marry his daughter. When it is revealed to be not the prince but Claudio who is the possible bridegroom, we don't see Leonato's exact reaction but, as the prince has wooed for Claudio, there's not much he can do.

Welding
Sandie ?

Much Ado About Nothing!

The play is concerned with three distinct and colliding groups of people. First the aristocrats returning from the war, with Claudio newly promoted to their ranks, Benedick, respected as a good soldier and popular as a witty companion, and Don John, also a prince, embittered both by being defeated by his brother and by having been forgiven but under surveillance.

Next come the civilians. The Governor and his household. Used to more domestic campaigns, like organizing the celebration supper for the returning heroes, and coping with a daughter of marriageable age and a niece who refuses to conform to the usual rules – disdaining the idea of a husband, preferring a vision of heaven where St Peter shows her the bachelors' compound '. . . and there live we as merry as the day is long'. In Brussels the audience recognized these rich bourgeois and their ambition to join the aristocracy, as did other European audiences on later tours to Switzerland, Vienna and Holland. In London, though, our audiences are too young to have reached the middle-aged comfortable world where money has been accumulated and only a title or a good marriage lends a glow to the future.

The third group is the military/civilian . . . Dogberry and his band of volunteer militia, who form the Watch policing the town. In their innocent zeal they thwart the wicked plot of Don John to discredit Hero. In the words of Borachio to Leonato in Act V, confessing his crime and arrest by the Watch, 'What your wisdoms could not discover, these shallow fools have brought to light.' In Dogberry we see a man dressed in a little brief authority, and, although the function may have changed, there are committees, town halls, trade unions and such who find the occasional Dogberry in their midst today. 'Our sexton hath reformed Signor Leonato of the matter' is straight from a memo or phone call in bureaucracy, 1976.

Benedick and Beatrice are usually examined as the main characters of *Much Ado* (or let us say the best known, because they are so attractive). The idea of the antagonists who are really in love with each other has sustained a few hundred Hollywood movies, but in fact Beatrice and Benedick are only part of the pattern of the play, and a very intricate pattern it is.

This play, like all of Shakespeare's, is filled with mirror images, ironies and practical jokes. Until I started to think about it, I hadn't truly realized how many of the plays are concerned with practical jokes or their very near relatives, disguises and assumed names and personalities. Even Hamlet, in inserting the scene into the play for the king, is playing a practical joke – no joke, perhaps, but certainly practical. Rosalind and Celia disguise themselves in the pursuit of love; Viola becomes the victim of her own practical (?) solution of dressing in her brother's clothes by being unable to tell the man she loves that she is a girl and the woman who loves her that she's not a man. I'm sure you can think of other examples.

Upon your opinion of practical jokes will depend your reaction to *Much Ado*. Do you think they're harmless giggles to pass away the time, or dangerous meddling in the life of somebody you don't really like or that you fear? It's easy to see Borachio's scheme of dressing Margaret, the serving girl, in Hero's dress and making the onlookers believe she's Hero and that he's her lover, as a vicious idea, destined to do mischief. But what about the so-called 'goodies' . . . Don Pedro, Leonato, Claudio, Hero and their plan to make two people, who apparently dislike each other intensely, believe each is in love with the other? Not to mention the way they go about it.

If you think that they were justified because the plot turned out happily, and believe it was just a merry way of passing a few idle days, don't read on. I think Shakespeare knew more about human nature than that. What makes this play a fascinating one for me is that it seems clear that nobody actually *liked* Benedick and Beatrice. Just think. Very witty, sharp people are fun to be with for five minutes or so at a party, but too uncomfortable and spiky to have around all the time. They seem to be popular, but people long for their downfall, and their very wit, which is usually based on pain, isolates them from the society which will either lionize them or ostracize them. Dorothy Parker? Lenny Bruce?

Have a look at the scene where the joke against Benedick and Beatrice is thought up, Act II, Scene 1. Beatrice has just left the company, having successfully disrupted the solemn moment of betrothal. When she's gone and they discuss her, the Prince says that 'she were an excellent wife for Benedick' (i.e. they deserve each other). The subject is dropped, until the question of how to pass the week between the betrothal and the wedding, and it's Don Pedro's idea to play a joke on Benedick (his apparent friend) and the niece of his host. He plans it with the speed and skill of a military campaign. The irony is that literally a minute later we hear Borachio, the nominal villain, planning his scheme in much the same way.

What is remarkable about the rest of the play is that we have the pleasure of seeing the biters bit. The very people we see daring to speak their minds about Benedick and Beatrice, knowing them to be helpless to reply for once, are confounded by the same sort of plan against themselves. Leonato, who 'acted' in the garden for Benedick's benefit, has to 'act' the grieving father in earnest later on, even though he knows his daughter is alive. Don Pedro and Claudio have just finished 'acting' their parts in the joke against Benedick when Don John arrives and does to them exactly what they've just done to Benedick, and they are just as taken in as he was. Hero, who hasn't much to say for herself as a dutiful daughter (maybe she was exhausted by all that laughing in the middle of the night – she shared a room with Beatrice), has the opportunity to say everything she's ever wanted to, in Act III, Scene 2, without fear of reprisal. 'I'll devise some honest slanders to stain my cousin with. One doth not know how much an ill word may empoison liking.' And ironically, on her wedding morning, she was to find the eyes of everyone she loved suddenly turned to the eyes of strangers, due to an exactly similar device. All these patterns are there to be relished.

It does seem to me that the only two people who behave like generous, loving human beings are Beatrice and Benedick. (Well, perhaps I'm a bit prejudiced . . . I played Beatrice.) True, they're sharp and beady, but mainly with each other, enjoying their 'merry war'; in fact it's clear that Beatrice is pining for her sparring partner at the beginning of Act I, but like lots of shy people she finds the shell of wit useful to hide behind. Beatrice as an orphan, Benedick as a non-aristocrat in noble company. The scene in which they declare their love for each other is one of the finest love scenes ever written. Shakespeare dares to place it after the church scene where Hero is accused. Beatrice and Benedick are alone together for only the second time in the play. As Ellen Terry wrote: 'This wonderful scene throws such a flood of light on Beatrice's character that an actress has little excuse for not seeing clearly what kind of woman she has to impersonate'. Quite right. And there is enormous tenderness at the end of the scene, when she realizes that the result of the duel between Benedick and Claudio needn't necessarily end in a win for Benedick. She has mortgaged the life of the man she loves, her future happiness, for a revenge dictated by the social code she has always mocked.

Well, maybe I'm being too hard on all the other people in the play;

after all, they're only human. And Shakespeare shows nature its mirror with timeless genius. There's all sorts of little delights to be found in the text – for example, the best stage direction ever written, 'look where Beatrice, like a lapwing, runs close by the ground to hear our conference'; all the angling images (that's a cruel sport!); the only piece of information about Leonato's brother, Antonio, is that he has a twitch . . . 'I know you by the waggle of your head'; Dogberry's advice to his Dad's Army, showing him to be the most peaceable of law enforcement officers; the delight of the eloquent outpourings of Benedick and Beatrice, which drive people mad . . . with their acrobatic intelligence; the revealing fascination of Don Pedro's answer to Claudio's question 'Hath Leonato any son, my lord ?'. Don Pedro knows exactly what's behind it and says 'No child but Hero, she's his only heir'.

It is Don Pedro who is the most interesting character in the play for me, though. He is the only person who is sad at the end. His brother has again shown his vicious nature, he has lost the young man from Florence who was such a delight to him, with his youth and high spirits, and, through his own plotting, he has lost Benedick, his jester and companion. Why does Don Pedro woo on Claudio's behalf ? Why does he suddenly propose a practical joke about people being in love just after the announcement of the betrothal ? He is the lonely one, who has to return to Arragon to continue his life without any happy ending, to face another family dilemma. An intriguing man to find in what is classified as a comedy. Of course in Shakespeare's terms a comedy simply means that nobody dies during the play, whereas in a tragedy somebody does. Elizabethan 'A' and 'X' certificates.

Much ado about . . . nothing ? Or a marvellously funny play with astonishing insight into human behaviour long before people analysed their motives or questioned their impulses ?

Enjoy the play, it's beautiful. And there's a last word from that most exquisite of Beatrices – Beatrice Lillie. There was a line of dialogue written for her in a movie in the thirties, in which she was replying to someone who questioned her classical theatrical experience. 'Of course I've been in Shakespeare', she retorts. 'Why, I played the part of Nothing in *Much Ado About Nothing*.' Ah, there's a Beatrice!

1976

The Merry Wives of Windsor

TERRY HANDS

I

'Wives in England . . . are not kept so strictly as they are in Spain or elsewhere. They go to market to buy what they like best to eat. They are well dressed, fond of taking it easy, . . . They sit before their doors, decked out in fine clothes, in order to see and be seen by the passers-by . . . their time they employ in walking and riding, in playing cards or otherwise, in visiting their friends and keeping company, conversing with their equals (whom they term gossips) and their neighbours, and making merry with them at child-births, cristenings, churchings and funerals . . . England is called the Paradise of married women.' *Van Meteran, 1575*

The Merry Wives of Windsor is Shakespeare's warmest and richest comedy. How Alice Ford and Margaret Page earn their 'Paradise' is played out against an acute and lovingly observed tapestry of Shakespeare's own country, Elizabethan England, its follies, strengths and new emerging society. It is the only bourgeois play Shakespeare wrote: it is perhaps the funniest.

This new society was a direct result of mercantile expansion. Before the late 1500s English society was still largely mediaeval, wealth was in land and inherited; peasants lived from the soil they tilled; barter was pre-eminent and only war could significantly vary the economy. With the new ships, trade on a large scale became possible. Merchants banded together to send off single vessels or sometimes small fleets, which might return with nothing or with a king's ransom in gold and spices. A newly-rich class developed; powerful not by birth but by acquisition – forever 'galling the courtier's kibe' – threatening the old landed aristocracy and finally forming the back-bone of the puritan revolution of 1640.

It is to this class that Page and Ford belong. They are rich – £1,400 is to be Anne Page's dowry (multiply by 15 for an approximate modern equivalent) – and proud of their centrality within the new system. They are instinctively puritan. Their values, however latterly sophisticate, are still close to peasant thriftiness and toil.

'Whosoever studieth the laws of the realm, who studieth in the universities, who professeth liberal sciences, and to be short, who can live idly and without manual labour, and will bear the port, charge and countenance of a gentleman, he shall be called master . . .' *Sir Thomas Smith, 1588*

Like a new centre of gravity, Master Ford and Master Page attract as a group the other classes of the play, each one rich in the individuality of an uncluttered England, though not all English. To educate their children they have Sir Hugh Evans, a Welsh parson, whose curious rendering of English is matched only by that of the Frenchman, Dr Caius. Obsessive, eccentric men, passionately attached to their love of learning or medicine, they are rivals for the sympathy and patronage of the new ruling class. The conflict between these two, their gulling by the Host of the Garter Inn, and their final victory over him, forms the manic sub-plot to the main action of the play. Here they are involved as protagonists and valued for the virtues which brought them to Windsor in the first place. Dr Caius, a distinguished man of medicine with important court connections, is a splendid catch for the hand of Anne Page. And Mrs Page – who has everything save position – pursues him fondly if snobbishly. Sir Hugh Evans, on the other hand, a pillar of puritan rectitude, adds weight to the claims of Abraham Slender, the choice of Mr Page. And Abraham Slender is the nephew of Justice Shallow, a worthy gentleman . . .

'A worthy gentleman . . . is a thing out of whose corruption the generation of a Justice of Peace is produced. He speaks statutes and husbandry well enough to make his neighbours think him a wise man . . . His travel is seldom farther than the next market town, and his inquisition is about the price of corn . . . Nothing under a subpoena can draw him to London: and when he is there, he sticks fast upon every object, casts his eye away upon gazing, and becomes the prey of every cutpurse. If he go to court, it is in yellow stockings, in a slight taffety cloak, and pumps and pantoffles.' *Sir Thomas Overbury, 1614*

Living rustically in Gloucestershire from his fields and what he grows, a stranger to cities – except in his mad young student days – Justice Shallow comes to Windsor to present his bumpkin nephew as suitor to Anne Page. But Slender is as out of place in Windsor as Shallow would be in London. Within minutes he has had his pocket

picked, and his country naivety is no match for the directness and
energy of the merchant's daughter Anne. His servant, the aptly named
Peter Simple periodically on loan to Sir Hugh Evans, completes the
Gloucestershire group. Defined by their names – slender, shallow,
simple – they are a formidably innocuous trio.

'The English are serious like the Germans; lovers of show, liking to
be followed wherever they go by whole troops of servants, who wear
their masters' arms in silver fastened to their left arms, a ridicule they
deservedly lay under. . . . they are vastly fond of great noises that fill
the ear, such as the firing of cannon, drums and the ringing of bells, so
that it is common for a number of them, that have got a glass in their
heads, to go up into some belfry, and ring the bells for hours together
for the sake of exercise . . .' *Paul Hentzner, 1598*

Then the Court, Falstaff and Fenton. The one old and reprobate,
the other young and dashing – both impoverished and looking to the
rich merchants for reparation. Falstaff through Mrs Ford, Fenton by
marrying Anne Page. The former learns a lesson, the latter to love.
Theoretically Falstaff is senior to the Pages and Fords, and certainly
they treat him – initially anyway – with respect. They expect him to
have the courtiers' accomplishments – 'the courtier's, soldier's,
scholar's eye, tongue, sword' – and Falstaff's gullibility to their
flattery is part of his downfall. More especially, however, he is the
victim of a new type of society. He expects the easily gulled landed
gentry of Shallow and company when he arrives in Windsor, but finds
a bright energized society, strong in class and family ties, with wits
razor sharp and values not only believed but practised. Fenton, in a
simpler way, discovers the same thing, and where Falstaff is chastened,
he falls in love:

> *Albeit I will confess, thy father's wealth*
> *Was the first motive that I woo'd thee, Anne:*
> *Yet, wooing thee, I found thee of more value*
> *Than stamps in gold, or sums in sealed bags;*
> *And 'tis the very riches of thyself*
> *That now I aim at.* III. 4. 13–18

With Falstaff come his London city-cronies, Bardolph, Pistol, Nym,
to meet Mrs Quickly another Londoner already installed. They are
remnants of the old war-booty system, landless, homeless, bearing
only their master's badge and condemned to poverty if Falstaff's plans

do not thrive. His inability to maintain them prompts his seduction of Mistress Ford; their scorn of his likelihood of success provokes their casting off. In revenge they inform Ford of his wife's temptation and the already jealous merchant embarks upon his series of private-eye catastrophes.

The play thus becomes the clash between old and new. The different groups, Windsor, Wales, France, Gloucestershire, London and the Court – all with their particular accents, dress and behaviour – whirl together to provide the central conflict. Windsor wins; but in winning it too has to be chastened. Just as Falstaff learns the true nature of Mrs Ford and Page, so the Page family have in turn to learn the true nature of Fenton. The acquisitive marriage-brokering of Mrs Page is defeated, so too the traditional matching of Mr Page. Even the jealous Ford – as finely drawn as Leontes or Othello – learns to undeceive himself. Virtue and love triumph.

It is impossible to enumerate all the delights of the play. But this structure of contrasts, with its concentration on accent and language, is the mechanism which, deadly serious in practice, makes the play so warm in appeal and hilarious in action. There is a further, mellower tone, which makes it quite unique.

II

'Merry England was merry chiefly by virtue of its community observances of periodic sports and feast days. Mirth took form in morris-dances, sword dances, wassailings, mock ceremonies of summer kings and queens and of lords of misrule, mummings, disguisings, masques – and a bewildering variety of sports, games, shows and pageants improvised on traditional models. . . .

'The seasonal feasts were not, as now, rare curiosities to be observed by folklorists in remote villages, but landmarks framing the cycle of the year, observed with varying degrees of sophistication by most elements in the society.' *C. L. Barber, 1959*

Opinions have differed on the season of the play. Theatrical tradition has tended towards the winter, scholarship towards the spring. It is impossible to be certain, but the latter seems least likely. The Garter passage (Act V. 5. 57–73) upon which this theory is largely based is probably an insert. The verse is structured differently, more sedately and out of keeping with the surge of the rest of the scene. Professionally it would be logical to insert such a passage in a performance before royalty at Windsor Castle, and equally logical to remove it in less distinguished company or more general circumstances.

The winter tradition is a little easier to justify, but the evidence is flimsy. One would expect precise descriptions for such a precise season, but the text offers only hints. Page refers to Evans in doublet and hose on such a 'raw rheumatic day'. Herne's oak is leafless; but Falstaff is thrown into cold water, not frozen and even '. . . my belly's as cold as if I had swallow'd snowballs' is qualified by 'if'. His evocation, at the end of the play, of rain, thunder, hail, snow and tempest could as well prefigure winter as be it. All these references, in fact, might as easily suggest autumn as winter, particularly when we remember that the buck Falstaff shoots at the beginning of the play was normally hunted in October. Above all neither spring nor winter provides a suitable festival to celebrate the play's ending. It is not Christmas, 12th Night or May Day and yet everybody – even Page and Ford – appears to be on holiday. It is a festal time. A time for visiting friends, hunting and wooing. A time which has as final ceremony an entire village running round at night dressed as fairies and hobgoblins, waving pumpkin lanterns and singing songs; an oak tree; the burning of a horned tree-spirit. Bonfire night. Suitably, perhaps, the clue is given by Peter Simple. Trying to specify a long time ago, he refers to it as 'upon All-hallowmas last, a fortnight afore Michaelmas'.

The only festival which makes sense of all the references is All-hallow Even or Hallowe'en, October 31st. It was the principal and perhaps oldest bonfire festival of the Celts; the night of the transition from autumn to winter and originally a pagan celebration, awesome and mysterious. The early Christians took over this ceremony and made it their own. The dark side may still have been there, with its puritan overtones of witches-sabbath; as Mrs Page says, 'No man means evil but the devil and we shall know him by his horns'. By the late sixteenth century all kinds of simpler village superstitions had humanized the legend. Some years later it moved up five days and coped with Guy Fawkes; hot chestnuts, potatoes and possets remaining the natural conclusion to the night's sports.

And the mood of the play is autumnal. Falstaff and the merry wives are no longer young. The latter's indignation at his advances is tempered by amusement and self-mockery. The temptation he presents, however doomed, is flattering and unexpected at their age. It serves to bind ever more closely the Page family and renews the deep love of Alice Ford and her passionate Frank. Even Falstaff has mellowed and talks of his physical attributes with a gentle despair. No longer a warrior in Boars Head battles, he seeks to woo – and in wooing reveals a depth of self-knowledge wholly seductive and a vulnerability wholly sympathetic.

> FALSTAFF *I do begin to perceive that I am made an ass.*
> FORD *Ay, and an ox too. . . .*
> FALSTAFF *And these are not fairies: I was three or four times in the thought that they were not fairies, and yet the guiltiness of my mind, the sudden surprise . . . drove the grossness of the foppery into a receiv'd belief . . . despite . . . all rhyme and reason . . . See now how wit may be made a Jack-a-Lent, when 'tis upon ill employment!* v. 5.

He is fooled by the wives and time.

'When the fire is low, collect the ashes in a circle and around the circumference put a stone to represent every one present; next morning, if any stone is displaced or injured, the person it represents will be dead before next Hallowe'en.' *Anon, sixteenth century*

III

Scholars have advanced various theories for dating the play. Madden suggests it was written somewhere between 1592 and 1596; Pollard, Hotson, Daniel, Green 1597; Wilson 1598; Bradbrooke 1601. Dennis, Gildon, Rowe all believed it was written in fourteen days to satisfy the queen's demand to see Falstaff in love.

In the theatre we cannot dispute dates, but we can discover through rehearsal that the text, albeit mainly prose, has a richness of imagery, a sureness of effect commensurate with the fullest period of Shakespeare's writing. Such richness, in fact, that the fourteen day theory seems hardly conceivable.

What seems more likely is that Shakespeare re-furbished either an old 'jealousy comedy', reworking its central character to fit Falstaff, or improvised, through performance and with his actors, upon several Stratford themes dear to his heart – he too had a daughter called Anne, who was courted by a doctor and Justice Shallow may be equated with the Sir Thomas Lucy who banished Shakespeare himself for deer-stealing – or he may have done both. For, on examining the so-called Bad Quarto of 1602, we seem to have an imperfect touring version, and looking at the Folio we find a compilation of several prompt copies repeating some speeches with only slight variations, and confusing the characters of Mrs Ford and Page. But this is only on the page, in rehearsal the texts mingle and clarify.

The Merry Wives of Windsor is perhaps Shakespeare's most professional play, worked out in performance and through performance, and it *still* works in performance when the Quarto and the Folio are used together. It is finally the language that triumphs, the words, images, ideas, perfectly expressing each several character.

Falstaff baited by Evans at the end of the play at last turns upon his tormentor:

FALSTAFF ... *Am I ridden with a Welsh goat too? ... 'Tis time I were chok'd with a piece of toasted cheese.*

EVANS *Seese is not good to give putter; your pelly is all putter.*

FALSTAFF *'Seese' and 'putter'! Have I liv'd to stand at the taunt of one that make fritters of English? This is enough to be the decay of lust and late-walking through the realm.* v. 5.

After all his trials and tribulations the English courtier-scholar re-emerges, however dilapidated, and indignantly brings everything into perspective. It is England that has been under attention. Its individuality, eccentricity, energy – all that may be conveyed in its language. And its warmth.

MRS PAGE *Good husband, let us every one go home,*
And laugh this sport o'er by a country fire,
Sir John and all. v. 5.

All is forgiven. It has all been a sport. The society portrayed has no extremes. People are cold – not frozen; hungry not starving; angry not psychotic. They are human, sympathetic villagers. And their play in performance burns with all the cheerfulness and comfort of the fire they gather round at the end to recall it.

'Put a candle in a turnip mask and frighten the cat.' *Anon, sixteenth century*

1974

Julius Caesar

GLEN BYAM SHAW

What is it that has made *Julius Caesar* one of the most popular plays that Shakespeare ever wrote? I suppose it is very often the first that young children study at school. How often must 'Friends, Romans, countrymen, lend me your ears:' have been the first Shakespearean line that a child has slyly smiled at, and remembered for ever? Also the historical story is strongly and clearly told, in spite of the fact that Shakespeare has, for dramatic reasons, considerably condensed the time in which the events portrayed in the play actually took place.

From the opening right up to the lynching of the poet Cinna the action sweeps along with the fierceness and pace of a forest fire; and, in any production of the play, it would be ridiculous to have an interval before the end of Act III. The last two acts have not the drive and vitality of the first three, but Shakespeare has sustained Act IV with the entrance into the play of Octavius Caesar, the great quarrel scene between Brutus and Cassius, and the appearance of Caesar's ghost. Shakespeare's ghosts are always intended to inspire awe and pity, and the intended effect here is the same as when the Ghost in *Hamlet* says to his son: 'Remember me'. Act V has a dying fall in tune with the disintegration of the Conspirators' army and the suicides of Cassius and Brutus.

The play is full of splendid parts for the men. Julius Caesar, Mark Antony, Brutus, Cassius, Casca, and Octavius Caesar need actors of outstanding talent, and there is hardly a character that doesn't give an actor real opportunity. Even such small parts as the second Citizen, the Soothsayer, Ligarius, Artemidorus and the poet Cinna are full of individuality and life.

On the other hand, the two female characters are rather colourless and far below Shakespeare's greatest creations. Although there is something to be made of the contrast between Portia and Calpurnia, no actress of importance would thank one for the chance to play either part. (While they were at school together, Miss Diana Wynyard and

Dame Peggy Ashcroft played Brutus and Cassius. Obviously the mistress in charge decided that such talent would be wasted on Portia and Calpurnia!)

For a really good group of actors it is possible to achieve something remarkable in the crowd scenes, with their tremendous variations of mood, and in the battle scenes towards the end of the play. This, more than anything, can make *Julius Caesar* so immensely exhilarating for any company (be it professional, amateur or student) to act, and it is certainly a play that needs to be acted for its great qualities to be fully appreciated. It is a Company play and cannot be sustained by one or two fine performances only; this I believe partly accounts for its popularity, as there is nothing more exciting in the theatre than to see a good company of actors in a play that requires real team work.

It has been said that most of the Christian characters in *The Merchant of Venice* are unpleasant or stupid. Bassanio is a sponger and a fortune hunter, Antonio a homosexual bore, Gratiano a foul-mouthed Jew-baiter, Lorenzo a seducer and a thief, Launcelot Gobbo a promiscuous glutton, the Prince of Arragon a nit-wit and the Duke of Venice a half-wit. These defects of character can all be supported by indications in the text; but it would be a foolhardy producer who decided on a production of *The Merchant of Venice* which stressed the despicable traits in the Christians to an extent that was not intended by the author, and who stirred up in his audience a feeling of contempt and hatred for them. The truth is, of course, that Shakespeare created human beings in his plays, not conventional stage puppets, and being human they have their faults as well as their virtues.

This applies, equally, to the characters in *Julius Caesar*. I must confess that, personally, I hate the Conspirators and am entirely on the side of Caesar and Antony. Brutus appears to be positively in love with his honour, but, frankly, I cannot see that virtue in his nature. To begin with he allows the bitter and prejudiced Cassius to abuse Caesar (his avowed friend) in the most futile way. Not even the most critical of British generals would, I think, question the greatness of Sir Winston Churchill because he had once had to give Churchill a helping hand when they were swimming together, or because Sir Winston, during one of his campaigns, had contracted malaria and asked, in a weak voice, for something to drink.

Then it appears that the only reason why Brutus decides that

Caesar must be killed is because he fears that Caesar may accept to be
king and 'change his nature'. But, having agreed to head the band of
Conspirators, Brutus is very insistent that Caesar shall be killed
decently:

> *Let's kill him boldly, but not wrathfully;*
> *Let's carve him as a dish fit for the gods,*
> *Not hew him as a carcass fit for hounds:*

but he is the first to plunge his hands into Caesar's wounds and cover
himself with his friend's warm blood. Worse than this is his stupidity.
He, and the other Conspirators, kill Caesar without having made any
plan for taking over control of the state once the tyrant is dead. His
speech to the populace, after the assassination, is the dullest sort of
stone-walling. No wonder that after such an innings, Antony can raise
the crowd to a frenzy of excitement with his brilliant and daring
strokes of irony and passion. Parenthetically, is it not also the height
of irony that Caesar, who had the practical ability to evolve the
calendar in approximately the form in which it is still used today,
should be murdered by a man who is so vague that he thinks it is the
first of March when in fact it is the fifteenth?

Brutus' wife, Portia, is an absurd neurotic, wounding herself to
prove her constancy, hysterically almost giving away the Conspirators'
plan to assassinate Caesar, and finally committing suicide for no reason
except that her husband has gone to the wars.

For me there is nothing praiseworthy in any of the other Conspirators, and although Caesar's genius is not fully drawn, he does at
least appear as a man of dignity, authority, courtesy and determination.

Whatever one's personal feeling about the individual characters
may be, it is, of course, all-important to try and realize the effect that
the author intended them to have on an audience, and I am sure that,
as in *The Merchant of Venice*, Shakespeare wanted his audience to see
all the facets of these characters, and understand the different sides to
their natures.

There is no hero and no villain, and if, when I produced *Julius
Caesar*, I had allowed my dislike of the Conspirators to upset the
balance that Shakespeare has so subtly achieved, it would have been
wrong and would have interfered with the audience's understanding
of the play. Ideally a production of *Julius Caesar* should be followed

the next evening by *Antony and Cleopatra*. Then, I think, one would realize the full scope of Shakespeare's intention.

At the start of *Julius Caesar* the people are on holiday. They are out in the streets with their families and friends, enjoying themselves. They feel secure in their trust and admiration for their great leader. Then we hear a crown has been offered to Caesar by Antony. Although he refuses it, the fear that he may later change his mind drives Brutus to join the Conspirators and to destroy him; but as soon as Caesar is dead the once happy and contented people become a mad rabble without sense or mercy.

At the end of *Antony and Cleopatra*, Octavius Caesar is about to become the first Emperor of Rome and take, in practice though not in form, the position and power that his uncle refused. Between these two events Shakespeare shows us what can happen to a great state when there is no supreme leadership.

'Motley' did the designs for my production of the play at the Royal Shakespeare Theatre during the 1957 season. The play was presented in two parts and the scenery was designed to allow each part to be performed without a break in the action. It consisted mainly of six large screens, each of which was a simple rectangular shape with an indication of classical detail. These could slide smoothly on and off stage as required and during the first part, which ended with the lynching of the poet Cinna, the different locations in Rome were suggested by altering the position and relationship of the screens. For the second part of the play they were opened to their full extent so that the stage was left clear for the camp near Sardis and the plains of Philippi.

The costumes were based on Roman dress of the 1st Century BC. The traditional toga of the Patrician was, of course, white, but to fit with the violence of the play and to help the audience recognize immediately the many different characters, the togas were made in the strong rich colours found in the Roman and Pompeian paintings of the classical period.

1962

Twelfth Night

PETER HALL

It is impossible to cut a word of *Twelfth Night*. Even its obscure jokes are brought alive by the exuberant rhythm of the scenes. It belongs to that small group of Shakespeare's plays (*Macbeth* and the *Dream* are others) that are sinewy and compact. They have no excess fat. *Twelfth Night* is complex, ambiguous, and heartbreakingly funny. It is the masterwork among the comedies.

It was written in 1600 – or so we think – the date is only important in understanding its place in the canon. Its mood is ripe and rich. It springs from a heart now fully capable of compassion – an emotion which is rare in the earlier works. *Twelfth Night* has a view of men which is objective and realistic. But it can be terrible in its honesty because it is so understanding – just like Shakespeare's presentation of that uncontrollable Vice-figure, Falstaff.

A Midsummer Night's Dream, As You Like It, and the national epic of the histories are in the past. We are moving into maturity; the great tragedies, the romances, and those plays of such ambiguity (*Measure for Measure, All's Well*, and *Troilus and Cressida*) that scholars have always found them 'Problems'. A bitterness of spirit is about to inflame the rest of Shakespeare's work.

Twelfth Night is significant as a transitional play, and there is something of this bitterness in its comedy. But the comedy is rich, because there is darkness and disturbance. The comedy is defined by tragedy, the folly and the illusions by sincerity, the joy by anguish.

The play deals with the theme common to all Shakespeare's comedies: the journey by means of experience to maturity – a maturity which it is necessary to crown by a marriage. *Twelfth Night* is a critique of illusions. A very young countess (Olivia), who is more in love with grief than with the true memory of her dead brother, is courted by a duke (Orsino) who is more in love with the idea of love than with the countess. Both of them have emotions which are modish and self-regarding. Their lives are invaded by a young girl (Viola), a realist who is in love with life, and has been freshly rescued from the sea and from the true anguish which she feels for the loss of *her* brother. Her presence when she becomes an illusion herself, a girl disguised as a boy, forces Olivia and Orsino, and all the self-deceivers who surround them into an understanding of reality. By the end of the play the deceivers have all suffered retribution for their faults. They are then capable of maturity.

This is the main and comic action of the play. It is set in a never-never land suited to such heady illusions, Illyria; a place, whatever its actual geography, that is a complete country of Shakespeare's imagination. It has music and flowers, buttery-bars, ancient monuments, box-trees, a very London puritan, Elizabethan court-jokes, and an abundance of cakes and ale. It has a relaxed climate in which sharp practice can easily disguise itself as friendship, and hypocrisy can masquerade as idealism. And it is all lapped by the sea, that image of opposites that haunted Shakespeare throughout his life. Tempest and sudden death are countered by calm seas, miraculous salvation and regeneration.

All Shakespeare's thinking, whether religious, political or moral, is based on his concept of Order. There is a just proportion, a necessary balance, in all things; Man above Beast, King above Man, God above King. It is the job of existence to seek out this order and abide by it. Revolution, whether in the family, the State or the heavens, breathes disorder and ultimate anarchy. Sometimes this chaos may be necessary, as the fever of rebellion is the way to health for the sick state, or as the young must repudiate their parents to reach maturity. But the action is still wrong, and some retribution will follow any act of disorder. Bolingbroke *has* to depose Richard II to weed the garden of England, but he and his family will suffer for the action.

For it is wrong to depose a king; just as it is wrong for the heart to rule the head, or for extremes in anything to be victorious. Balance is the only sure basis of life. Cakes and ale are just as dangerous in excess as the intolerant zeal of a high puritan.

It follows, then, that Man must govern himself as precisely as an army or a state, and strive for the just balance of opposites, the mean:

> *Take but degree away, untune that string,*
> *And hark what discord follows.*

All the characters of *Twelfth Night* save Viola are creatures of excess, agents of disorder. Orsino is in love with love, Olivia is in love with grief, and Sir Roby is overdrinking, behaving merrily below-stairs, and gulling a fool of his money. Sir Andrew is blinded by pretension, and Malvolio by egotism and hypocrisy. Even the cryptic Feste is self-indulgent in his bitterness and his melancholy. Sebastian is unwittingly churlish to the man who loves him and does not know how to express it. And we feel some criticism of Antonio because of the secrecy of his private and public life. Fabian and Maria lack tact; they behave out of their station and are thus disorderly.

All the main characters are treated critically, even Viola herself, overzealous to disguise herself as a man, suffers from the reality. But none of the critical spirit kills the joy of the comedy. It is for the audience to enjoy and then judge. For these characters are rich and complex. They are not simple Jonsonian humours.

I have space only to talk of one character in depth. I pick what is to me the most important character in the play – Feste. He is a deliberate enigma, poised uneasily between the two worlds of the court and the great house:

A fool that my Lady Olivia's father took much delight in.

He is bitter, insecure, singing the old half-forgotten songs to the Duke (for nostalgia is predictably the Duke's favourite musical companion), his jokes now tarnished and not very successful. He is the creation of a professional entertainer, and we may perhaps remotely relate him to John Osborne's Archie Rice, or to that fearful misanthropy which overtakes most comics when they begin to despise their audience. He is suffered by all, and liked by few. He is the most perceptive and formidable character in the play. Viola brings reality to the play by her instinct, but Feste could often do it if he wished by his shrewdness. I believe he penetrates Viola's disguise:

Now Jove, in his next commodity of hair, send thee a beard!

He is left alone at the end of the play singing bitterly, and more obscenely than most people realize, about the transient nature of life.

And he is the main character of the play's most extraordinary scene. He is a strange kind of fool, when disguised as Sir Topas he cruelly tortures the imprisoned Malvolio. He is very perceptive about Orsino, and offers a penetrating judgement:

Now the melancholy god protect thee, and the tailor make thy doublet of changeable taffeta, For thy mind is a very opal.

Feste is the critical centre of the play, the Thersites, the Jacques without eloquence, the malcontent, the man who sees all and says little, the cynic. It takes an idealist to be such a cynic.

I would like now to speculate. It is known that many of the professional fools were, in fact, defrocked priests. If the poor boy who was educated up to be a cleric failed to get a benefice, or if his reason or his morals dragged him away from the true faith, there was not much open to this medieval outsider except professional foolery. The education, the mental agility, and the Latin tags could all find a professional use. The destructive resentment of the failure could help his professional personality. Such a hypothesis is impossible to prove, but it is certainly a useful background to the actor playing Feste. It leads him without difficulty to the malice of Sir Topas's scene. Men are very bitter about the professions that fail them.

Only one of the other characters of the play, in my opinion, lacks three dimensions, and the life-enhancing inconsistency with which Shakespeare regularly surprises us. This is Malvolio – after Viola, the most famous character in the play. I find the character drawn from the outside and slightly caricatured. The plot makes it appear a great part – or at least offers an actor of genius the opportunity of making it flesh. But it is two-dimensional. Shakespeare's professional enemies were plagues and puritans. Perhaps he could not be objective; perhaps his hatred was too intense.

The structure of *Twelfth Night* repays careful study. There is no play with a surer exposition. In forty lines we meet the Duke, learn of his frustrated love for Olivia, and savour his court of music and flowers. His opening speech is justly one of the famous lyrics of our language. But when it is spoken by Orsino, the love-sick character in action, it is ironic *because* it is so beautiful. This capricious man ('Enough. No more! Tis not so sweet now as it was before'), with his indulgent love of fancy, is hardly fit to rule a state when he cannot rule himself. The excessive beauty of this first scene reveals all.

There is, in fact, very little that is *purely* lyrical in dramatic Shakespeare. Henry VI's pathetic yearnings to be a shepherd on the battlefield, or Oberon's lustful and malicious 'I know a bank', are critical of the characters who utter them.

In the second scene of *Twelfth Night*, the storm delivers a grieving and sincere Viola to this country of false love. But she has courage, and springs quickly to new life. She resolves on disguise – as a man. Then, with the tempo of the play still racing, we meet the sunshine comedy of Sir Toby and the foolish Sir Andrew (a contrast to the stormy sea coast). The tone is reckless, dangerously irresponsible.

One scene with Viola in the court hoist with her own disguise –

> *Yet a barful strife!*
> *Who e'er I woo, myself would be his wife,*

and we are back in Olivia's house meeting the strange clown, Feste, the superior Malvolio with his promise of a comic fall to come and Olivia herself.

The comic exposition is now complete. Shakespeare has dealt himself a perfect hand for misunderstanding and complication. We expect the arrival of Viola's twin brother, and a pattern of misunderstanding, just as we expect the pretensions of these comic characters to be exposed.

Let us also look at the last scene, where predictably all the follies come home to roost, and all the misunderstandings are cleared up. Everything can then end in the fullness of marriage, and only Feste is left outside with his bitter song.

Shakespeare relishes denouements. His last scenes in which order is restored have the counterpoint and balance of music. In *Cymbeline*, indeed, he permits himself the delights of some two score discoveries. This is no incompetence. Information is withheld and arranged so that the dance can go on as long as possible.

The most beautiful thing in the last scene of *Twelfth Night* is the twin recognition of Viola and Sebastian. Each knows that the other is truly their nearest and dearest, yet their joy is deliberately prolonged while they confirm to each other what each already knows.

This is the lyrical heart of the scene, and around it is woven a comic pattern of discovery and retribution until all is known:

> *and golden time convents,*
> *A solemn combination shall be made*
> *Of our dear souls . . .*

The imagery of *Twelfth Night* is as rich as its humanity. It is drawn from music, from the appetites (their yearnings and their uneasy surfeits), and, of course, from the inevitable image of human love, 'the worm i' the bud'. The imagery is sensual but transitory. The predominant image is that of the sea. It is an image of life and love, ranging from 'capacity receiveth as the sea' through the colloquialisms of 'board her', 'hoist sail', the prose precision of 'determinate voyage is mere extravagancy' and finally to the joy of 'share in this most happy wreck'.

The play is deliberately and delightfully erotic. We must remind ourselves that the original Viola and Olivia were boys, and that Shakespeare conceived his play in these terms. The pattern is then as follows: a boy playing a girl disguised as a boy is sent on a mission of love to a boy playing a girl, when his real emotions must be centred on playing a girl who is in love with Orsino. The second boy-girl then falls in love with the boy-girl-boy. Aphrodite can ask for no richer situation. Shakespeare had explored the possibilities of such a situation in *The Two Gentlemen of Verona*, but here he uses it to the full. It is hard on a modern actress to find this deliberate ambivalence.

The play bored Samuel Pepys, but in spite of this has held the stage successfully ever since. There are three dangerous traditions of the stage. Malvolio is by custom played by the leading actor. But the star in this role cannot help playing for sympathy, and even if he wishes to avoid it his public will insist upon giving it. A sympathetic Malvolio raises questions which should never be asked. We must still laugh at his final exit. The play only works if a brilliant actor can play the part in order to be completely detested, laughed at, and finally understood.

Olivia is generally played too old: doubtless a tradition which comes from the stock companies where the part belonged by right to the character lady who also played Gertrude. *Twelfth Night* is a play of youth and Olivia must be much younger in wisdom and experience than Viola.

The other dangerous stage tradition prevents us from clearly seeing Sir Andrew Aguecheek. He is always played as an effeminate. The text would rather indicate the opposite. He is a man with manure on his boots rather than ribbons in his hair. He is an unattractive, pretentious knight from the country – a man of money who loves dogs and hunting and who yearns to make a good match, though he is too much of a coward to try. Elizabethan literature is full of such empty roaring boys, such gentlemen bumpkins.

But the stage has not dealt badly with the play, and assuredly the play has always brought joy to the theatres. If the comedy is kept true to character and the lyrical emotions are expressed clearly and music-ally, but with no false resonance or oversentiment (unless the char-acter positively demands it), then the miracle will always work. The period of the play should not be specific. But in Shakespeare's Illyria you must not think it strange to meet Sea Captains and Puritans, Counts, Priests, Fools, Country Parsons and English aristocrats.

These ideas of mine cannot pretend to be original, I write this short essay from a study of the play over more than twenty years, and the happy experience of three stage productions. I cannot honestly re-member whether the ideas I have expressed are my own or somebody else's. But I do know they have stood the test of experience. To those that I have pillaged, I therefore offer my apologies and thanks.

1966

As You Like It

PETER BROOK

I imagine someone picking up the Folio Society edition of *As You Like It*: Folio – the word conjures up ancient manuscripts, echoes of scholarly discussion, the study of the methods of the Elizabethan theatre, of Shakespeare played in Shakespeare's way: he opens the book, there are designs by Salvador Dali, the notorious surrealist: one who is famous for his intimate knowledge of the anatomy of spiders but not for his interest in the structure of the sixteenth-century playhouse. What can he and Shakespeare have in common? So he has designed a production of *As You Like It*! This may give our imaginary person quite a surprise. How right, he may exclaim, or even how wrong! If he is an innocent abroad in the world of the theatre, he may wonder whether such extremes as Dali and a Shakespeare folio can ever meet. How should one stage *As You Like It*, he may wonder. As we imagine Shakespeare did in his time? Or as we imagine Shakespeare would do in ours? In this age of chaos, no chaos is greater than the theory of Shakespeare production – if one can use the word 'theory' to cover the jumble of styles and manners that are inflicted on the plays. In every country they are performed in a different way: I have heard Shakespeare's characters quote Voltaire, I have seen a Cleopatra flash a diamond bracelet and say of Enobarbus 'Ah, quel numero!': the plays are done in arenas, or reconstructions of the Elizabethan stage, in modern dress, in ancient dress: in crinolines, in dinner jackets: I have myself been responsible for staging one play in the manner of a painter who lived a hundred years after Shakespeare died: and another as though it were part of a newsreel in the Middle Ages . . .

Where are we going with all this? Is there any connecting thought in the work of the producers? Or do they just take the plays and 'put them on' as they feel inclined. Is there anything that is universally accepted as 'correct'? In fact, which way should someone picking up this *As You Like It* turn were he to wish to stage the play: towards the Folios, or towards Salvador Dali?

The conflicts and tendencies in Shakespeare production are two-fold and eternal: they stem from the simple fact that as a building the theatre has developed since Shakespeare's day. On the one hand, there are the resources of the modern theatre, its scenery, its lights, its machines: on the other hand there is the naked beauty of the text that thrills even in the simplest performance. There is elaboration, tempting to the producer, diverting to the audience, yet often a distraction, harmful to the play: there is simplicity, tempting in its austerity, manna to the purist, a revelation often helpful to the play, yet all too easily drab and boring to the audience.

At the moment a period of elaborate experiment has passed, and the trend is towards simplicity: study of the Elizabethan theatre has shown us how many of the plays' greatest virtues have been masked from us. It is now universally accepted that the cumulative effect of scenes following one another in an unbroken flow is an essential part of Shakespeare's method and that complicated scenery which adds a pictorial effect at the price of continual scene changes is energy mis-directed. The growing understanding that Shakespeare's characters are not naturalistic studies, that they need playing with sweep and line, not with observed or invented detail as in a modern character part, is leading to a simpler and swifter acting that makes the action clearer and more direct.

With all this we have not found the true Shakespearean way: it seems to elude us, for style can turn on itself. We may stage our Shakespeare with simplicity and love, with diction and care, allowing the text to speak for itself: this is not quite enough. The critics may praise us and we ourselves may be delighted until one day we realize that in our purity we become dullards while our audiences shift in their seats and yawn. It seems to me increasingly that in seeking a single style we are wrong, in tolerating a multiplicity of styles we are equally mistaken, but were we to recognize a twofoldness in Shake-speare's work, then all would fall into place.

Broadly speaking, the whole of the world's theatre falls into two vast categories. There is the High theatre, covering the formal, the ritual, the conventional, the poetic, the tragic, and there is the Low theatre, covering the natural, the real, the conversational, the literal and the comic. Each of these calls for a totally different approach from the producer: in fact, he must possess two styles to which every-thing he does can be referred.

The way to stage the plays in what I call the High theatre is very rigidly governed by the plays themselves. Aeschylus or Seneca, Otway or the great French classical school of Racine and Corneille can all be staged in one manner only, which is essentially appropriate to them and which can hardly be varied from producer to producer or from one period of history to another. In these plays every word that the dramatist uses is consistent with a self-imposed and disciplined unnaturalness: every form of behaviour or cue for movement conforms to rigid laws. If the dramatist bars himself from the natural, if he makes it impossible for any one of his characters to utter a spontaneous 'Hallo!', then any form of producer's invention that ignores the protocol in movement or behaviour, any relaxing of formality in setting furniture or actors' positions would be ineffective, tasteless and wrong.

The plays in the Low style have their feet on the ground, they are plants that flourish with mulching, the more the producer brings to them the more they yield. The vulgar theatre needs vulgarity, it needs embroidery and expansion to complete itself. The realistic text needs to have realistic detail imagined and added in the staging to achieve an effect of real life, and a production which does not contribute is inadequate. Tragedy may need simplicity, but comedy does not exist without comic invention: what the comedian calls 'business' is part and parcel of his art. The rarer the material of which a play is composed the rarer must be the material of the production: as in the heavens, the higher one gets the lighter the air, and the purer everything becomes. So with Fra Angelico all is simple and clear while with Rubens the canvas overflows with earthy detail, and so the producer, confronted with any play, instinctively assesses the 'rarity' or 'density' of its atmosphere and elaborates or simplifies accordingly.

Of course the two categories are neither clear cut nor constant, and the school of playwriting that in no way conforms is that of Shakespeare and the Elizabethans. For although Shakespeare's work can be divided into tragedies and comedies never once did he write a work all in one key. Not one of his tragedies remains consistently elevated in manner, nowhere does poetry continue without a break, nowhere is the metre of the verse itself unbroken for long. Shakespeare's technique is to heighten the truth to make it more vivid, and to pull it down to earth to make it more real. The most lyrical line is broken by the flash of character: the torrent of speech is followed by the inarticulate monosyllable: the purple patch is pitched against the slang of everyday speech. This technique is what gives the plays their breadth and excitement: it gives them the power to crowd the stage with real life, and yet unlike all the naturalistic plays, enables them to fly up to the heights reached only by poetic means. Shakespeare uses a film realism to surround his tragic moments, offsetting each with the other and achieving by this simultaneous use of two styles a level of expression that towers above Aeschylus and Racine on the one hand, and Ibsen and Shaw on the other.

So to stage any Shakespeare in a manner that reflects the intentions of the plays, the producer must be ready with his full range of implements on the two levels and prepared from moment to moment to switch from one to the other. He must face the fact that not every word Shakespeare wrote is of equal power: were they so, we would be choked by riches in the first pages. On the contrary, if one counted lines, the vast proportion of Shakespeare's work is filled with as many stock phrases as that of any hack writer. As in the works of Mozart, where the stock phrases and eighteenth-century clichés vastly outweigh the passages of genius, as in a modern poster where the great portions of featureless blank are the most vital part of the design, so Shakespeare spaced out his poetic moments with the language of everyday life, thus making the poetry more telling. The production that treats the wrong portions with reverence is in effect irreverent to the great moments. The Shakespeare producer must search for, recognize and discriminate between the places where he is working in realism: where the more he colours, the more detail he invents, the more Shakespeare's effect is heightened, and the times when without warning Shakespeare heightens the verbal effect and achieves a change of state. Then all at once the producer is dealing with poetic utterance, where simplicity and concentration are necessary, where the word is all-expressive, and extraneous invention a destroyer.

Furthermore, he must distinguish between the plays – not between the stock divisions of Comedy and Tragedy, for *The Tempest* is labelled a Comedy and yet is written in terms so high and rare as to call for a production of the most poetic nature, and *Richard III* which is labelled a Tragedy yet belongs to the earth and is made more vivid by rich invention. He must make his own divisions and must gauge for himself the level and the climate of each play.

There are some who see in *As You Like It* a hidden philosophical intent – some meaning in the contrast of country and court that the surface does not show. I myself see none of this. To me, *As You Like It* seems written purely to please. It is an entertainment, a gay youthful enchantment, a play of the physical world full of all the external physical things that give pleasure in the theatre: fights, songs, dances, movement, adventure, disguises, high spirits. A production of *As You Like It* stands or falls by the success with which these elements are staged. No academic point avails, the fact that the play is by Shakespeare cannot mean that it should be done less fully than were it by some other lesser author. It is no use producing it correctly 'as in the Elizabethan theatre' if any of the external requirements are inadequate. And the external standards are high: they are those of the best popular theatre of wherever and whenever it is performed. How often can such standards be applied: how often are our Shakespeare clowns as good as the best clowns of the commercial theatre, how often is the singing as accomplished, the dancing as imaginative and fresh as in the best musicals ? Yet these things are the very stuff of this play: its psychology is simple, and its heroes must be good: its villains are black and must be formidable: above all its comics must be funny. The play starts with a bang and to stage it correctly it must be played swiftly, in a strong, clear-cut way. In the second scene, Shakespeare notes 'A fight'. Shaw would have given two pages of detailed instructions: Shakespeare did not need to do so, because he knew that in his playhouse his stunt men would not let the crowd down. A producer, however loyal to Shakespeare, who does not see to it that the wrestling is terrific betrays his author.

It is only after all these external elements are completely under way that the moment comes for the producer to look deeper into *As You Like It*. Then he finds that, unlike the modern musical, it calls for the most accomplished comedy playing from all its performers. To make things harder, much of the spirit comes from the juxtaposing of scenes written in different keys. Here the producer must sense the different levels of comedy, the different degrees of artifice and realism they require, and play each one fully for what its manner dictates. He must not be afraid of inconsistency – everywhere Shakespeare sacrifices consistency for his own inner unity and the producer must follow suit. The realistic country girl Audrey must not be a music-hall joke, she must not be stylized to fit some arbitrary conception of the play, she must be a truly observed, realistically played character. At the same time the pastoral lovers must not be made more realistic:

they must behave and speak on the elevated plane of the pastoral play.

The virtues of any production of *As You Like It* are theatrical ones: it should have all the magic of the greasepaint world. If the production is alive, brilliant and diverting, then it is most likely both a good and a Shakespearean one. If the production is boring, then whatever theoretical loyalties may have brought it into existence it will be totally un-Shakespearean. In *As You Like It* the spirit of enjoyment should colour decision. Even the problem of scenery which can be so thorny a one in other plays is simpler here.

In *As You Like It*'s neighbour, *A Midsummer Night's Dream*, the more attractive the scenery the more it takes away from the magic of the words, for they only make their greatest effect in the simplest of settings. But *A Midsummer Night's Dream* is a high poetic play: *As You Like It* has no lyrical magic; and the problem is simple. Against a background of beauty and cunning design the play will be more joyous. Against a background such as a reconstructed Elizabethan stage that to modern eyes is featureless and austere this happy play might seem a little sad. That is why in going to Dali for his sets for *As You Like It* the Italian producer Visconti showed what to my mind is completely the right approach to this play. I did not see the production but it clearly showed that he wanted to give to the play all he could of fantasy and theatrical magic. Had he done so for *Hamlet* or *Lear* I might have disagreed. But in *As You Like It* the producer who, taking his cue from the title, reconciles the vivid excitement of Dali with the sober responsibilities of the Folio is, I am sure, on the right track.

1959

The Tragedy of Hamlet

RICHARD BURTON

An actor who is playing Hamlet should, perhaps, not write about the play. He has formulated his own opinions in order to portray the character as best he feels able. This means that, for the moment, he is set in his ideas about a character on the analysis of which the finest brains of critics and actors have been bent for three hundred and fifty years: so it may seem presumptuous of him to drag the cloak of his opinion in so vast an arena.

To speak of any man with other than superficial judgement requires more than a few moments, or a page or two of print. To speak of Hamlet quickly, summarily, is more unwise still – for Hamlet is not a person but a quintessence.

It has been estimated that some ten thousand books, articles and theses have been written on *Hamlet*, which indicates that it is by far the most controversial play in the canon. It would also suggest that there can be very little left to add. Certainly an actor would prefer to simplify, rather than further complicate the issue, if only for the reason that there is a very definite limit to the number of these subtleties, suggested by generations of learned critics, which an actor can embody in one performance.

Why this controversy? Perhaps chiefly because each reader who discovers the play for the first time, and for the first time wonders at the strange, almost unworldly, and yet most human Prince of Denmark, will hold in his mind yet another – if only very slightly different – picture of him from all others held before.

Charles Lamb felt that there was a little of us all in Hamlet. Here is a character in whose sufferings we can all of us feel the throb of our own; in whose gentleness, or rage, fear, horror, in whose very love of life, or bewilderment in its difficulties, we can often hear an echo that is sadly or gladly personal.

But does that of necessity give rise to controversy on such a scale? The plot of the play, baldly considered, is simple enough. It is with the convolutions that result in the final hecatomb that the writers on

Hamlet concern themselves; but there are many plots as complicated in contemporary dramatic writing, many plays with a more fearsome list of dead at the final curtain. It is, in the final analysis, the weird light that follows the young prince through the windings of the story that so fascinates the commentators. For the character of Hamlet is unique in all literature – a portrait of such depth and breadth, of such tender subtlety, as, filling the minds of watcher or reader, can create in each a different picture. The mirror that is here held up to nature flashes fires of infinite colour and intensity.

The questions to be asked are almost limitless; their answers multitudinous, and none of them satisfactory to everyone. It is certainly not within the scope of this introduction to attempt to answer them, and certainly an actor faced with the part is wisest to look for his own answers not in the critical Tower of Babel that looms over the play, but in the text of the play itself.

John Barrymore, one of the memorable Hamlets of the century, said: 'Not only does every actor play Hamlet provided he live long enough, but every member of the audience plays it, each in his own unyielding fashion . . . you can play it standing, sitting, lying down or, if you insist, kneeling. You can have a hangover. You can be cold sober. You can be hungry, overfed, or have just fought with your wife. It makes no difference as regards your stance or your mood. There are within the precincts of this great role a thousand Hamlets, any one of which will keep in step with your whim of the evening.'

Sir John Gielgud, probably the greatest Hamlet of the contemporary theatre, gave us a Hamlet poetical – sensitive – illogical. Here was the beautiful, effortless, tenor voice, soaring from the early depths of misery, through the antic hysteria of a torn mind, to the exquisite resolution of death – faced and accepted. Here Hamlet shrank from immediacy with a mind too fine to cut through the tangle of his fate with a bloody sword; a mind driven to near-lunacy by his mother's carnality, and pathetically finding horror even in the simplicities of Ophelia.

This was a definitive performance, but, in an indefinable part, not exclusive.

It is still possible for an actor broad of face, wide of shoulder, thick of thigh and robust of voice – in brief, too solid for such a sensitive interpretation as Gielgud's – to advance his own definition, survive the onslaught of the adverse, and attempt some of the many facets of so versatile a character.

I strongly recommend that readers of *Hamlet* should, for their own enjoyment, also read some at least of the writers about the play – bearing in mind that some of the flashes of the mirror may only be will-o'-the-wisps.

A modern reflection upon *Hamlet* is that it is the tragedy of a man who could not make up his mind. To chase a possible will-o'-the-wisp, to risk death by drowning in its pursuit, let us postulate that there is 'within the precincts' a Hamlet who not only could make up his mind, but who knew very well what he was about.

Hamlet vows vengeance in the presence of the Ghost. On only one occasion in the play does Hamlet find the king unattended, and, therefore, vulnerable. He comes upon him praying, alone. Now might he do it, and now he'll do it – 'that would be scanned; a villain kills my father, and for that, I, his sole son, do this same villain send to heaven'. His withdrawal from action is strongly reasoned, according to the doctrine of an eye for an eye. He must not, in killing the king, be kind, take him in prayer and 'season'd for his passage'. He must wait until the king is again vulnerable, but in 'some act that has no relish of salvation in 't', and pay home the debt of his father, who was killed in the full flush of his unrepented life.

The next time that Hamlet thinks Claudius may be within the shadow of his sword is in the Closet Scene. A cry from an eavesdropper behind the arras draws his blade in deadly thrust, and his cry of hope, 'is it the king?' It cannot be laid at the door of Hamlet's vacillation that the over-zealous Polonius should be the first fortuitous victim.

From then on Hamlet is defending his own life; his companions on the enforced voyage to England, who are to hand him over to death, are sent to their own death by him, as the result of his immediate decision. Their death is fortuitous, but results from the mounting tide of evil that stems from the first sinning of the king, not from a by-blow of Hamlet's indecision. He kills them to return to Denmark alive. Once back, he is faced with the culminating horror of evil in the Laertes plot, so that he is forced to final action. The king is killed, and with him his instrument, Laertes, and in the welter of evil Hamlet himself has to die.

There is a brief to be upheld on such a line, that is to say, there is a possible Prince of Decision who can hold the interest. The play may not be one of weakness, but a portrait of strength in its finest most certain form. Horror is pulled upon our heads perhaps by the initial horror of murder, gathering way and reflected in Hamlet's mind, not in the weakness of that mind.

The epitaph for the writer of a thousand pages or a thousand words on *Hamlet* is forever the same: the reflection from one facet of the jewel took the eye, but let no one think that there is only one colour in the diamond.

Take the play. Read it. The greatness is there in the bald, printed line.

1954

Troilus and Cressida

BOHDAN KORZENIEWSKI

Any account of the contemporary fortunes of *Troilus and Cressida* reads very much like the story of many war-torn European cities. I was brought up in Warsaw. I lived through her destruction and her rebuilding; it is therefore easy for me to understand a process that is echoed in my own personal experience. When they began to excavate among the mountains of rubble which smothered so much of the oldest part of the city, called the Old Town, some completely unknown fragments of ancient architecture were suddenly revealed.

In Poland, as everywhere else, the enterprising nineteenth century adapted whole towns to its own advantage and convenience: above all, advantage. Hastily, because capital must earn dividends, buildings which in earlier centuries had been erected after long and careful forethought, were adapted to a new use. How the nineteenth century appreciated an older love of beauty is only too well known! That which was in the way it razed, that which was still of use it converted. Parts of the barbicans, the watch towers, the defensive walls, even the fine houses of the nobility all met the same fate when it paid to incorporate them in the walls of new houses designed to be profitably rented. If these houses were intended for people in the higher income bracket, entitled to a certain comfort, statues *à l'antique* were added, painted in oils and perched on steps of imitation marble. If an ancient bas-relief was discovered in a wall destined to become the interior wall of some drawing-room, the mason either obliterated it with his hammer or slapped a coat of plaster over it.

This brash nineteenth century, bursting with energy, enterprise and an unshaken faith in the purposeful existence of man, likewise discovered Shakespeare for itself. There was nothing strange in that: every epoch – except those which choose to ignore him – has made the same discovery. But here the 'for itself' might well be underlined, as the nineteenth century so coloured Shakespeare that, like Lady Macbeth with her bloodied hands, we have not been able, to this day, to wash away the stain. It treated the lowering, bloody, savage drama of

Shakespeare like a tale about robbers, told at evening round the fire-side. The fable evoked a pleasant shudder or two of awe because it was wholly improbable, and so gave the participants in such pastimes a feeling of superiority over the people of other ages, now fortunately remote, when to win possessions, favours and riches one hired paid brigands to slit the throat of one's political opponents. In the nine-teenth century political opponents were overcome in a parliamentary manner by the counting of votes, and around twilight a well-brought-up policeman watched over passers-by so that law and order in public places should be decently preserved. There were country-wide mas-sacres, of course, in some Congo or Nepal, which spared neither women nor children, but these were trivial mishaps associated with the white man's burden and it was not done to talk about them out loud. It was even more not done to link Shakespeare with such minor incidents. It was understood that the specialists in spreading civiliza-tion sometimes had to fall back on violence when it became difficult otherwise to persuade those being civilized that it was all being done for their own good. It was simply not a tragedy in the Shakespearean sense. This had to depict events so terrible that civilized people could sigh with relief and say to themselves, 'We live in times when such things are not possible'. It served to brighten their lives, like other amusement. The theatre was, after all, amusement.

How far the past century (indeed, until the outbreak of the First World War) adapted Shakespeare to its own taste is witnessed by the improbable fact that it found it possible for obese singers in velvet costumes to warble the sentiments of Macbeth or Othello amid the painted canvas walls of mediaeval castles. History, which thriftily amasses all evidence of human criminality and of bad taste, has bequeathed us a photograph album of singing Shakespeare murderers – hardly a creditable testimony!

The time came, however, when the bombs fell on the houses of those people who thought that their way of life was so secure. In Warsaw it was the same as in London; the only difference was one of degree. In Warsaw, twice reduced to ruins to an almost fantastic ex-tent, it was possible, among the uncovered staircases, for the eye suddenly to light on a painted ceiling. One particular example, of which there were many, etched itself on my memory. Dressed in diaphanous robes, Aurora was flying through an azure sky, a torch in her outstretched hand. For the first time the imagined sky merged with the reality and the induced reaction was one almost of terror. In the real sky aircraft threatened. In their descent, the bombs accomplished a very efficient confrontation between reality and the art that went with the conviction of people that they controlled reality. Hand in hand with the destruction of buildings went the destruction of a morality whose cornerstone was complete self-confidence.

In destroying illusions the war discovered another Shakespeare. That knowledge of the world which informs all his work was not out of date at all. Shakespeare became contemporary again. Not after the manner of Beckett, Sartre or Genet; such comparisons, which were in fashion a few years ago, are too much like science fiction fantasies where the authors try, on the basis of a superficial knowledge of earth, to imagine civilization on Mars. The image of mankind that pervades Shakespeare's plays has no need of such analogies to underline his astonishing modernity. If he does not address us from the stage in the language of today, it is only because the majority of theatres have continually been concerned with the forms of the past century. After all, we are not free of them yet. It is hardly surprising that people, appreciating the topicality of Shakespeare, reach out for plays that the past has slighted. The war uncovered in Shakespeare something that the previous century, in rebuilding culture, had plastered over, reckoning it completely useless for spiritual needs.

In the post-war world two universal classics have suddenly met with startling success. For a score of years now Molière's *Don Juan* and Shakespeare's *Troilus and Cressida* have been the two plays that have most tempted those people who longed to use the stage to project post-war anxieties. Both these plays were rejected by the previous century. It condemned them for having been based on times of moral degeneracy, for having been written when the well of creative imagination had run dry. A cursory glance at what some of the leading critics of the day had to say, shows in what little esteem both these plays were then held. Underlining the severe and sometimes even offensive judgements was the feeling that both these works were entirely foreign to the spirit of the times. They offended most of the principles by which people then wanted to be governed; their view of the world appeared black, their courage in laying bare the impulses behind human achievement was taken for cynicism, and the ruthlessness of their approach to the very foundations of the social structure – and here was the main stumbling block – was held to encourage the spread of anarchy. It needed a war and the total ruin it brought to certain doomed countries before it penetrated to man's conscience that in those, as it were, moments of refraction, both these authors of the modern theatre had dared to look truth in the eye, even though, like Medusa, their opaline gaze turned the hearts of men to stone.

In *Troilus and Cressida*, in those post-war years still full of horror at what had happened, we were attracted above all by its evident and cruel knowledge of life, a knowledge so cruel that it is utterly devoid of illusions. Hamlet's unease and revolt, born in the discovery that 'the time is out of joint', is replaced in this play by the conviction that the world is not out of joint at all through a momentary disturbance of the order of things, but that this is its natural state. *Troilus and Cressida* is built on the discovery that the world, and at that the world as organized by man, is not governed by the moral laws which mankind through long centuries has inclined to regard as the foundation of Creation.

The Crakow setting of *Troilus and Cressida* emerged in 1960 from a Europe full of despair and dissension. Even then it was a little behind the times. Over the first post-war years the characteristic tensions induced by bitterness had slowly lost their power. No longer were bearded youths meeting at the 'Deux Magots' to air their collective despair over a nonsensical world. The abstractionists, after scoring a resounding victory in nearly every continent, had already begun to recognize the first signs of weariness in an art which longed to forsake truth. In short, the smoke from the cremation ovens, which had poured forth like a black cloud over our country in particular, had by then dispersed. Admittedly a belt of radiation had drifted over the earth, bearing witness to numerous tests of atomic bombs, but it had passed out of sight and become invisible, needing the imagination of the student in the nuclear laboratories to conjure up the terror and the threat.

The reason why we were behind the times lies in the nature of the theatre. Essentially the theatre involves collective operation and common decision, and for this reason any given production seldom appears in due season. In this case the setting for *Troilus and Cressida*, although ready on paper, had been a good five years forcing its way on to the stage. The path lay through almost virgin country. Intimate though our relations with Shakespeare had been – for close on twenty years he had almost been our national author, continually re-translated and re-acted – *Troilus and Cressida* had lain fallow, as it had everywhere else in the world, England not excluded.

It had only been performed once in the Polish theatre, again in Crakow and again in time of war. It was produced in 1916 through the initiative of Tadeusz Pawlikowski, one of the most independent of men in this poor man's craft, who traded his family lands and fortune for the pleasure of tackling something difficult in his own theatre. A caricature of that time showed him at the first night of a new play, sitting alone in a hall seating a thousand. Accustomed to struggling with audiences, he did not shrink from joining battle over Shakespeare's most pessimism-saturated play. He did not, however, live to see the first performance. According to his notes, the play was produced by others. In resurrecting this malignant version of the Homeric legend, there was no question therefore, even had the need arisen, of falling back on any Polish tradition of presentation.

But the need did not arise. Dislike of what predecessors had done with Shakespeare made it essential to seek for a new solution.

Inevitably, however, this idea of a new solution was faced with insuperable problems. Many of the theatre buildings had weathered the war and where the shell remained every possible care was devoted to re-creating the theatre as it had been; no country displays a greater affection for the old forms of art than one consumed by revolution. Several years went by filled with dreams of a truly new Shakespeare, but when the chance of a production offered, it had to be in a typical nineteenth-century theatre with three tiers of velvet-covered seats. Consequently many excellent ideas had to be abandoned, only faint traces of them remaining in the theatre programme.

I have always encouraged audiences to bring their imaginations to the theatre, and that theatre could – though, as yet, it does not – really present a Shakespeare of our times, if only people knew how to take advantage of the fruits of today's civilization.

'In Shakespeare,' I have written, 'there are always undiscovered possibilities. Until now, humanity had produced no poet who can equal his skill in projecting faithfully both man and his destiny without stooping to an imitation of reality. . . . A theatre accustomed and adapted to imitations, however, does not lend itself to a portrayal which seeks to emphasize his relevance to the present day. The wealth of wisdom with which his poetry abounds – where both the grotesque and the tragic are expressed with a clarity that even our most daring approaches have so far failed to achieve – can only be fully realized in a new theatre. Here the actor could come out to his audience, could almost be one with it, and fiction and reality could regain that missing unity without which there is no true theatre: the oneness of stage and audience.'

'Please therefore imagine' – this time I was addressing an audience seated as of old in plush seats and thus conditioned to the old-time reception of plays – 'that this performance of *Troilus and Cressida* is being enacted in a theatre where the traditional division of stage from audience does not exist. The audience are sitting in the various seats of a hall designed with the necessary imagination – which today can be translated into fact. The experience of recent years has shown that in this sphere the mastery of man over matter, his freedom from material limitations, is something to be proud of. Today we can create buildings the shape we want. There is no line, however freakish, in an architect's sketches which cannot be given form in a building made of the new materials – aluminium, concrete, glass. In a theatre serving the new Shakespeare, the actors, like the audience, use different parts of the hall which change according to the needs of the play. For the stage can be everywhere, wherever the actors appear. At one moment they will be restricted to only one area or staircase, where they are intended to form the pre-arranged group demanded by taut dramatic construction. At another, where the construction is freer, they will move from place to place. They position themselves among the audience or mingle with it just as freely as the play itself mingles with life.

'In *Troilus and Cressida* many parts of the theatre are used, in tune with the fantasy in which Shakespeare embroils human destinies. The Greek tents, faded by many years of use, stand in the middle of the arena. Among them Thersites hobbles from one group of lounging soldiery to another, choking with impotent rage at the stupidities of mankind. From the arena wide steps, partly occupied by the audience, lead up to a first platform. Here, between the Greek camp and the walls of Troy, the leaders of the warring nations meet and wage their battles. The next level serves as the walls and turrets of Troy from which a series of new levels leads into the garden where the lovers meet...'

Some discerning person once said that only the overcoming of difficulties can produce true art. Having approached the experiment of a production of Shakespeare at the beginning of the atomic era in conditions appropriate to Queen Victoria, I doubt whether this remark is always true. I shared this doubt with the audience in the programme. 'In a theatre where the stage is set behind a proscenium arch,' I said in the preface, 'Shakespeare will be a compromise. In politics (as the English do not need to be told) compromise often leads to victory. In the drama it invariably leads to defeat, or else to a seeming victory more fraught with dangers than any defeat.'

In the act of creating any work of art, doubts and fears are obviously omnipresent. The shaping of the final form is a continuous process involving continual struggles with resistant material. In all spheres of art except the theatre these struggles between Jacob and the angel take place in creative solitude. The theatre is different in that its battles were waged by a group – the fiercest being those fought by the actors. However, before it comes to the final confrontation that results either in victory or defeat, preliminary trials of strength are conducted by the producer and the designer. In the modern theatre these two people shoulder the burden of giving shape to what does not yet exist. They must therefore visualize the production through the eyes of the imagination, having only an opened copy of the play in front of them.

Then – and this is the moment of truth – they have to decide how to present dramatically to the realistic world of people something that only possesses as much real existence as the printed word has been able to catch. Only a man devoid of artistic judgement would be tempted, for instance, to put the Iliad on the screen. Imagine how it would look to capture on film Zeus rebuking Aries, Hermes winging through the air with a message from the gods, or Thetis, with a caress, wheedling a shield for her son from Vulcan! The reaction must be one of complete horror. The stage producer and designer, however, have to succeed in doing just this. Admittedly the drama of *Troilus and Cressida* is not Homer's epic poem, although it borrows material from him. Shakespeare does not provide gods. In this elaboration of a myth, the sky over Troy is empty. But, for the designer who has to create the setting for the words there remain more than enough intransigent problems full of equally dangerous and insidious pitfalls.

At first, the obvious but not universally perceived fact that a play of this size is not just the sum of worldly knowledge, tends to disguise these pitfalls. If the purpose of the theatre were merely the presentation of knowledge of man and his quarrels with his environment – or with himself – this particular art-form would not demand any special talents. It would appeal to publicists for its political or social comment, to sociologists dissatisfied with the disciplines to which they are submitted, to psychologists longing to give impetus to a more extreme fantasy than that science permits, and finally to people who just feel that the organization of a spectacle is as good an occupation as any other. On the basis of a good deal of observation, I suspect that many theatres throughout the world do understand their calling in this way. It keeps both audience and producer happy and, in progressing from success to success, does achieve something. It is, without any doubt, a success well merited when a theatre satisfies the so-called 'paying public', or gives a lot of people what they want. It is a disturbing fact that, today, a lot of people do not want poetry. They get along perfectly well without it. The hunger for poetry is not nowadays that of a man tormented by defeat. The vast majority of people are distinctly undernourished in this respect, but this has not up till now excited alarm at the United Nations.

Troilus and Cressida is a poem. Its greatest value lies in its poetry. Cruel, predatory, sardonic, tragic poetry, like that which the poets of today speak more to themselves in solitude than to the world outside. The play communicates the author's deeply felt alienation which is, at times, tinged with horror, but mostly springs from simple rebellious despair. Realizing this, the begetters of the Crakow production were faced with a task that involved elements of wizardry or devil-worship.

The costume designs by Andrzej Majewski for the Crakow production show the degree to which he succeeded in conjuring up this magical atmosphere. At the same time, they give an insight into the creator's mind at a time when his creations were still intangible, unrealized. It is, perhaps, because of this that, if there can be said to be an abstract aspect of a production, it is this aspect that they represent, an aspect which usually disappears for ever when the final curtain falls. Through them the Shakespeare lover will see what happened when one of his greatest works was staged in Poland. As with a messenger's speech in Greek tragedy, the value lies in the essential truth that it conveys.

1968

Othello

Senate and
street scenes

The Tragedy of Othello

IVOR BROWN

Othello is one of the Shakespearean plays which can be dated with some confidence. There was a Court performance given by the King's Men in the Banqueting House in Whitehall on November 1st, 1604. There is an obvious allusion to the title-part ('More savage than the barbarous Moor') in a play by Dekker and Middleton called *The Honest Whore*, which was printed at the end of that year. There may, of course, have been previous public performances during the summer season at the Globe. It was evidently liked, for it was kept in the repertory of the King's Men. We know that the Prince of Wurtemburg saw it at the Globe in 1610 and it was one of twenty pieces chosen for production at the Great Revels, preceding the marriage of the 'Princes Highnes the Lady Elizabeth' with 'the Prince Pallatyne Elector' in 1613.

The first Quarto edition of the play (1622) described it as 'diverse times acted at the Globe and Black-Friers by His Majesties Servants'. In the early records the play's name is usually given as *The Moore of Venice* (or More of Venis or Venise, with spellings assorted), and not as *Othello*. The chief part or parts began to be increasingly used as the titles of plays; for example, *Much Ado* had become *Benedicte and Betteris* in 1613 and *Twelfth Night* was *Malvolio* in 1623. Nowadays we are faithful to the brief *Othello*.

There are further mentions of performances in 1629, 1635 and 1636. At the restoration *Othello* was one of the first pieces to be revived at the reopening of the theatres. Pepys saw it at The Cockpit and noted that 'a very pretty lady called out to see Desdemona smothered'. Killigrew, in the same year, introduced a woman, Margaret Hughes, to play Desdemona, and this may have been the first appearance of a professional actress on the public stage. Court ladies had long ago played for sport (or exhibitionism) in Court Masques.

Several leading roles in Shakespeare's plays have been ascribed to Richard Burbage without contemporary evidence, it being assumed that the leading actor of the King's Men always took the leading part. (Did he never have a rest?) But we have proof that he played Othello in the verses written after his death in 1619.

> *No more young Hamlett, ould Heironymoe,*
> *Kind Leer, the grevéd Moore, and more beside,*
> *That lived in him, have now for ever dy'de.*

'Kind Leer' must surely be a misprint for king, unless the reference is only to the play's piteous end. The assumption that the role of Othello, like the others, was for ever dead was a gracious compliment to the mighty Richard, but a singularly inaccurate prophecy. There has been no farewell to Othello's great farewell to occupation and to glory. Its trumpet notes have immortal echoes.

Burt was the Othello seen by Pepys in 1660. Since then our great tragedians have been smothering their Desdemonas down the centuries, provided they felt they had the physique and primitive passion necessary to undertake the part. If they did not care to risk the role, there was Iago for their talents. Garrick played Iago to Barry's Othello, and Laurence Olivier, at the Old Vic in 1938, was Iago to Ralph Richardson's Moor. Sometimes the two leading actors have exchanged these parts after a while as a display of expertise. Matheson Lang and Arthur Bourchier did that in 1920.

During my time I have seen the following Othellos: Matheson Lang, Godfrey Tearle, Paul Robeson, Wilfrid Walter, Ernest Milton, Abraham Sofaer, Ralph Richardson, Donald Wolfit, Frederick Valk, Jack Hawkins and Anthony Quayle; all these on the professional stage. There have been amateur productions which I do not care to re-member: this is not a play for undergraduates. Of the Iagos I have most vivid memories of Ralph Richardson and Bernard Miles.

Some of the Othellos were, as Costard said of Sir Nathaniel when the latter was cast as Alisander, 'Alas, you see how it is, a trifle o'er-parted'. The physique might be right and yet the bearing wrong. Paul Robeson, for example, with no need 'to black himself all over' had the stature, but not the stance and carriage, the flow of feeling but not the technique to convey it. A man does not become a Shake-spearean actor overnight and Robeson, a stranger on these perilous heights, was also handicapped by an absurd Iago and incompetent direction. The part, too, was an odd choice of Ernest Milton's, showing more courage than prudence in the selection. Of him James Agate wrote, 'In place of the noble, perhaps vacant and certainly slow, unblinking majesty of the King of Beasts, [he] exhibits the eager, nimble-witted watchfulness of one of the lesser and more apprehensive cats'.

It was generally held at the time that Godfrey Tearle's first Othello (1921) was the top of his performance: to try again, nearly thirty years later, was to bring a ripe experience but not to add emotional impetus; his rendering was momentous but lacked what J. C. Trewin has well called, in assessing Tearle, 'the arched fury of the breaking wave'. Agate, who never saw the second venture, was enormously impressed by the first.

There are, as everybody knows, two sides, two well-nigh contradictory sides, to the Moor. He must have a soldierly splendour: he must seem to be descended from 'men of royal siege': he must merit the high regard of Venice; he must be a likely fascinator of Desdemona: he must have that nobility without which his collapse into the extremes of savage barbarism fails to be tragic; yet, when goaded, he must have the latent bestiality of one who, provoked in the extreme, can vow to chop his so recently beloved wife into 'messes'. Tearle had the splendour in full measure and he made as good a show of brutish frenzy as art, working on and even against nature, could contrive. A crumbling greatness, the ruin of nobility, came to him more easily. His Antony in *Antony and Cleopatra* was, for me, the summit of his work, because there was more in him of the lust-betrayed Roman than of the lust-ensavaged African. But both his appearances as Othello had their magnificence.

It can be argued that the part defies the English temperament, except when the Englishman is altogether out of the ordinary, as Kean must have been, with the lightning-flash of power that set Drury Lane a-tremble and must have caused far more pretty ladies to cry out at seeing Desdemona smothered than occurred when Pepys had his eye on the fair ones in 1660. There must have been a demon in Edmund Kean, a demon peeping out with all the luridness of evil suddenly uncaged. 'His eye, who can forget that eye?' wrote G. H. Lewes of Kean's transformation from the dignified to the demonic.

We have had thunderous Othellos – Mr Valk not least. He presented more of the goaded bull than the lion tormented. Thunder must be linked with poetry and there has to be lightning too. Donald Wolfit has been so much praised for his Lear that his Moor has been less regarded, somewhat unjustly. We have had believable soldiers turned to madness and I have not forgotten Anthony Quayle; and it must be remembered that the same actor has also given us one of the most plausible of recent Iagos.

Both parts have one thing in common, the mixture of a hidden diabolism with the outward look of a good fellow. If there is too much of the latter in Iago, he may so convince us of his honesty that we can never believe that he would turn to villainy or to cruelty unparalleled. On the other hand, an Iago seeming crafty at all times would never have held his place with the Moor or been so recklessly believed by him. Bernard Miles as the Ancient was admirably sly, twisted, and capable of evil, but hardly honest-seeming. Perhaps Olivier, Richardson and Quayle have been most effective in this blend of Iago's qualities: Leo McKern, a most versatile Shakespearean actor, won very high praise during the Stratford company's tour of Australia and New Zealand. Knowing the range of his work, I can well believe that the plaudits were amply justified. A judge of high quality whose death in January 1955 was a tragic loss to criticism, T. C. Kemp of *The Birmingham Post*, praised the Stratford production with its 'beautifully designed all-purpose setting' by Tanya Moiseiwitsch; he commended also the 'remarkable intensity and inwardness of Quayle's Othello' and the way in which McKern's Iago 'hid his designs behind a hearty, back-slapping approach, but allowed a pretty fiend to emerge in private'. I did not see McKern, but I can endorse the other two valuations.

Many find *Othello* the least acceptable of the great tragedies, and I myself do not welcome another call to Venice and Cyprus as eagerly as I do to Elsinore, Inverness, Lear's blasted heath, or Cleopatra's Egypt, with its marvellous motion from the bed-soft to the battle-scarred. Nobody can possibly deny the sublimity of the writing of *Othello*, even when the action is the least sublime in its portraiture of character in ruin. Nor can one withhold admiration from the extreme efficiency of the narrative. Shakespeare never tightened the strings of a plot more cunningly: the pace and the impact are terrific. The time-scheme, as is often pointed out, is chaotic, but Shakespeare was obviously writing in a flood of excitement. What were hours and days to him then? And what have they been to spectators and auditors ever since? We are too closely gripped by character and calamity to be fussed about the calendar. The pedantic reader can bring a stop-watch to the text, if he cares to: in the theatre time is irrelevant to the surge and the gallop of Othello's journey to disaster.

What none the less hampers a complete surrender to *Othello*, at least for me, is the excessive folly of the man in trusting Iago so easily and the excessive brutishness in the subsequent fury. That mess-chopping roar, the likening of his wife to a fly in the shambles, may not have disgusted the Jacobean public as much as it grates on modern ears. The handkerchief episode, or rather episodes, may surely be deemed trivial for the gigantic theme: the proof of infidelity by such tokens is proper to a comedy of intrigue, not to a tragedy of all-powerful emotions. It is impossible not to be swept along by the word-music of *Othello*, but it is also impossible not to be dismayed by the slightness of motive and the horror of the conduct. Can all be quite redeemed by the mastery of verbal magic? Mention of word-music sends my thoughts back to Godfrey Tearle; there have been others in our time more ready with the cataract of passion, none better gifted with a full diapason of sound and with a vocal beauty matched with the beauty of the lines.

Since Mr Ridley's text has been used for this volume, it would be courteous, as well as instructive, to quote him.

'From the purely dramatic point of view this play may well appear the summit of Shakespeare's achievement. It is not so profound as *Hamlet*, nor so overwhelming as *Lear*; in general emotional impression it more nearly resembles *Macbeth*. It is superb theatre, with the severest economy and concentration, and it is by far the most intense of all. There is no relief, none of that alternating increase and decrease of strain that is so clearly marked in the others, none of those periods in which, even though there is no comic relief, the action seems for a few moments to stand still while we recover ourselves. From the moment of the landing in Cyprus Shakespeare has the fingers of one hand on our pulses and the fingers of the other on the levers of the rack. It is the most cruel play he wrote, and the most pitiful.'

He is right. And so to the torture-chamber – and, for consolation, to the music-room.

1955

All's Well That Ends Well

OSBERT LANCASTER

It would, manifestly, be foolish to try to maintain that *All's Well That Ends Well* is among the more successful of Shakespeare's works. While not wholeheartedly subscribing to the view put forward by certain critics that it is, in fact, a straight 'potboiler', it is difficult to avoid the conclusion that for once the dramatist has succumbed to the temptation, from which not even the greatest are wholly immune, to give the public what he thought it wanted.

The plot, creaking and groaning with improbabilities, which can only be resolved by that hammiest of all Elizabethan gimmicks, the GREAT BED TRICK, can barely have sufficed to hold the reader's interest in the original Boccaccio *conte*; transferred to the stage it demands of the audience a suspension of disbelief which even Shakespeare's skill and language are powerless to achieve. Nor, with one exception, are the characters sufficiently interesting or sympathetic to enable us to overlook the nonsensical circumstances in which they find themselves.

Not all the author's partiality can for one moment persuade us that the heroine, Helena, regarded dispassionately, is anything but a tough and ruthless little operator, determined at all costs to marry the boss's son. For an actress the role must be one of formidable difficulty as in order to maintain some sort of balance she has to endow the character with an overweight of personal charm, with little or no support from her lines, to compensate for the invariably unattractive nature of her actions.

From Bertram, on the other hand, who is presented as an obstinate young snob, incapable of realizing where his own best interests lie, it is impossible wholly to withdraw our sympathy. Admittedly a fool, there is still no denying that he finds himself in an intolerable situation, for which, as far as we can see, he is not in any way responsible. Why should he wed this bossy little orphan with whom he has been brought up and of whose company he is by now, likely enough, heartily sick? Particularly at a time when he has not yet had an opportunity of judging what alternatives the Court of France might offer. But finally, and with a scarcely credible inconsistency, by the tame way he accepts his fate, and the drivelling ineptitude with which he conducts his interview with the king, he succeeds in changing our pity to contempt.

If the character of the countess is perfectly consistent and skilfully presented it is certainly no more attractive. One needs no Freudian support to appreciate the significance of the lines with which she opens the play. 'In delivering my son from me I bury a second husband.' She provides throughout the perfect case history of the dominating mother figure. Determined at all costs to retain her son as a substitute for her departed husband, the ceaseless repetition of whose virtues encourages the belief that in life he had had a pretty thin time, she is prepared to force Bertram into marriage with her beloved protegée, who is in many ways simply an extension of her own personality. The teasing aspect of the case lies in the ambivalence with which her creator regards the old monster. For it would be foolish to suppose that Shakespeare was unaware of the deeper motives which underlie her actions, although he gives us no hint either of disapproval or extenuation.

The king presents no such problems. He is simply a lay-figure, a necessary part of the machinery of the plot, and nothing more. Adversely to criticize the Old Vic production of 1952 for making him a hypochondriacal figure of fun, mumbling unexceptionable platitudes, seems therefore, unjustified. Without some such element of the farcical the tedium of the Court scenes would be almost unbearable.

Nor can it be said that the secondary characters add much to the excitement. Lafeu, that stock Shakespearean figure 'an old Lord', is a more sensible, less garrulous, and therefore less theatrically effective, Polonius, and Lavache must come very high on the list of the more intolerable of Shakespeare's clowns, the majority of whose wise-cracks are always likely, mercifully, to be abandoned in production.

Fortunately there remains Parolles. While the rest of the cast, with the partial exception of the countess, have little or no relevance to life as we know it today, and must, even within the accepted conventions of the Elizabethan stage, always have seemed remote, Parolles is vital, three-dimensional, timeless. He is the eternal fixer, whose *combinazioni* are always doomed to go wrong; the wide boy so sharp that he must always cut himself. Fertile in invention, tireless in name dropping, forever wearing a club tie to which he is not entitled, he is far too familiar a figure for us to feel for him in his hour of humiliation the embarrassed pity which Malvolio excites. Parolles we know will always bob up again, for Malvolio there can be no real future.

Moreover, like Falstaff, Parolles has the gift of self knowledge, and his great speech in Act 4, 'Simply the thing I am shall make me live', is certainly, given an actor of Mr Hordern's merit, the most effective moment in the whole play. But the comparison with Falstaff, although inevitable, can be pushed too far; Falstaff for all his cowardice, trickery and self-indulgence remains a gentleman by birth, to whom some tattered vestiges of dignity still cling, even when exploding the whole concept of 'honour', but Parolles' claims to nobility are not for one moment to be believed either by him or us, and could not possibly carry conviction with anyone less dismally stupid than Bertram.

The difficulty created by the tameness of most of the characters and the overwhelming vitality of one are not unfortunately resolved or redeemed by any outstanding poetic merit in the text. In this play Shakespeare is at his most gnomic, and the verse varies from the tiresomely-elaborate to the distressingly trite. In particular, there is an over-abundance of the flattest rhyming couplets.

> *More should I question thee, and more I must,*
> *Though more to know could not be more to trust,*
> *From whence thou camest, how tended on: but rest*
> *Unquestioned welcome and undoubted blest.*
> *Give me some help here, hoa ! If thou proceed*
> *As high as word, my deed shall match thy deed.*

After a few minutes of this sort of thing one begins to wonder whether, in fact, 'Savanarola Brown' has not had a hand in the composition.

It will be readily appreciated that *All's Well That Ends Well* is not, therefore, an easy play to mount. The overriding problem which faces the producer is how best to retain his audience's attention in the long sections when Parolles is off-stage. To accomplish this he is surely perfectly justified in using every trick of the trade and every elaboration of setting, for of all Shakespeare's plays, *All's Well That Ends Well* is the least likely to suffer from over-production.

There is, however, one line of approach for which sufficient justification exists in the text and which the intelligent producer – and his designer – will exploit to the utmost – the contrast of the two main settings. On the one hand Rossillion and the Court of France, medieval old fashioned, hierarchic; on the other Renaissance Florence, tough, realistic modern. The whole ridiculous situation can only receive some degree of rational support if we conceive of it – as Shakespeare well may have – as a conflict between two ways of life, one doomed, the other expanding. The static, strictly-graded world of sixty-four quarterings into which poor Bertram was born, controlled by a semi-sacred sovereign with absolute power to interfere in the private lives of even the most exalted of his subjects, and the go-getting, uninhibited world of swift-moving *condottieri* where all actions are judged by results. The only possible theatrical justification for Helena is that she provides the link between the two; while paying lip-service to the conventions by which the countess and the king are guided, she is, nevertheless, a sufficiently contemporary character to have no hesitation in employing stratagems for which Parolles is soundly condemned. Seen in this light her move to Florence acquires a symbolic significance. In the same context moreover, Parolles himself becomes more meaningful; he is no longer an isolated 'character' in the Jonsonian sense but one whose attitude can be regarded as providing, by way of contrast and exaggeration, a sharp commentary on that of his noble companions. The little stratagem over the lost drum fails ludicrously; Helena's impersonation trick comes off. But in both cases the object of the exercise is purely selfish and the means employed unquestionably ignoble.

Fundamentally *All's Well* is therefore a profoundly cynical play, and is best treated as such. Unhappily, the producer's task is rendered almost impossible by Shakespeare's reluctance openly to define his attitude. The happy conclusion so firmly proclaimed in the title and so unconvincingly arrived at must be accepted at its face value; all doubts must be implied, never stated. On one plane we must not question the assumption that all *is* well that ends well; on another we must remain uneasily aware that it is highly questionable whether this end does justify these means. But the fact that a perfect balance is unlikely ever to be achieved in performance, that the underlying ambivalence cannot properly be stated in theatrical terms, is hardly the fault of the producer.

1963

Measure for Measure

HAROLD HOBSON

The Stratford on Avon *Measure for Measure* in the 1962 season continued a tradition recently established when, just before the outbreak of the 1939–45 war, George Robey played Falstaff. In the late 'forties Stratford brought another famous star of musical comedy and the halls, Jay Laurier, to give breadth and a sort of vulgar humanity to some of Shakespeare's more clownish parts. In *Measure for Measure* Norah Blaney, who had appeared in some of the most celebrated musicals of the 'twenties, such as *Oh, Kay*, was engaged to provide a very juicy performance as Mistress Overdone. This, however, as it turned out, was only a small point of antiquarian interest. What made John Blatchley's production memorable was something quite different from the introduction into Shakespeare of players formerly famous in the world of song and dance shows. The striking thing about it was its exaltation of the Duke.

There was, it is true, no ducal splendour about John Bury's setting, which was impressive, but very simple. At the back of the stage there was an enormous wall of what looked like grey rough stone. There was a rough stage surface of a similar texture, across which ran a wide wooden platform diagonally. This facilitated the swift movement of the Duke. It enabled him to pass rapidly from point to point, to dart hither and thither, to be (almost) omnipresent. This swiftness, this speed, this ubiquity, were established against the darkness and gloom of Vienna under his notorious deputy, Angelo. And throughout the evening this deputy – it is a vital fact of the production – remained a deputy only: nothing more.

From his first appearance this Angelo was a man who was cowardly afraid of his soul: he had no worldly authority, no joy in the glorious pageantry of ducal existence, in the possession of wealth, or of power over the lives and deaths of men and women. He was played by Marius Goring, an actor who began his career at the Old Vic with a fine, rhetorical and romantic panache. He was an Old Vic Romeo in *his* twenties and the age's thirties. Behind this early picturesque glow, however, was a mind keenly interested in historical developments. There are few players who have studied as deeply as Mr Goring the sordid history and the appalling terrors of our times. This knowledge has marked Mr Goring. As an actor he is as accomplished as ever, but his old frank welcoming of rich emotions has disappeared. He is an expert now in the neurotic, the morbid, and the brilliantly unbalanced.

All this was evident in his Angelo. Mr Goring played Angelo with unseeing, staring eyes. His face was blanched. Wherever he was, on the platform of justice, or in the secrecy of his candle-lit and concupiscent chamber, he stood frozen in fear. He was ever in the midst of appalled silences. It was impossible to believe that anybody, the weak, dark, poetic Claudio of Ian Holm, or the strangely bouncing Isabella of Judi Dench, rosy from the flesh-pots of the world, could be at his mercy.

Long before he felt the least temptation towards Isabella he was plainly at the mercy of a being more terrible than himself. From the beginning his nerve had gone. Neither he, nor Miss Dench's robust Isabella, more fitted to the breezy pastures of East Anglia than to the cold seclusion of a convent, dominated the play. They were both dwarfed by the alarming phenomenon of the meddling Duke. For the first time in my experience the Duke, and not Angelo or Isabella, was the principal figure in the play.

This man, played by Tom Fleming with eager authority, zestfully disguising himself as a monk, teaching Isabella how to trap Angelo into bed with another woman, popping up in prison to decide whose head is to be chopped off today, ranking as blasphemy any joke made at his expense, punishing sin, rewarding virtue, playing cruelly with his creatures till his moment comes to dispense final judgment, grew larger, as the play progressed. At the end he was everywhere, on the magistrates' bench, in gaol, in robes of state, under the monk's cowl, all-interfering and omnipotent.

It was thus that Mr Blatchley brought the audience to consider the problems and paradoxes of religion. Who is this Duke? Is he indeed a man, or a god? He has in his area of activity all power. He can bring about his aims by a wave of the arm. Why, then, does he not give the immediate signal that would end all ills? Why does he choose to accomplish his desires by means so unnecessarily tortuous, so unnecessarily torturing? Why does he achieve the happiness of his people only through their pain, when pain could be dismissed by one

straight word from his lips? Through Mr Blatchley's direct and un-
equivocal vision Shakespeare posed a problem which has vexed all
theologies that accept the reality of evil: how can the continuance of
this evil be reconciled with the universal and irresistible goodness of
God?

Shakespeare himself gave his answer in another play. It was a bitter
answer. The gods, he says, enjoy our torture. It is not an answer we
are bound to accept. In philosophy, whatever may be the case in
literature, Shakespeare abides our question as much as most, and
more than Berkeley.

It is easy to see why Mr Blatchley did not adopt the conventional
approach to *Measure for Measure*. The change which has taken place
during the twentieth century in our ideas about morality has made
this one of the most difficult, the least obviously and superficially
viable, of all Shakespeare's major works. It is founded upon an extraordinary reverence for chastity. It regards physical purity as the
greatest of virtues. It accords to virginity a mystical importance. In
terms of human happiness I am not by any means sure that it is not
wise to do so. But wise or not, it has a view of chastity which few
people anywhere hold today, and practically no one in the theatre. I
do not think that it is too much to say that no living actress could make
acceptable as the central feature of the play Isabella's single-minded
preoccupation with her bodily integrity.

If chastity cannot any longer be relied on to furnish the play's *raison
d'être*, what about the thing against which chastity is a protection,
namely, sex? It was sex that Peter Brook's production of the play
emphasized, also at Stratford, a few years ago. There was a hot flow of
lubricity in Mr Brook's presentation which undoubtedly gave to the
play a powerful vitality. Isabella's impossible purity was subordinated
to brothels and bawds. But this is the kind of interpretation that
cannot be done twice. It is not a thing that wears. John Blatchley
perceived this. He began the production, true enough, in a puddle of
sex. In his interpretation the act of sex rode the imagination of
Isabella as powerfully as it did that of Angelo, or of Lucio, or of
Pompey the bawd, who talks about it all the time. But Mr Blatchley
saw that these were horses that would not a second time run to the
end. Whereas normally Pompey and his companions in all classes of
society are life-sized people whose problems and preoccupations are
intended to horrify, to perturb, and to melt the hearts of the audience,

at Stratford in 1962 they gradually diminished into nasty-minded children, dwarfed by the frightening Duke. In these difficult circumstances Mr Blatchley chose a quite new interpretation: an interpretation that brought up the question of government and of evil still continuing despite the existence of incontrovertible moral power.

I dwell in some detail on the circumstances and attitude of the 1962 production at Stratford because it is the beautifully characterized costumes designed by Alix Stone which are illustrated in this volume. But there is also another reason. The advent of Peter Hall at Stratford, and the subsequent invasion of London at the Aldwych Theatre by the Royal Shakespeare Company is a major development in the history of the British drama, and especially in the interpretation of Shakespeare. Mr Hall has brought about a new attitude towards the production of Shakespeare in this country, and this attitude is brilliantly illustrated by the *Measure for Measure* which was presented under his auspices.

Britain of course, has always had a great tradition of Shakespearean acting. It has been a tradition built up by stars. There is no reason to suppose that Shakespeare himself would resent this. He did much of his work – much of his finest work – to the measure of a particular star of his own time, Burbage. After Burbage we have had Garrick and Edmund Kean and Irving and, in our own age, John Gielgud and Laurence Olivier. The old tradition of Shakespearean playing – the old tradition at its best, a tradition that paid enormous and intelligent tribute to the proper speaking of the verse – still held sway when I first began to visit the London theatre. It yielded some magnificent things. In the 'thirties there was a production of *Twelfth Night* in London – it was called the black and white production, because the scenery and costumes were in those colours only – in which Cecil Ramage spoke with such nobility and repose the lines beginning 'Mark it, Cesario, it is old and plain, the spinsters and the knitters in the sun Do use to chant it' that I went to see it over and over again. Or, to be absolutely exact, I went over and over again to hear Mr Ramage speak those particular lines. The feeling of peace which they gave, the balm, the surcease to all anxiety and strife was something I shall carry with me all my life.

A little before this I saw Gielgud's Richard II. Here was not peace, but a sword: not calm, but an almost intolerable tension. This was the performance of a man stretched to the very limit of his nerves, yet preserving in his agony a luscious enjoyment of his own misery expressed in lambent and self-indulgent verse of unsurpassable loveliness. Gielgud standing aloft on the battlements of a lonely castle and speaking through clenched teeth to the rebellious Bolingbroke, 'We are amazed; and thus long have we stood To watch the fearful bending of thy knee', all his majesty outraged, yet finding a masochistic enjoyment in so magnificently marking the depth of his humiliation, is a memory that cannot be forgotten. Shakespearean playing before Peter Hall was full of such superb achievements.

It is now the fashion to view such matters with misgiving. We have come back to the Macaulay view that the mind of Shakespeare is our triumph, not a dozen lines of rhetoric. We no longer believe Shaw when he argues that Shakespeare is a master musician, but a poor thinker. We now rate the thought above the music. Only we are not absolutely certain what the thought is. We go behind the lines in order to see what the lines mean. The development of modern psychology is such that we are quite ready to believe that Shakespeare, for all his unrivalled mastery of words, was often saying things of which he himself was quite unaware. It is thus that we find that the most admired, the most popular, and the most accomplished Shakespearean productions of our times are remarkable, not for the performance of the principal character, not for the general beauty of the treatment of the verse, but for an interpretation of the meaning of the play which would have astonished our predecessors. We have a *King Lear* from Peter Brook which shows that Lear was a tiresome old man, against whom Goneril and Regan had many legitimate causes of complaint: he petulantly knocked over tables which had been set for a dinner, a habit which no hostess could be expected to endure. We have from Peter Hall himself a *Twelfth Night* in which the grief-stricken Olivia is a comic character; and we have from Mr Blatchley the *Measure for Measure* of which I have been speaking.

I do not believe it is possible to say that the one method of Shakespearean approach is better than the other. The pre-Hall method is a thing of dazzling, isolated, sensuous effects; the Hall method achieves an integrated, intellectual and emotional interpretation that is all of a piece. One sends a shiver, many shivers, down the spine; the other feeds and stimulates the mind. One is outside time; the other speaks directly, through Shakespeare, to the fears and feelings of the contemporary world. The Royal Shakespeare Company makes Shakespeare relevant to the problems of our age. The best productions that preceded the Royal Shakespeare revolution made us for a moment forget our problems, and so perhaps increased our strength to deal with them. All this is a matter for argument. My own feeling is that the older method of playing Shakespeare had had a long innings, and was becoming a little weary. It was time for it to retire to the pavilion after knocking up a very large score, and for a new batsman to emerge. But he, too, will tire in his time, and there will be need either of a successor or of a restoration. But at present the Royal Shakespeare approach to Shakespeare, of which *Measure for Measure* is a very sound example, is hitting hard all round the wicket.

1964

Timon of Athens

PAUL SCOFIELD

Of Shakespeare's plays, *Timon of Athens* seems to be the one at the point of his life when he had 'of late lost all his mirth'; when, in the face of all his expressed delight in mankind, he saw it as a 'quintessence of dust'.

The play is that of a man mentally and spiritually scarred by a betrayal of trust, and Timon's experience of such a betrayal is the most bitter and painful denunciation of man's cupidity and cruelty and faithlessness.

When I attempted to play Timon at Stratford-upon-Avon in 1965, the play was a blank page in my knowledge of Shakespeare. I had seen it only once, in a very ingenious modern-dress production in 1948 at the Birmingham Repertory Theatre. Timon had been played most movingly by John Phillips, and in that immediate post-war atmosphere the modern settings and costumes gave a sharp point and edge to the tragedy.

But when, some eighteen years later, I was faced with this formidable play, I felt myself to be in a state of open ignorance, by which I mean that I was prepared for anything and that I still had to begin the physical process of rehearsal and performance which is perhaps the actor's most reliable means of informing himself. So began for me a marvellous journey of discovery, fraught with difficulty and often quite harrowing.

How to make credible the indiscriminate generosity and reckless sociability of the man in the early part of the play and then how to find some dignity in his hysterical resentment at the realization that his friends were only interested in his money? Not, on the face of it, a major tragic situation. It was certainly not the great human statement that *King Lear* was, but it seemed possible that the two plays were closely related, that the slough of despair had to be explored just as the mountain had to be scaled – that the claustrophobia and sense of imprisonment of Timon found its release in the freedom and peace that came at last to Lear.

It represented the predicament of a man poised above an abyss, unable to move forward or back, surrounded by evil winds and the proximity of foul water, his passions full of poison and with no promise of eventual forgiveness or compassion.

So it is not surprising that I was, as an actor, afraid of monotony, of the one insistent note of complaint. However, the scenes with Apemantus provided, if not exactly comedy relief, then a certain grim and grinding wit. The two men strike very lively sparks from each other, and with Paul Rogers playing the part, they came to life quite early in rehearsal. Other scenes were more troublesome. Dr Johnson found that there were many passages in the play that were 'perplexed, obscure and probably corrupt', but found an attractive aspect of Timon's character in the obvious affection and zeal of his servants; certainly the undemanding loyalty of Flavius provided the only moment of real tenderness. These, then, were the comparatively sunny strands in a fabric of unrelieved melancholy, and the actor's problem remained.

John Schlesinger, the director, saw neurosis and mental unbalance or abnormality as the only logical motivation for Timon's behaviour, but I came to agree with this less and less, and at long last to find in it instead the knife-edged pain of a betrayal which Shakespeare himself must have experienced as keenly as did his hero. It must be true that a man's life illuminates his work, and that its darker, more shadowy aspects can be traced to his life's experiences. Timon's laceration of himself and his world has a shocking conviction.

This discovery, transparent though it may appear, came to me with the force of a fact, and I began to play Timon, whether successfully or not, not only as the Athenian but also, in a very restricted sense, as Shakespeare himself. Only then did the exquisite passages in the second half of the play have real meaning for me, as well as a violent beauty, and the play became a journey of expiation and finally reconciliation. An expulsion of hatreds and disappointments and black despair; a last purged emptiness and nothingness; an extreme of human experience; and the moment at which Timon became free to reconcile himself with his Maker –

My long sickness
Of health and living now begins to mend;
And nothing brings me all things.

The actor must be presumptuous and to come close to the heart of a writer is perhaps uniquely his opportunity. Speaking these lines made me feel very close indeed.

1976

The Tragedy of King Lear

DONALD WOLFIT

It seems probable that there have been more performances of this, the greatest of Shakespeare's tragedies, in England in the last twenty-five years than at any previous time since the play was written. It has appeared with great regularity in the repertoire of both the Memorial Theatre, Stratford upon Avon, and the Old Vic. My own company of players have given more than two hundred performances. Perhaps this is not so remarkable if one remembers the two world-wide and gigantic wars through which we have passed, comparable to the titanic struggle that went on in the mind and the soul of Lear, conflicts based on greed, ingratitude, jealousy and self-aggrandizement. No one can read or hear the speech of Gloucester, the ineffectual elder statesman, without marvelling at the universality of Shakespeare, the forerunner of existentialism:

Though the wisdom of nature can reason thus and thus, yet nature finds itself scourg'd by the sequent effects: love cools, friendship falls off, brothers divide: in cities, mutinies; in countries, discords; in palaces, treason; the bond crack'd between son and father. . . .

We have seen the best of our time: machinations, hollowness, treachery and all ruinous disorders follow us disquietly to our graves.

Never since the Puritan closure of the theatres in the middle of the seventeenth century has the full text, with a minimum of cutting, been so consistently played before audiences as during this last quarter of a century. In 1681, less than twenty years after the Restoration of the Monarchy, a version of the play was published in Quarto, *The History of King Lear* by Nahum Tate. This astonishingly impertinent idiot not only seized on the jewels of poetry and tortured them out of all recognition, but he also twisted the plot to make Edgar in love with Cordelia, to restore the king to sanity and to provide the play with a happy ending. Could anything be more removed from the majestic Greek quality of the original? Tate described his procedure in these words:

'It was my good fortune to light on one expedient to rectify what was wanting in the regularity and probability of the tale, which was to run through the whole a love betwixt Edgar and Cordelia; that never changed word with each other in the original. This renders Cordelia's indifference, and her father's passion in the first scene, probable. It likewise gives countenance to Edgar's disguise, making that a generous design that was before a poor shift to save his life. The distress of the story is evidently heightened by it, and it particularly gave occasion of a new scene or two, of more success (perhaps) than merit.'

Such was Tate's modesty in describing his own mutilations of the original, statements worthy of the illiterate script writers of many a Hollywood epic. The Fool was eliminated from the text, and, according to the theatre historian, Genest, there seems to have been but one solitary performance with the original catastrophe in a score of revivals between 1681 and 1829.

Even David Garrick at the height of his fame dared not hazard the bold attempt of reinstating the Fool into his place in the play, though he intended the part for Woodward, who promised to be very chaste in his colouring and not to counteract the agonies of Lear.

Thus for nearly one hundred and fifty years the version by Nahum Tate held the stage, and in it appeared Betterton, Booth, Quinn, Garrick, Barry, and Mrs Siddons (as Cordelia) with Edmund Kean as Lear.

This was the garbled version which called down the dictum of Charles Lamb:

'So to see Lear acted – to see an old man tottering about the stage with a walking stick, turned out of doors by his daughters on a rainy night – has nothing in it but what is painful and disgusting. But the Lear of Shakespeare cannot be acted.'

The answer is, of course, that Charles Lamb never did see Shakespeare's tragedy *performed* – but a truncated, deformed imitation of the original majestic work, which has come down to us in what is known as the Pide Bull Quarto of 1608 and the Folio of 1623. The latter is the shorter of the two, and is probably nearest to the play as it was ultimately established in the repertoire of the Lord Chamberlain's Men under Burbage and Shakespeare.

At last, in 1838, Macready restored the original text to the stage and, greatly daring, reinstated the Fool, but played by an actress, Miss Horton, as a sort of fragile, hectic, beautiful-faced boy. The revival was a great success, and succeeding generations owe a debt of gratitude to Macready for his adventurous policy.

Sir Henry Irving's acting version was published in 1906. To the Shakespeare lover this has little to recommend it, for enormous incisions are made in the text to allow for scene changes and intervals. Today the theatre seems to be moving back to the Elizabethan form, with fewer intervals, and some attempt at a permanent setting which will not obtrude between the playgoer and the play. With no wait for scene changes, a more or less full text can be presented in the same playing time as the over-mounted productions of the nineteenth century, and the speeding up of the action makes for a clear unfolding of the tragedy with all its subtleties.

Anyone embarking on even the briefest preface to this great tragedy, and most of all an executant in the world of the theatre, cannot fail to be conscious of his tremendous indebtedness to Harley Granville-Barker, whose insight into the whole play is comparable only to the description of Edmund Kean's acting – 'illuminating the text by flashes of lightning'. His ripostes to Lamb and Bradley, both of whom found the play unactable in the theatre, are unanswerable. Indeed, it is largely owing to the encouragement of Barker, and behind him, William Poel, that producers in recent times reconsidered the play for production and found it full of superb stagecraft.

Many critics have complained of the opening scene – of the unreason of the king – even going so far as to claim that Lear is mad before the play opens. But a stage play is not a riddle, and *King Lear* least of all. The dramatist was attracted by a striking but improbable situation – that of a king, not in his dotage, undertaking to apportion his territory among his three daughters, according to their protestations of affection, and because of laconic honesty, casting off his dearest, Cordelia, only to discover that the others were wholly false and she divinely true. Against the bidding of his heart he disowns her; and in the end his heart is broken by her death. To argue against this crystal-clear statement of Shakespeare's is to indulge in sophistry and erudition for its own sake: structure is turned into psychology, and ever-mounting drama is flattened into biography. It blurs the contrast to indulge in speculations as to what Regan and Goneril, two icy-minded, haughty women, had suffered at the hands of Lear.

This approach withdraws much of our admiration and sympathy from the heroes and heroines and bestows it on the villains, sets the structure awry and goes back to Nahum Tate's version of the play. The tragedy rests firmly on the opposition between paternal love and filial ingratitude; in the contrast between Lear's thoughts of the two whom he has cherished, and of Cordelia whom he has cast off.

There was no chance division of the kingdom – it had obviously been the subject of great debate, and never did Shakespeare put more importance into the opening lines of a play than in this one. The two earls, Kent and Gloucester, expected Albany to be preferred to Cornwall: Cordelia was to marry either France or Burgundy, but preferably Burgundy: but all goes awry, owing to Cordelia's honesty and her refusal to descend to flattery, and the tragedy is on its way. From this moment there should be no interval, scene should follow scene with unerring rapidity until we are presented with the madness of Lear, his departure in a litter to meet Cordelia with the army of France at Dover, and the blinding of Gloucester by the butcher, Cornwall. With those two crises the wheel comes full circle. The destruction of Lear's reason and Gloucester's eyes are parallel forces which propel the tragedy to its sublime end, the downfall of Edmund and the two sisters, and the ascension of Lear's spirit to the empyrean to rejoin Cordelia there after their earthly reconciliation.

It is remarkable to note how Shakespeare preserves the pagan atmosphere throughout the play. The invocations are all pre-Christian. Lear's opening pronouncement:

> *For, by the sacred radiance of the sun,*
> *The mysteries of Hecat, and the night,*
> *By all the operation of the orbs,*
> *From whom we do exist and cease to be,*

and Gloucester's speech on Dover cliff beginning:

> *O you mighty gods!*

are two examples of this.

One or two practical discoveries may find a place in this Introduction. From countless rehearsals and two hundred performances, I have stumbled across two points in the text which make, I think, some contribution, one of major and the other of minor importance.

To take the minor one first.

In Act IV, Scene ii, line 68, Goneril replies to Albany's justifiable criticism of her conduct with:

Marry, your manhood mew.

This last word, MEW, has been altered by some commentators to NOW. Yet in the earliest Quarto, as Aldis Wright states, the word MEW was followed by a dash. This line of Goneril's is immediately followed by the entrance of a messenger and Albany's line 'What news?' It is my contention that MEW is a printer's error in the Quarto and should have been NEWS, not followed but *preceded* by a dash, and that it is in fact the voice of the messenger off-stage before he enters.

The passage would then read as follows:

> GONERIL   *Marry, your manhood——*
> MESSENGER   [entering] *News.*
> ALBANY   *What news?*

This undoubtedly makes sense, and furthermore it sustains the action of the scene. The word MEW spoken at that moment by Goneril is nonsense, as indeed is NOW, and, regrettably, it has become a dangerous schoolroom joke, which any juvenile in the audience wants to hear. Misplaced laughter in tragedy is an unforgivable thing, especially when it is caused by obscurity.

The major point is more far-reaching, and concerns the re-entry of King Lear in Act I, Scene iv. Kent has arrived at Albany's castle in disguise. The king, returned from hunting, is subjected to the insolence of Oswald, the first of a series of carefully planned indignities by his eldest daughter, and with the demand that he shall disquantity his train of one hundred knights.

As the text stands at present, Albany enters, and Lear, after cursing Goneril, makes an exit, only to re-enter four lines later to deliver a second curse. I have always felt the text to be faulty here – Shakespeare seldom reduces his dramatic tension with a feeble exit and a return in such a short space of time. In the performances I had witnessed before putting the play into production under my own management, this passage had always worried me. Perhaps what I experienced was primarily an actor's, and not a scholar's instinct. In performance, so wrong did I feel the text to be, that in making some essential excisions I had removed lines 312 to 332, and in discussion with Mr Ridley (who was preparing a broadcast version of the play), I expressed considerable doubts as to the veracity of the text. Knowing that the Quartos of the play were hastily printed, I reached the conclusion that here two speeches were placed in the wrong order. Although this does not conform to the actual lining of the Quarto pages when printed, it is quite possible that when the original draft was taken to the printer, two sheets of manuscript bearing the two speeches were muddled and the order reversed.

Mr Ridley will not go so far as to agree with my theory of an accidental transposition, though he does agree that my dramatic instinct was right, and that the first speech: 'Hark, Nature, hear, dear goddess!' is far more impressive and dramatically correct if it follows rather than precedes the second speech, as given in the Pide Bull Quarto. The re-entry of Lear and his line, 'What, fifty of my followers at a clap, Within a fortnight?' to me has no ring of truth about it and I believe was added in performance by the actor to bridge the gap and thus came to be included in the Folio. It may well be that on purely scholarly grounds this transposition cannot be supported, but I think there is food for thought here for the textual expert.

In over one hundred performances since this discovery I have therefore removed the re-entry of Lear and the cumulative effect of the scene has been heightened beyond any words I can find to express. The greater curse of Lear upon Goneril now succeeds the lesser, which my instinct tells me was Shakespeare's dramatic intention.

The scene therefore runs as follows from line 269:

LEAR　　　　　　　　　　　　　*O Lear, Lear!*
　　Beat at this gate, that let thy folly in
　　And thy dear judgement out! Go, go, my people.
ALBANY *Now, gods that we adore, whereof comes this?*
GONERIL *Never afflict yourself to know the cause,*
　　But let his disposition have that scope
　　That dotage gives it.
ALBANY *What is the matter, sir?*
LEAR *I'll tell thee. Life and death! I am asham'd*
　　That thou hast power to shake my manhood thus,
　　That these hot tears, that break from me perforce,
　　Should make thee worth them. Blasts and fogs upon thee!
　　The untented woundings of a father's curse

Pierce every sense about thee ! Old fond eyes,
Beweep this cause again, I'll pluck you out
And cast you with the waters that you make
To temper clay. Yea, is't come to this ?
Yet have I left a daughter,
Who I am sure is kind and comfortable:
When she shall hear this of thee, with her nails
She'll flay thy wolvish visage. Thou shalt find
That I'll resume the shape which thou dost think
I have cast off for ever: thou shalt, I warrant thee.
ALBANY *My lord, I am guiltless, as I am ignorant*
Of what hath mov'd you.
LEAR   *It may be so, my lord.*
Hark, Nature, hear, dear goddess !
Suspend thy purpose, if thou didst intend
To make this creature fruitful;
Into her womb convey sterility,
Dry up in her the organs of increase,
And from her derogate body never spring
A babe to honour her ! If she must teem,
Create her child of spleen, that it may live
And be a thwart disfeatur'd torment to her,
Let it stamp wrinkles in her brow of youth,
With cadent tears fret channels in her cheeks,
Turn all her mother's pains and benefits
To laughter and contempt, that she may feel
How sharper than a serpent's tooth it is
To have a thankless child ! Go, go, my people !   [Exit]

I think that my devotion to Shakespeare's text has been made abundantly clear in my productions of his plays, and I can be exonerated from the accusation of tampering unnecessarily. Here is, to me, a clear case of faulty text in the original binding of the Quartos. How happy we should all be if Heminge and Condell had preserved in some archive or another the tattered prompt copies from which they made the Folio edition, which has none-the-less earned them the gratitude of the entire world.

I am touched with gratitude at the honour which has been paid to me in being invited to write a preface to *King Lear*. The final paragraph of the address to the Folio of 1623, written by Heminge and Condell, would seem to be a fitting conclusion to my thoughts:

'But it is not our province, who only gather his works and give them you to praise him. It is yours that read him. And there we hope, to your divers capacities, you will find enough both to draw and hold you; for his wit can no more lie hid than it could be lost. Read him, therefore, and again and again: and if then you do not like him, surely you are in some manifest danger not to understand him. And so we leave you to other of his friends, whom if you need, can be your guides: if you need them not, you can lead yourselves and others. And such readers we wish him.'

1955

The Tragedy of Macbeth

LEWIS CASSON

This preface is based, not so much on literary study, as on practical experience of acting in and producing *Macbeth* under all sorts of conditions and in many parts of the world, ranging from Charles Fry's Costume Recitals, in St George's Hall in 1900, to the Old Vic tours in the coal valleys of South Wales during the last war. My suggestions are offered with diffidence rather than dogmatism, in the hope that they may throw some small light on the play's magnificence.

The universal opening gambit to any preface to *Macbeth* is to remark on the extraordinary corruption of the text, and our complete dependence on the Folios, since no quartos, good or bad, are extant. The Folios were edited for publication as a sort of authorized memorial collection, while the good quartos are reputed to follow the theatre prompt-books, and the bad quartos to be pirated, written down from memory, either by members of the audience, or more probably by actors. Yet the text of *Macbeth* always seems to bring one nearer in feeling to a stage performance, which actually took place, than any of the other plays; not indeed of a *new* play, but of a revival of a play already well known, furbished up for some special occasion.

Mr Ivor Brown has lately drawn a vivid picture of the conditions and atmosphere in which the new commercialized Elizabethan theatre had its birth and life; the confusion of poetry, romance, sordid cruelty and ribaldry amidst the stench and clamour of the London slums and bear gardens. And he has drawn on his own knowledge of modern back-stage conditions to point out the confusion of improvisation, invention and vital creation that go to the making of any stage production. But even he has not sufficiently emphasized this eternal characteristic of the theatre. I have myself produced a play for which the author had to write three last acts before he and I were satisfied. I remember Mr Somerset Maugham writing overnight a new last act for an American adaptation of a novel of his, after we had been rehearsing a fortnight. I can recall scarcely a single new play that has been performed word for word as it was written; and the subsequent printed book was usually a hotch-potch of both versions.

In Elizabethan times it must have been far worse. Every source was being hurriedly tapped to feed the new entertainment industry. Old plays, chronicles, fairy stories, Court pageants, and pastorals from the aristocratic houses – all were grist to the Shakespeare and other mills. Plays were adapted, written and re-written, cut and expanded by others, and revived in their original or revised form. *The Booke of Sir Thomas More*, about 1590, the only play we have in manuscript that can probably claim Shakespeare's authorship even in part, is reputed to have had at least four contributors or revisers, including him.

A further cause of possible error and uncertainty is that the actors of those days depended far more on ear than on eye for memory. Quite probably many of them could not read, and had their lines read to them to learn them (Snug's 'Have you the Lion's part written?' points to this), and they possibly took as much liberty in the use of the actual words as the 'booth' actors of a hundred years ago, to whom the general sense and rhythm, and the cues, were the only essentials. The text of *Macbeth* and the bad quartos may, therefore, well represent what the audience actually heard better than the author's original scripts.

It is generally considered that the play, as we have it, was largely based on an earlier one, possibly not Shakespeare's, which closely followed Holinshed's *Chronicle*; that at some later time the 'hand of glory' re-wrote much of it, including the vital scenes between Macbeth and Lady Macbeth (which always suggest they were written in a single feverish night), and that, later again, most of the Witch scenes, including the appearances of Hecate, were added by Shakespeare or another. The only witness we have of a contemporary performance says the play began with the entrance of Macbeth and Banquo on the heath, which would make the play even shorter than it is now. As this seems improbable, it would appear that much of the version he saw has been since cut, carelessly and hurriedly too. Why then should our version include so much inferior stuff, both old and new? My own suggestion is that in our text we have, assembled largely from memory, the prompt book of a gala revival of the play given before King James, with the Witch scenes specially written up for his benefit, and the scene of the Bloody Sergeant restored, to include a famous speech of some well-known old actor (who may also have spoken the Hecuba speech in *Hamlet*); and that the play was slashed to make room on this occasion for the 'improvements'. That plays, if already well known, could be thus drastically cut is shown by Mrs Siddons' own copy of *Douglas*, a piece popular for fifty years before she played it, where the plot is rendered almost unintelligible by the vigour of her blue pencil. The study of this eighteenth-century play for the Edinburgh Festival of 1950 threw another light on our problem. Written by a Scottish minister, but in his best English, it contains such phrases as 'a language taught among the shepherd swains', where the context clearly demands *talked*. This points to the fact that even as recently as that, scriveners were working from sound, not sight; for the Scottish *talked* might well be misheard as the English *taught*. *Macbeth* is full of such possible mistakes. A good instance is 'this push will cheer me'; for right up to Victorian times the word *chair* was pronounced *cheer*, among educated people. This is shown in *Trelawny of the Wells*; and also in the true story of an old stage-manager of those days who, during a quiet scene, asked his property man for 'three cheers' with disastrous results!

Another aspect of the question of errors of sound may well have affected the text. Many actors and most prompters, in course of rehearsals and playing, come to know the lines of the whole play without much attention to their meaning, like a well-known song, and can reel off scene after scene; but they frequently are unable to ascribe the lines to the particular characters. An actress who re-wrote from memory the whole of Laurence Irving's version of *Crime and Punishment*, after the script went down with him in the Gulf of St Lawrence, had the same difficulty. If *Macbeth* has been written down from memory we shall expect to find these errors of ascription.

I have dwelt on these possible sources of error for the reason that, while in reading or studying a play we can entertain doubts and uncertainties, and consult notes and glossaries, the producer and actor are in no such position. They must decide firmly on their view of the author's intention at every moment, and expound it clearly to the audience. If they conscientiously believe that the existing text interferes with or misrepresents the author's intention, either through possible errors or a vital change in the meaning of essential words, it is better service to the author to change the text than slavishly to follow it. To deny this while accepting rearrangement of scenes, distracting pageantry, intervals, and deliberate misreading of character is mere pedantry. The addition or substitution of the word *expediency* to elucidate *commodity* in *King John*, as Peter Brook did at Birmingham, is in my view a legitimate case in point.

The play's theme, to me, is vaulting ambition 'o'erleaping its saddle' and falling on the other side; the tearing apart of the marriage of a heroic soldier and his loving wife, not by ambition, but by the deliberate choice by both of them of evil means to a legitimate end; with the result in the one partner of the growth of the power of evil to heroic stature, till it is finally crushed by heroic good; and in the other the evil 'worm i' the bud' eating its way to the parallel disaster of gradual decay and death.

The opening scene sets for us the darkness and sense of immanent evil that pervades the whole play. The second gives us the atmosphere of violence, conspiracy and blood, in which its action is to pass, and pictures for us Macbeth and Banquo as the noble valiant soldiers whom we meet in the third scene. It is difficult, in a play as well known to us as this, not to *anticipate* our knowledge. We tend to regard both Macbeth and his wife as criminals from the first, and so lose much of the poignancy of the drama. When we first meet Macbeth, we are meant to see him as a hero returning in triumph from a battle with his king's enemies, confident that he has deserved well, his mind filled with hopes that the king will reward him with the succession to the throne, to which, according to the old legend, he had good claim. He may be ambitious and may love power, but these are not necessarily criminal attributes. In this mood he suddenly receives from the Weird Sisters the threefold greeting of Glamis, Cawdor and king hereafter, and, while in the wonder of it, the startling confirmation by Ross of the Cawdor prophecy. He is filled with fears and horrible imaginings, but surely he does not yet so far yield to the suggestion to 'catch the nearest way' as to admit the word *murder* to his thoughts (Act I, Scene 3). This must be a mishearing by an anticipatory scrivener for *matter*. In any case, Macbeth rejects the temptation later though we see in the same scene the beginnings of his jealousy of Banquo, who is to 'get kings', though never himself to be king.

It is in the fourth scene, when Duncan, in the very instant of praising and thanking Macbeth, dashes his hopes to the ground by suddenly naming 'the boy Malcolm' as his successor, that Macbeth yields to the temptation to take the way of violence as a short-cut to

power. Duncan's 'fatal' decision to pass beneath Macbeth's battlements seals the king's fate and his own.

In Scene 5 we see, in her reading of her husband's letter, Lady
Macbeth's reaction to the prophecies. Here again it is important not
to anticipate. There is nothing in the text to justify the view that she
is naturally cruel, bloodthirsty, or lascivious; all these attributes
weaken rather than add to the tragedy. She is practical, and of limited
imagination, unscrupulous in her ambitions for her husband (as many
good wives are), but not a mere villainess of melodrama. We should
note that the letter was written before the critical meeting with
Duncan, and contains no hint of previous conspiracy. The letter read,
she coolly and dispassionately analyses her husband's character in
relation to the promise of the kingship, and decides that he is 'too full
of the milk of humankind to catch the nearest way' (*kindness* is
obviously wrong in sense and scansion), though she is herself clearly
tempted to do so. But it is only when Fate takes a hand, announcing
the actual coming of Duncan beneath her battlements, that she yields
to the temptation, and then deliberately prays for cruelty, to steel her
to carry out the deed herself ('My keen knife'). This terrible prayer to
the powers of evil was rightly marked by Mrs Siddons 'to be
whispered'. Its full horror is lost by declamation. The ensuing scene
between husband and wife (after the greeting 'My dearest love') is a
fencing match between them, each accepting the idea of murder,
without admitting it to the other. It helps the scene of Duncan's
welcome (Scene 6) if Macbeth, unseen by the king, is visible to the
audience in a balcony above; and surely the martlet speech (Act I,
Scene 6) should be spoken by Duncan. Was it taken from him because
the old actor could not do it justice?

Before the feast given to Duncan in Scene 7 there must have been a
scene where Macbeth 'breaks the enterprise' to his wife, and they
agree to it. This scene has been cut, if it was ever written, for when we
see Macbeth again he is repenting of the plan and finding excuses.
Only his wife's passionate taunts restore him to his purpose. His
soliloquy here is so confused and obscure that Bernard Shaw, who gave
us much help in our 1926 production, suggested considerable cuts in
it. I feel that it would be clearer if it read:

> *If it were done, when 'tis done, then 'twere well.*
> (*It were done quickly if the assassination*

Could trammel up the consequence, and catch
With its surcease, success). If but this blow
Might be the be-all and the end-all here
(But here, upon this bench and school of time)
We'd jump the life to come.

'Bank and shoal of time', though now hallowed by age and senti-
ment, are improbable accompaniments to the ideas of judgment and
teaching, and *mentor* would make more sense than *inventor*.

Of the great scene of the murder, which constitutes Act II, little
need be said. I agree with Bradley that in the opening scene Banquo
is definitely suspicious of Macbeth's purpose, but has 'the wisdom to
act in safety'. Their dialogue is a fencing match of mutual suspicion,
ending in Banquo's ironic 'The like to you'. In the dagger speech, I
read 'There's no such thing' as a flash of brave defiance, which
banishes the fatal vision as surely as later it banishes Banquo's ghost.
Note too the courage of Lady Macbeth returning to the murder-room
with the daggers to smear the grooms with blood, though she faints
with horror later, when their murder follows the king's. I think the
apostrophe to his bloody hands in Scene 2 should be taken in wild
hysteria, not with the solemnity that most actors give it. The Elizabethan punctuation of 'making the green-one *red*' then becomes
possible. Actors often take famous speeches much too portentously.
Another common fault of actors is to take Macduff's re-entrance from
the murder-chamber much too loud. 'Horror' is not a word to be
shouted. Tongue cannot conceive it. Its intensity is beyond noise.
'Awake! awake! Ring the alarum bell' should be spoken to the dozing
porter, rousing him to action. 'Banquo, Donalbain' should be the first
loud shout (should it not be Malcolm instead of Banquo?), and the
bell starts soon after. It is worth noting that Banquo's 'Dear Duff' is
the only clue so far to Macduff's identity! At the end of the scene
when they go off to arm, Macduff should delay long enough to over-
hear Malcolm's 'I'll to England'. We shall recall this in his fencing
with the careful Ross in the Old Man scene, which closes the act. I
believe that there is a slip in the text here, and that Ross should leave
the stage at 'Adieu', so that Macduff says 'Farewell, father' to the Old
Man as his own farewell to Scotland. The Old Man's reply then
becomes a riddle, pointing to the purpose of Macduff's flight, and
foreshadows the summoning of help from England.

MACBETH
ACT V Scene III
onwards.

Banquo's soliloquy that opens Act III marks further his suspicions of Macbeth, and we see the growth of Macbeth's jealousy to hatred. The punctuation of this passage suggests that the dismissal of the guests finishes at 'sweeter welcome'. The rest, 'We'll keep ourself till supper-time alone', if addressed to Lady Macbeth only, marks the separation between them that now widens throughout the play. The scene beginning 'Is Banquo gone from Court?' vividly shows the progress of this separation. Unfortunately it is marred by more gaps and corruptions than any other. The verse rhythm of the scene is particularly strong, yet missing words rob it of much of its effect. In our Ainley-Thorndike production in 1926, I added (and have done so ever since) certain suggested words to complete the sense and rhythm, and made further changes. I cannot recollect any critic ever noticing any of them, except James Agate, and he approved. So they must be reasonably acceptable, and they are certainly helpful.

> *But let the frame of things* become *disjoint*
> *Both the worlds suffer* dissolution.
> *Whom we to gain our* place *have sent to peace*
> > *Nothing*
> *Can touch him further.*
> Come my lord, *come on.*

From experience I know that the next passages seem to have a truer ring if these lines are given to Lady Macbeth, thus:

LADY MACBETH *Gentle my lord, sleek o'er your rugged looks*
Be bright and jovial among your guests to-night.
MACBETH *So shall I, love, and so I pray be you.*
LADY MACBETH *Let your remembrance apply to Banquo.*
(Macbeth shudders)
Present him eminence, both with eye and tongue.
MACBETH Our place is still *unsafe the whiles that we*
Must lave our honours in these flattering streams ...
Disguising what they are.

I find it hard to believe that Macbeth, although he keeps his guilty secret from his wife, would quite needlessly prescribe her behaviour towards a man whom he knew she would never see again. They are not, as yet, as far apart as that; and *her* 'Let your remembrance' would link up with her previous 'Has Banquo gone from court?' to the servant. Surely the advice formed the 'few words' she urgently wanted to say to the king. Some words are obviously missing at the end of this scene, and its rhyme and rhythm are so vital that I have always used the suggested addition 'makes wing to the rooky wood *in due arow*'.

In the concluding line, a riddle in which Macbeth half warns his wife of Banquo's end, the emphasis should be strongly on *ill*. Then her first lines and his last, in the scene, mark the contrast between the two protagonists in the effect on them of their first crime.

> LADY MACBETH *Nought's had, all's spent, when our desire is got without content.*
> MACBETH *Things bad begun make strong themselves by* ill.

How heroic is Macbeth's courage at the feast, when Banquo's ghost has already appeared and vanished, in the challenging 'Would he were here', and how magnificently Lady Macbeth supports him.

On the question of the allusion to Macduff in Act III, Scene 4, I agree with Ridley that the meaning is 'What do you make of Macduff's denial of his presence?' The purpose of the line, I am sure, is to give Lady Macbeth a chance of showing her horror at the prevision of yet another murder. She echoes this in the sleepwalking scene.

There is some confusion in the characters of the next two scenes which suggests that the spectator had been unable to identify them. The 'another lord' of Scene 6 is an important character to be so labelled, and he might well be Ross, whose later appearances in Macduff's castle and England point to it, in spite of his last line; and it can hardly be the secretive Lennox of this scene that hears, and reveals to Macbeth in the next, Macduff's flight to England. I have usually given this task and also that of the Messenger who warns Lady Macduff in Scene 2 to Macbeth's body-servant, Seyton. The Cauldron scene (IV, 1) and the Hecate scene raise the question of the Weird Sisters (never in the text called witches). They were, I feel sure, originally intended as seers of the future and as symbols of the evil powers of the world, but not as instigators of evil. But later inferior additions, and the opportunity that these scenes give to producers for pictorial and musical mumbo-jumbo, has given them too great an importance; with the result that they tend to blur the human tragedy that is essentially one of will and character.

Scene 3, the long Holinshed-in-blank-verse scene between Malcolm and Macduff, is always pretty dull, and cutting makes it unintelligible and so duller still. It can be quite effective if Malcolm plays it as fairly broad comedy, taking the audience boldly into his confidence as he pulls the leg of the simple honest Macduff. Malcolm is the Caesar Augustus ruling type, and callously uses Macduff's grief for his own, and Scotland's, purposes. This attitude, more marked if Macduff leaves the stage at 'Heaven forgive him too!' tends to make us discount his description (in the final scene) of Lady Macbeth as fiendlike, and so may even produce a reaction of sympathy for that wretched woman.

As to the last Act, the first thing I want to note is that after the Cavern scene Macbeth is off the stage completely for some 450 lines, i.e., at least twenty minutes, probably half an hour. This is a far longer rest than the actor of Hamlet or Lear or any of the great parts ever gets. Is this not an indication that an immense physical effort is expected of him in the four short scenes (amounting only to 160 lines in all) that remain? Is it not a pointer to the way this act should be played? That Macbeth, growing in physical power as his moral stature falls, becomes in the last act the incarnation of triumphant evil, inhuman, callous, and utterly defiant of the forces of retribution gathering to crush him. The rapid alternating scenes, Macbeth within the castle and the nemesis approaching without, if played with passion, speed and energy, build up to a tremendous climax in the final combat between Evil and Good. The effect is marred by any interruption through changes of scenery, however swift; but it is still more marred by slow or sentimental playing. The key is in the reading of Macbeth's response to 'The Queen . . . is dead'. So often the actor, either lured by the sonority of the vowels of the thrice-repeated 'Tomorrow', or out of a craving for sympathy, turns this challenging devil's creed of nihilism and atheism into the solemn hymn of a repentant sinner; and the reading of the whole Act has to be tamed to suit. 'Life's but . . . a tale told by an idiot, signifying nothing' is the supreme blasphemy, and it is answered at once by the Jove's thunderbolt of the Birnam Wood messenger. In panic and final defiance of fate, Macbeth then commits his fatal blunder – a sortie from the castle, 'Arm, arm and out!' Staking all on the third prophecy, he goes to meet his end, defiant still even when that last reed breaks and betrays him.

The double stage directions for the final duel are interesting. The first 'Exeunt fighting' raises the dramatic tension by leaving the issue doubtful all through the quiet of Old Siward's touching scene, until it is revealed by Macduff's entrance with the head, and the greeting to

Malcolm: 'Hail, *King*'. This direction is generally followed today, and is probably the original. The second 'Enter fighting, and Macbeth slain' was probably added when the play and its end became well known, and the effect of suspense was therefore lost, to give both actor and audience in compensation the pleasurable opportunity of a stage death.

A suggestion given me originally by Mr Bernard Shaw, which I have always since adopted, concerns the contrast between the two messengers in the last Act. While the first, the cream-faced loon in Scene 3, should be a panic-stricken youngster received with jeers and laughter by Macbeth and the soldiers, the second should be an elderly and dour Scot, gravely and imperturbably reporting the strange phenomenon of a moving wood, with no inkling of its terrible significance for Macbeth.

I have never had the opportunity of trying a last Act suggestion of Mr Laurence Housman, which is worth recording, that during the arming scene (Scene 3) Lady Macbeth should enter 'above', and, unseen by the soldiers in the general confusion, abstract a weapon. It would certainly elucidate the doctor's phrase 'means of all annoyance' and make clear at an earlier point in the play the end of Lady Macbeth.

1964

Antony and Cleopatra

LAURENCE OLIVIER

As one plods diligently through the more comprehensive histories of the various performances of *Antony and Cleopatra*, one may smile at the innovations created to divert the public according to its adjudged taste, or applaud the more earnest adherences to the text, but one is conscious of the fact that general approval seems never to have been gained, and, as at all times it has been a heavy and expensive piece to put on, it must always have been a hazardous venture. Yet the eulogizers of the play have been numberless, and with all of them one has nodded gravely in assent to their appreciation of its glories, even if few of them can do much more in its praise than quote passages from it.

It was therefore with mixed feelings, feelings mixed by the confusion of thoughts, thoughts confused by the study of the play, the play studied together with its history, its history haunting us like a warning spectre, that we decided to produce the play for the Festival of Britain Season in 1951.

When I was first asked to write this introduction I could see no possible reason against it; I was in the throes of preparation for production to be directed by Michael Benthall, and by comparison with the dread of the opening performance, the thought of writing a preface for a new edition of the play held no terrors for me; there were quite a few months to think about it, by which time I felt sure I would have something practically useful if not illuminating to say. Besides, I reminded myself, I had done a similar job for the Folio Society's *School for Scandal* and, despite a little critical censure, I still felt quite pleased with the result.

So, like a swimmer about to attempt the Channel, having a mental plan of all the tides, currents, swells and hazards of the journey, I nodded airily to the last press reporter at Cap Gris Nez and waded in, quite confident that after a given number of hours' swimming the opposite shore would be in sight and I should soon be emerging from my struggle, tired no doubt, but, also no doubt, quite garrulously informative.

Well, the 'given number of hours' have passed, and I can nowhere see the opposite shore; those tides and currents are still at grips with me, my whereabouts in the channel I do not know; I can only feel very much on the unhappy side of half-way. The trouble is that though I have known the play for most of my life, as well as most people know plays they have acted in, seen two or three productions, read it through three or four times, turned up favourite passages many times, studied several commentators, lately worked intensively for three months of preparation, and now played in it for twenty weeks, I still feel anything but satisfied that my understanding of the play is complete.

The main impediment to my progress has been the problem of the inner working of the minds of the play's two main characters, for what goes on in the minds of the rest of the characters is adequately described by themselves. I feel, therefore, that it may be of some value to the reader if I pose this problem, even though I still feel unable to elucidate it with any certainty.

At the outset there seem to be two major peculiarities. The lack of character drawing in the beginning of Antony's story, and the extension of character drawing at the end of Cleopatra's. The first is like a major dominance in the opening of a symphony that is taken for granted, the second is like an unexplained variation of an earlier motif used to heighten the sublimity of the climax.

The lack of any nobility in Antony's behaviour throughout the first half of the play presupposes a knowledge and an acceptance of the fact that the man had been a great man before the play started; the gossips give it to the audience in the first and last speeches of the first scene.

From the beginning, when a 'Strumpet's Fool' is an almost kindly judgement of his demeanour, to his last gasp in the arms of Cleopatra, Antony hardly performs an honourable action. There is an occasional flash of infinite sweetness and gallantry – 'Fall not a tear I say', after the debacle at Actium; touching, human flashes of optimism, which to his old intimate, Enobarbus, are transparent –

> *and I see still*
> *A diminution in our captain's brain*
> *Restores his heart*

and the marvellous lover's generosity when he learns that Cleopatra's 'death' was a wile to see how he would take it – no bitterness, no self pity, just 'Bear me, good friends, where Cleopatra bides', followed by a flash of reawakened manliness to his followers,

> *Nay, good my fellows, do not please sharp fate*
> *To grave it with your sorrows; bid that welcome*
> *Which comes to punish us, and we punish it*
> *Seeming to bear it lightly*

and, at the final meeting, no word of reproach to his queen:

> *I am dying, Egypt, dying; only*
> *I here importune death awhile, until*
> *Of many thousand kisses the poor last*
> *I lay upon thy lips.*

These are the only kind of instances that call from our emotions a sense of admiration. Yet deep human interest and understanding are always with us, and, despite some moments of horror and disgust, our sympathy never flags, nor at any time does he fail to awaken our compassion.

That Cleopatra loves Antony there can be no doubt and her glowing glorifications need no explaining; but, for the rest . . . ? Every reference to Antony throughout the play is on the same note, regretting the past, deploring the present. He is, in fact, something like Romeo, a character bolstered up into an artificial heroism by popular misconception; 'He's no Romeo' a young girl may be heard to say about a young man, implying that the latter lacks prowess as a lover; the same young girl is naturally bitterly disappointed when one day she finds in the play that the poor Romeo was by no means the kind of lover she had been led to believe by the illustrations on cigar boxes, and that only when he learns of Juliet's death does he attain manhood at all. The very titles, 'Romeo and Juliet', 'Antony and Cleopatra', promise a romanticism which makes all the more bitter-dry the irony, the human disillusionment, the cunningly observed philosophy, in the plays themselves.

Right from the beginning the study is one of a man already gone to seed, who only half believes in his own reclamability, and after a few disastrous tests to prove it, he, like so many others of Shakespeare's men, becomes intent on his own destruction; the lion tearing himself to pieces, taking advantage of every circumstance to lay the blame outside himself – in Antony's case, as in many others, on the thing he loves. 'This foul Egyptian has betrayed me', he shouts to all who may hear, after the last disastrous battle. He has no reason to think so, Shakespeare offers us none, Plutarch none, history and tradition twist up a lip in non-committal surmise. Shakespeare's Antony must *speak* these words, to give himself an excuse for his own end. He is, I feel, quite prepared to bring this about, and indeed is already at the point of doing so, the moment before Mardian brings the news of the queen's 'death'.

Riding him down hard, all this time, has been Antony's dreadful jealousy of his rival 'the *boy* Caesar'; 'this novice'

> *He at Philippi kept*
> *His sword e'en like a dancer; while I struck*
> *The lean and wrinkled Cassius; and 'twas I*
> *That the mad Brutus ended . . .*

– two claims not substantiated by Shakespeare in the earlier 'Julius Caesar'. – Even his early prowess, then, is coloured now by exaggeration and wishful thinking; Ventidius has a word to say about the quality of his sportsmanship; and as with so many who pride themselves on a sense of sportsmanship, as most certainly did Antony, there was a limit to what he could take:

> *The very dice obey him*
> *And in our sports my better cunning faints*
> *Under his chance.* (II 3).

This realization is the turning point for Antony; this, and a breath of Egypt from the soothsayer, decides him to turn his back on the last chance of 'going straight' and 'living decently' offered by the new marriage with Octavia, and on the hope of a better relationship with Caesar. I believe that although he was palpably coerced by Caesar, Antony welcomed and desired the new marriage for the health of his soul. It appeased his guilty feelings and pleased the side of him that properly wished to be the respected triumvir, the 'decent chap', the side that prompted the 'Roman thoughts', that Cleopatra tells us were apt to strike him while in her coils in Egypt,

> *These strong Egyptian fetters I must break*
> *Or lose myself in dotage.*

But the cure did not work, the disease had taken too strong a hold, and a new complication was added to it, his jealousy of Caesar. He had to get away, away from the dreadful sense of rivalry that the partnership gave him. He dismisses his last bid for straightforwardness as a 'Marriage for my peace', and away he goes giddily running, staggering and crashing to his doom.

Cleopatra is at once more simple and more complicated. She is like a portrait sketch of a woman about whom the artist knew a great deal more than he cared to show; therefore she is a woman about whom the observer may guess and the impersonator may feel. She cannot be explained, she can only be felt; by 'she' I mean the woman about whom the artist knew more than he was giving away. He meant, then, his portrait to be an enigma, and an enigma it certainly is; its very power is in its inscrutability. Cleopatra is meant to be realized rather than understood, apprehended rather than comprehended. To explain Cleopatra you must take a line on her and this you cannot do because the line twists itself into impossible complications. (There are those who feel that a really amoral serpent was intended, a cruel siren, but one who loved Antony – loved him next to herself, that is; Antony of course loving her first and himself second. How nice and simple that would be.) Those who wish to find this line pin their faith on the extension of character drawing at the end of Cleopatra's story to which I referred earlier – the much argued and frequently cut Seleucus scene in Act V, Scene 2.

Referring to the source of the play, we learn that Plutarch himself did not believe that Cleopatra had much other motive at this time than to fool Caesar that she wanted to go on living, so that he would be sufficiently reassured to leave her the opportunity which she desired, that of taking her own life.

'Caesar was glad to hear her say so, persuading himself thereby that she had yet a desire to save her life. So he made her answer, that he did not only give her that to dispose of at her pleasure which she had kept back, but further promised to use her more honourably and bountifully than she would think for: so he took his leave of her, supposing he had deceived her, but indeed he was deceived himself.'

The most diligent study of this scene in Shakespeare will reveal no more than that which Plutarch wrote, in fact most of it consists of Plutarch's words quite thinly (for Shakespeare) transcribed into verse. I can nowhere find the smallest hint that Cleopatra was attempting to ensnare Caesar with her charms, or even that she was trying to feather her future nest; everything and more than she could ask was promised by Caesar before he left her; after which she promptly sent for the asp.

It would seem, therefore, that her intention of suicide was as strong before her meeting with Caesar as was Antony's before word came to him of her 'death'. In other words, unless a reading is forced upon the scene that is not indicated, it is as well to regard it as 'an unexplained variation of an earlier motif in order to heighten a sublimity of climax': the first rendering of the motif being the scene with the messenger who brings the news of Antony's marriage, an earlier character whom she 'haled up and down' but more effectively and much more richly in choice of language.

It would seem to be dramatically unwise of Shakespeare to repeat such a mood at this point in the evening, but Shakespeare knew his business and it is that undoubted fact that prompts the search for hidden meanings. For me the scene remains a mystery.

Any attempt to whitewash Cleopatra would be as fortuitous as painting her black. In life she husbanded her country better than is indicated in the play; so well, in fact, that after all was ended Augustus, as Octavius was to become, was able to feed the whole of his empire from all that she had garnered, cultivated and stored in Egypt. She was cowardly, cruel, irresponsible and most damnably capricious. At the same time, she was capable of infinite tenderness, had obviously more charm than has been allowed to most other mortal beings and was gifted with a shrewd, fascinating, if sometimes bawdy wit. One feels in her a delicious person who could on occasions be 'the greatest fun'. She had what has been described as 'a genius of femininity'.

She followed her instincts like a cat, and a cat's instincts are as easy to observe in life as Cleopatra's are in the play – but what of her premeditations, her calculations? I remember a cat once, when I was small, that ran up a tree in order to avoid my too boring attentions. I followed it up the tree and when for a second it looked as if I would achieve my purpose of catching her, she started to purr and rub herself against my outstretched hand in order to give me false confidence. I put my hand back on the branch to steady myself for a second, and the cat was down the tree and across the field before I realized what was happening.

This kind of cunning is patent in much of Cleopatra, in her buoyant variations of opposites according to Antony's moods, in varying degrees of subtlety and obviousness throughout the tragedy, and most blatantly in her pretended death; but on the whole it is the enigma that tells, the enigma that holds us. What is she *really thinking* when, for instance, Thidias first comes on with the sweet offer from Caesar; is she condoning the fact that this is the game that she must play even if it means the sacrifice of Antony, to save her kingdom, her children and her own life? Or does she notice Enobarbus stealing from the room and deliberately flirt with this rather obviously too likely young fellow, in order to achieve the jealous fury that will seize Antony when the scene meets his eyes, galvanize him into some kind of action and recall in him some semblance of soldierliness? If it is this, it works perfectly, though not permanently. Or is she just playing for time? Or, and I think this is nearest, is she experiencing a strange mixture of all three?

What does she *mean* when, watching Antony marching off to his pathetic little victory in the first day's skirmish of the last great battle, she says:

> *He goes forth gallantly. That he and Caesar might*
> *Determine this great war in single fight !*
> *Then Antony – but now –* Well on

We must remember that Cleopatra eyed every situation with an insatiable curiosity; it is one of the most fascinating things about her, and a small mark of greatness too. This shows even in her smallest actions. When the eunuch admits to her that in spite of his neuter state he still experiences passionate affections, 'Indeed!' she says; it is not a disinterested sound, she is rabidly interested, just for a moment. She was able to detatch herself from any and every situation as well as being part of it. It is only through this quality of curiosity that I can make sense of her prevarication in the first (and last) meeting with Caesar, taken in conjunction with the consequent scene with Seleucus.

Cleopatra remains a character about whom one dares not take a stand, about whom one can have convictions, but must allow oneself no authority. I am certain, though, that no matter what moral or psychological tests are applied, the subject beyond the portrait will ever be found to be a human, not an inhuman, woman. The portrait itself, transfigured, as it is, by Shakespeare's most rapturous poetry, will ever be an enigma.

1952

Coriolanus

MANFRED WEKWERTH and
JOACHIM TENSCHERT

Manfred Wekwerth and Joachim Tenschert were responsible for the production of Coriolanus at the National Theatre in 1971. They came to this Shakespeare play via many years of intensive work with the Berliner Ensemble and an intimate knowledge of Brecht's version of the play. Brecht had a very special interest in Coriolanus, *going back to the Twenties but crystallizing in the Fifties with his own realization of the text, and in a couple of peripheral plays which stemmed from it. He saw in the subject a vehicle for his ideas on social and political change.*

But, while working on the original text of Coriolanus, *Wekwerth and Tenschert decided to recover that which Brecht had lost in his various treatments. They shifted the balance from Brecht's stress on the lower classes, on the revolutionary elements – which had produced a fascinating social experiment in theatre, but which was far removed from Shakespeare – and, instead, conceived the play as a conflict between the liberties of a great individual, a hero passionately alive, and the liberties of the social entity which he threatened, the State. In such a conflict, the greater good of the greater number inevitably triumphs.*

The National Theatre production was therefore a reassessment of Shakespeare's great play viewed through Brechtian glasses, re-ground by experience.

Man verses Mankind: aspects of a contemporary interpretation of Shakespeare's *Coriolanus*.

Elizabethan drama powerfully established the freedom of the individual and then left him as powerfully to exercise his passions; his passion to be loved – King Lear; his passion to rule – Richard III; to love – Romeo and Juliet, Antony and Cleopatra; to punish or not to punish – Hamlet . . . and so on. Our actors are able to assist their audiences to indulge these freedoms even further. But at the same time, and in the same way, as the

freedom of the individual was established, the freedom of society was also
founded, its freedom to change the individual and to make him productive.
For what is the use of removing the chains, if the unchained individual
does not know how to produce, in which lies all happiness?

BERTHOLD BRECHT, *c.* 1940

The twentieth century shares a common theme with Shakespeare's
Coriolanus – the relation of the individual to society. Our production of the play had to search for the means to represent this contemporary issue realistically and explore it logically, both from the
point of view of the individual and that of society. We tried to avoid,
in every way we could, creating a 'classic' production – or perhaps a
better word would be 'classicistic' – not that we wanted merely to
loose a polemic against the accepted, classical, performance, but
rather because we wanted to set against it a more powerful presentation, richer in meaning, simple yet exciting.

At this point descriptions and criticisms of past German productions came to our assistance, though we would normally have avoided
studying them. Our researches showed us that many productions,
otherwise having very little in common, all shared a peculiar similarity
in that they either eliminated the big battle scenes altogether or cut
them drastically. But it is by means of the solid, down-to-earth nature
of these very scenes that the almost god-like rise of the hero is
demonstrated. He is proposed as consul because of the hope that he
will behave in Rome with the same decision that he manifests on the
battlefield – and on the battlefield he is an unsurpassed master. For
his greatness does have a very practical side; he is a superb fighter.

With this in mind, we moved the often deleted battle scenes to the
focal point of the production. We tried to show them as the crowning
achievement of two great warrior experts, Coriolanus and Aufidius.
Their behaviour in peacetime is only understandable when it is clearly
shown that they are *instinctively* bellicose. Off the battlefield, just as on
it, they cross swords with everything and everyone that opposes their
lust to fight. War, for them, is also the setting for their idiosyncratic
passions; the two great warrior-heroes must have their duel, even if it
imperils the whole world. This is the impelling force behind the story,
driving it to its relentless end. All the implications inherent in this
force, implications which the heroes, obsessed by their trial of

strength, ignore, must occupy our interest. Who is to foot the bill?
Over whose bodies do these two heroes fight? Who are the real losers?

The battle scenes are not conceived as mere ballast to fill out the
play, nor to give the chance for idle revelling in history for its own
sake, but they exist to provide solid proof of the value of the hero's
abilities. In other words, it is in the battle scenes that the audience
witnesses the formation of Coriolanus, and does not have to accept the
unfounded premiss that he is a hero merely because heraldic blood
flows in his veins. If that were all, it would make him quite useless as
the pivot of Shakespeare's historical scheme. For Shakespeare was not
interested in having a ready-made idol for the Roman Plebs, but
preferred to have his heroic qualities develop, even during the action
of the battle scenes. Only thus can the shifting opinions of the Roman
crowd become really believable. In the fifth line of the very first scene
of the play, Marcius is called 'chief enemy to the people'. When, later,
he asks the crowd in the Forum for their votes, they say –

SIXTH CITIZEN *He has done nobly, and cannot go without any honest*
man's voice.
SEVENTH CITIZEN *Therefore let him be consul. The gods give him joy,*
and make him good friend to the people!
ALL *Amen, Amen. God save thee, noble consul!*   II, iii

Here is the dividing line for every production of the play. Either one
allows a variety of events to develop between these two scenes, so that
the Plebeians' change of mind becomes explicable, or one allows no
development at all in the interim and so provides the mob with an
almost negative attitude which thus relegates the first half of the play
to the category of unexplained historical events.

It is also important to avoid a so-called 'modern' interpretation that
tries to make us forget the great historical gulf that lies between our
generation, which condemns war as morally wrong, and the era of
those whose daily way of life it was. It is easy to denigrate Coriolanus
simply for being a man of war. There are too many performances
today which no longer take pains over the recreation of greatness.
Because from the start they underline the ordinariness of the hero –
in a manner as abstract in its own way as is the classicist's – they only
succeed in fitting him out with all the trappings of a modern war
criminal. With such an approach to build on, the play automatically
translates itself into contemporary terms; but, by such an imposition,

its valid statement about the modern world gets lost: namely that one individual, armed with his achievements – and they are very real achievements in Roman terms – can blackmail his society with the threat that he is irreplaceable. If a production is based on this broader view, it will not only take sides against the war-hungry Coriolanus, but also indict every man who misuses his achievements.

It was in this attitude that the kernel of our argument and of our production lay. We tried to show in *Coriolanus*, not only that great men are replaceable, but the corollary, that a great man can use the belief in his own indispensability to coerce his society. That is what destroyed Coriolanus and robbed the community of a worthwhile leader. The plain fact is that society cannot submit to the doctrine that any single man is indispensable without risking its own downfall. In this context, we were constantly reminded as we worked on our production, that there is one dominant feature that marks Shakespeare's hero-figures – they are all men who do not fit into their worlds.

Keeping this idea in mind, we tried to get at the concept which underlies it. Does Shakespeare think the world too cheap for a man like Coriolanus, or does he conceive Coriolanus as too expensive for the world?

For the actor playing Coriolanus, the foremost task is to equip the character with all the traits of a great and, for his period, invaluable warrior. It is from this point that true and measurable greatness must grow. Measurable, too, for the Plebeians, who hail him not simply out of blindness, but from a realization of his value to the State. It is from this point, too, that the actors playing the Tribunes can derive stimulus for their interpretations. They must not continually condemn Coriolanus out of an abstract aversion for him, but be forced to reassess this Commander-in-Chief of the armed forces with every new turn of events. Naturally, they can assess wrongly both his value to the State and his potential threat to it, for neither the value nor the damage that he could cause are mutually exclusive. His usefulness *becomes* destructive when he turns his skill in war upon his fellow citizens, when he cannot stop the war and when he employs against Rome herself those very qualities for which both Patricians and Plebeians had so valued him when he used them against the Volsci.

Brecht once postulated that, since the Individual is the subject

matter of Shakespearean drama, then his behaviour provides its passion and his aims shape its events. Following this idea, we built on
Coriolanus' passionate rivalry with the Volscian leader, Aufidius,
stemming from their mutual, deadly obsession with victory. Further,
we tried to let all Coriolanus' political undertakings derive from simple,
personal causes. (He will do something just to please his mother; he
will blurt out exactly what he thinks, purely because he has learned to
speak his mind; he is angered when, in the teeth of critical times, the
people will talk of corn shortages . . . and so on.) Coriolanus maintains
his dignity because he has never become a tactical politician. He
remains a tragic figure because he keeps an historically conditioned
blindness with regard to his own actions and because, in spite of his
'Tudor' mentor, his mother, he cannot renounce his breeding. We
found, too, that the character of Coriolanus received a shimmer of
humour, perhaps for the first time, from the fact that if only he could
have kept his mouth shut once, the tragedy would have been averted.
If this version of his personality is accepted, then the poetic quality of
the hero's exhausted isolation becomes immediately accessible to experience, because it is no longer totally inexplicable. From fear of
civil war, those who originally urged him to use his talents against the
revolting Plebeians withdrew their support from him, leaving him
isolated and adrift.

The stage is a battlefield where the hero has to prove his ability – not
only in war, but in peacetime too, even to the brink of destroying the
whole city. The action which takes place on that stage must demonstrate vividly that the behaviour of all the characters, even of those
who are apparently peaceful, is in fact the behaviour of fighting men.
The dialogue must be conducted like a series of mini-battles, the
twists and turns of the plot should come across like the fluctuating
fortunes of war. The contrast which we saw between the mobility of
the tides of action and the monumentality of the cities, creating a
shock as of surging seas breaking on cliffs, led us to place a huge arch
on a revolving disc. Although it was too large, really, for mobility, its
each succeeding *volte face* did further integrate it into the movement
of the play. Here, too, the visual impact made capital from the battle
scenes, for the revolving stage presented each confrontation of battle-
breaker and city-cliff to the audience like the changing aspects of a
trial being submitted to a judge. It permitted, too, echoes of war,

when the turning disc showed Coriolanus inside Rome canvassing for the Plebeians' votes. Today's audience may well realize what those Roman Plebeians failed to realize; within the city there was war, too.

Much is talked about the verbal beauty of Shakespeare in both 'classical' and 'modern' approaches to the play. Some directors exploit it, others deny it; some let the verse flutter like blazoned banners high over the events on stage, others let the images hide themselves in the crowd. The language, or more accurately the verse, is not merely a lyric addition to the story. The verse is not a language by itself, nor does its beauty stand alone, but, like every other element in the play, it has to contribute its dramatic weight to the whole. One should not think of the lines of verse as poetic forms in themselves, but as the current coin of a human society. The verse of any Shakespeare play is not an unchanging pattern, common to all the characters in that play, but, like the rhythm of breathing, it changes with the personalities and conditions involved.

Yes. The verse is the expression of changing circumstances, or, to put it another way, the characters select their word patterns according to their situation. The way the verse is shaped suggests that if, in the interests of the flow of the argument, of the 'fight', some of the text were to be cut, then the actor would still have a distinct character to present. Menenius, for example, would still be idiosyncratically himself in the 'belly' speech even though some of the lines were to disappear. The individuality of his thought, of the way the lines break, would still appear. Which rather goes to show that in the richness of his part lie many pearls thrown before swine. On the other hand, the Tribunes would show that the real motive force behind their lines is a searching for expression. They think as they speak. The verse structure helps Cominius to deliver his battle report with the brevity and exactness of a successful warrior, one whom laymen like the Tribunes dare not contradict. And where the Plebeians have lines, they should echo with big empty phrases because they are such little people; noise is all they have.

In such an environment the simplicity of Coriolanus, who simply says what he thinks, must have the effect of a blow on the face, the kind of challenge that only a major figure can afford. Where, with the other characters, the verse comes as the result of consideration, Coriolanus delivers his as he does everything else, without thought,

achieving thereby stunning effects. . . . 'I banish you'. He knows, from
his experiences in battle, that he must act instinctively, forestalling his
opponent by that vital fraction of a second.

All the same, the great battles and fighting set-pieces, so popular at
the time when Shakespeare was writing his Roman plays, should be
shown as events that we, children as we are of this scientific age, do
not want to accept as the normal course of affairs. It is a difficult
balance to hold for, just as it is wrong to criticize the kind of events
that glorify *Coriolanus*, calling them immoral for peaceful human
beings, so it is also wrong to portray them as acceptable, natural and
simply immutable.

A final word about the music. In our production of this great work,
music, sister art of drama, took on an individual function. It was used
to invest the events on that passionate scene with a barbarous element,
deriving from a bleak era. The roaring of the victorious and the vanquished, of the swordsmen and their victims, with the aid of music,
seemed as something not of our age when, generally, killing is an
avoidable event. But it is only avoidable through struggle, through the
struggle of human beings against barbarism, against the man of blood
in authority, against oppression in the name of irreplaceability.

And the victory in this struggle will be a victory for reason.

1975

Pericles, Prince of Tyre

RICHARD PASCO

My first and immediate reaction on being invited by the The Folio Society to write an introduction to *Pericles* was – 'Why ever me? – it was all so long ago!' But the process of recollection brings reward, and revising my work and the remaining written accounts of the production I was involved in, has been a chastening, and indeed a tranquillizing form of therapy. How much had I learnt in the intervening years? Would I approach the part now, as I did then? These, and numerous other questions, passed before my mind's eye.

The play was performed most recently by the Royal Shakespeare Company in 1969, and many critics, scholars and 'experts', to say nothing of the leading actors and directors of that production, would be more immediately involved with the play than I am. I have to go back in time to 1954, the Birmingham Repertory production by Douglas Seale, under the watchful eye of the late lamented Sir Barry Jackson; the part of Pericles was really my first attempt at a major Shakespearean role and I can remember quite clearly how I was asked to do it. Casting time at 'the Rep' was always one of those frightfully anxious times in any repertory theatre, where gossip, bitterness, rivalry, hope, ambition and cynicism abound. The plays were usually known before the actors were named for the principal parts, and *Pericles*, of course, was the biggest plum on the tree that season. I had been waiting since the summer of 1952, when I first joined the company, for the crack of the whip, and when it came, like any number of momentous occasions in one's life, it was presented to me at a time when I least expected it. At lunch break on most days, during rehearsals, actors would repair to either the 'Company pub' (long since demolished in the Birmingham improvement scheme) or to the 'Market Hotel' near the theatre. Douglas Seale asked me to join him for a drink at the 'Market'. With drinks poured, and immediately after 'Cheers', he casually dropped the remark – 'How do you feel about doing Pericles for us?' Anyone interested enough, must contact Douglas Seale for what my immediate reaction was, but in retrospect,

I think I was delighted, astounded, embarrassed and downright frightened! 'Pericles – ah Pericles' – 'Emboldened with the glory of her praise' – 'The Romantic Hero' – 'The Ingenuous Prince' – 'A Hamlet character' – 'A minor Lear' – where to begin?

I suppose one's method of approach to a major Shakespearean role, or for that matter to any role or characterization, is part and parcel of the actor's innate sensitivity, instinct and craft; to divulge the method is not the point of this introduction. In my opinion, the actor should have his own 'copyright' on his ways and means, and unless he cares to write a textbook on the subject, those methods are private and personal and for his senses alone. I will say, however, that in repertory conditions – despite the luxury then of three weeks rehearsal and four weeks of performances – methods are somewhat different from those involved in the longer period of preparation and rehearsal now enjoyed for example by the artists of the Royal Shakespeare Company. 'Learn the lines – speed and pace – and go home afterwards to learn the lines of the next play due to open in the following three weeks' – could be said to be a fair guide to the inner workings of the actor in repertory. Obviously even worse conditions prevail under weekly and fortnightly working.

What can I remember therefore of that first venture into what must be a lifetime's dedication and devotion – the perfecting of the body and intellect towards cohesion – the creation of character, the interpretation of a major Shakespearean role?

I turned back, I read the comments of many classical scholars, diarists, critics and indeed actors. With Douglas Seale's guidance, discovering *his* ideas of presentation and method, and with Paul Shelving's open black permanent setting, surrounded by a cycloramic vista and with brilliant costumes, I tried to form a picture in my mind's eye of the possibilities of timelessness and the exploration of a man's destiny inherent in the play.

'No other play in the Shakespearean canon, with the possible exception of *Titus Andronicus* has aroused so much keen controversy as to its authorship' – such questions I had to leave to the scholars and pundits to cope with. It should be considered as a romantic, allegorical fairy story. In its movement, with such rapidity, from place to place, it is so much more a play of today than the neglect it appears to enjoy would warrant. (More valid even in 1972 than in 1954, the time of the Birmingham Repertory production.) It was an extremely popular play in Shakespeare's own time and it offers greater imaginative scope to the director than many of the other plays because of the very nature of its ambivalence and, with the linking chorus figure of Gower, its constant change of scene and focus. In the 1954 production, therefore, Douglas Seale directed the play in much the same way as it might have been directed in the Elizabethan Theatre, with a permanent setting and an almost didactic method of presentation to the *audience's imagination.*

> *To sing a song that old was sung*
> *From ashes ancient Gower is come*
> *Assuming man's infirmities,*
> *To glad your ear and please your eyes:*
> *It hath been sung at festivals*
> *On ember-eves and holy-ales*
> *And lords and ladies in their lives*
> *Have read it for restoratives.*

Gower's opening chorus and an implication of the play's intentions and hopes . . . the beginning of the eternally vibrant and engrossing allegory.

Ben Jonson, however, described it as a 'mouldy tale' and it was, later, rarely performed. In 1900 at Stratford it was bowdlerized and rewritten by John Coleman, who both produced it and played the title role. Robert Eddison was Pericles at the Open Air Theatre, Regent's Park, in a 1939 production. In 1947, under the aegis of Sir Barry Jackson, Paul Scofield played the part at Stratford and again in the Under Thirty Theatre Group revival in 1950. It then appears to have been neglected until the 1958 production at Stratford with Richard Johnson in Glen Byam Shaw's production. So my performance was 'sandwiched' as it were between two major Stratford productions. A further eleven year period of neglect ended with the Terry Hands – Ian Richardson production at Stratford in 1969.

In 1954, I was described by a Birmingham critic of the day, Claude L. Westell, as 'a young actor who has long been knocking at the door for a *full length large scale part.*' An apt description: the play does not deserve such infrequent performance. The same critic after seeing the play wrote: 'Mr Pasco established beyond question that he has the makings of a very good Shakespearean actor. He demonstrated a most convincing passion, he gave the hint of nobility, he caught the majesty of the lyrical passages and most important of all, he not only convinced us that he was feeling deeply, but he made us feel with him . . .' What more stirring encouragement could any young actor of twenty eight in his first 'large scale part' want ?

But it was the play that stirred me with its rich romance, its sense of adventure and its childlike-dream quality. It was like the first time one heard of King Arthur and his Knights, or the first magic delvings into Keats, Shelley and the romantics. My response to the play then, in preparation, was purely instinctive and geared to a romanticism which would perhaps not be acceptable today – neither to me, nor to an audience needing to reason logically about every line that Shakespeare wrote. But at that time, such an approach, in the limited time available, would have led me into the realms of turgidity and boredom. The play must sweep the audience into the world of the archetypal fairy-tale, almost entertaining disbelief to sustain the sometimes outrageous situations and characters. One can't sit down and rationalize *Pericles* – it must pass on the clouds – though it could possibly, today, bring back or rather contribute to bringing back the spiritual qualities that, sadly, seem to be missing in our daily rounds and common tasks. It is a soulful play – the recognition scene between Father and Daughter at the end is on the same emotional level as that between Lear and Cordelia. The 'anti-Pericleans' will say that it stumbles along from improbable incident to preposterous coincidence very much in the manner of a very old man telling a half-remembered tale. So be it.

Its mixed authorship, the identification of what Shakespeare actually wrote and the additional interest of Professor Allardyce Nicoll's suggestion that some textual alterations were derived from George Wilkins' novel *The Painful Adventures of Pericles, Prince of Tyre* which appeared in 1608 and preceded the unsatisfactory quarto, are all pointed out in Mr Philip Edwards' excellent article in the 1952 *Shakespeare Survey*, but the author then adds: 'For all this possible erudition and scholastic debating of the study, its proper medium is the immediacy of the Theatre with all that actors, musicians, designers and directors can bring to equate the intellectual appreciation of the play with the aforementioned magical quality akin to the *Arabian Nights* and the gentle effluence of a dream.'

As an actor, it was an initiation into the realms of creative exploration, the juxtaposition of emotion and intellect, the fusion of mind and body into complete characterization that becomes so much more difficult as one grows older and the actor's self doubts and weaknesses are more vulnerable to criticism or mis-direction.

> *Thou God of this Great Vast, Rebuke these surges*
> *Which wash both Heaven and Hell* (PERICLES)

> *Blow winds and crack your cheeks, rage blow* (LEAR)

> *I am great with woe, and shall deliver weeping.*
> *My dearest wife was like this maid, and such a one*
> *My daughter might have been:* (PERICLES)

> *Do not laugh at me:*
> *For, as I am a man, I think this lady*
> *To be my child Cordelia:* (LEAR)

It is a play with so much to offer the actor and audience: romance, poetry, bawdry (the brothel scenes would lend themselves well to the permissive society), humour, pathos – all ingredients for the magical theatrical bran-tub. 'The Purple violets and Marigolds shall, as a chaplet, hang upon thy grave, while summer days do last.'

Of many letters gratefully received by the Birmingham Repertory Company, was one from a 'Mr F.J.' of Birmingham who wrote: 'On Saturday night I had one of the greatest surprises of my sixty-five years of theatre going. As a lifelong lover of Shakespeare, I had heard with interest that Sir Barry Jackson was presenting for the first time at the Repertory Theatre, the rarely played *Pericles*. Though I knew that the amount contributed by Shakespeare was problematical, I seized what was almost certainly a unique opportunity of seeing the play performed, frankly from a desire to improve my knowledge of literature, even at the risk of rather a boring evening. But what did I find? *A play of absorbing interest*, magnificently acted, produced and staged, a packed house giving the players an ovation such as I have rarely witnessed in any theatre. There was no doubt that the applause was a genuine expression of delight at a pleasant evening's entertainment. The Repertory's performance of *Pericles* is no dry-as-dust exhibition of a museum piece, but one that any intelligent theatre-goer will enjoy and the object of this letter is to induce others *to share with me a unique experience*.' (My italics.) This public spirited praise perhaps sums up the attitude of the audience to that never-to-be-forgotten month in 1954 when I was fortunate enough to be given the gentle push over the abyss into a full-length large-scale part. I have never forgotten it.

I have always kept my working copy of the play and the hurriedly pencilled notes from Douglas Seale's encouraging guidance and direction gave me a pang of nostalgia when I re-read them recently for reference in compiling this introduction. Meaningless symbols, possibly, to the reader, but to the actor incorporating thought into the imaginative structure or scaffolding in the building of the character.

'The two great moments made by Shakespeare, the soliloquy over his new born daughter during the storm at sea, and secondly, the sight of the grief-stricken prince slowly but joyfully realizing that both his wife and daughter are still alive . . .' Pericles – 'a Medieval Ulysses' . . . and then rehearsal notes such as 'Wait for music to finish after "Rise I pray you Rise" . . . a later entrance in the Simonides scene . . . start "Thou God of this Great Vast" etc. after the scream . . . Let noise subside before "There will I visit Cleon" . . . "This is Marina" – a plain statement of fact . . . Nobility in early stages, Dignity latterly . . . *control* feeling from youth to age, joy to abject sorrow and from sorrow to joy again . . . The depth of *true grief* combined with a stoical reticence in expressing it . . . the simplicity of "Oh heavens, Bless my girl" . . . Nobility and charm; Melancholy; Hope; Reflection; Suspicion and Defiance; Grief and Joy.'

These notes taken out of the context of the gradual progress of rehearsal would perhaps appear to be more than running the actor's gamut of emotion, but this is all grist to the mill of *Pericles* – this strange confection of a play, so memorable to me with its scene 'Dispersedly in various countries' and the swift even passage of flight through Antioch, Tyre, Pentapolis, Ephesus, Tarsus and Mitylene.

So on your patience evermore attending,
New joy wait on you !

1972

CVMBELINE
Sebastian Shaw

Cymbeline

IAN RICHARDSON

Cymbeline is a confusing play to tidy minds which like to label things, falling easily into none of the three categories our scholars have seen fit to create for the placing of Shakespearean plays. History it is not, in spite of glancing references to Julius Caesar and the actual existence of a British leader with a name resembling the title; tragedy only seems to be applied to plays in which the hero, or the heroine, or preferably both, die; and it is a good deal too serious both in intent and treatment to be legitimately classed as comedy. The very title is a red herring, as the eponymous hero is far from being the subject of the piece, and emerges – when he emerges at all – as weak, vacillating, easily put upon, and neither good nor bad enough to be very interesting. In fact his only positive virtue, as exhibited in the text, is that he, alone of all his court, displays impeccably good manners when talking to his Roman enemy.

The play itself, which should more properly be called 'Imogen' or possibly 'Posthumus', is long, sprawling and uneven; part fairy-tale and part Morality Play, with hints of the old sagas. There are patches of exquisite poetry, and thought as original and beautifully expressed as any in Shakespeare, there are characters as alive and wonderful as human beings may be, but there are also some passages which seem to belong to an older, inferior convention, and people who appear to be no more than ciphers, or vehicles for plot advancement and dramatic device.

The principal story, that of the hard-done-by heroine battling through terrible odds to win her man, is a familiar theme in mediaeval romance, from Chaucer's Patient Grizelda to the Nut-Brown Maid, and was obviously a favourite with the audience. These stories, of which there were hundreds, mainly in ballad form, were all basically the same; the heroine, of unparalleled goodness, chastity, and fidelity underwent the most terrible hardships both physical and mental in the process of nailing her man, who was usually one of the principal instruments of torture, and who had to be convinced of her transcendent merit before he stopped being the sadistic brute of the first twenty-five verses or so, and turned into the smiling husband of the last. To the modern reader, these heroines appear at the best blinkered and pig-headed, and their escapades downright masochistic, although the success of *The Perils of Pauline* earlier this century shows that the genre has not lost its popular appeal. It took the epicene Shakespeare to get under Imogen's skin and transform her from the hackneyed stereotype she could have been, into a breathing, loving, human woman.

Imogen (a compositor's error for Innogen, implying innocence) is in the best tradition of Shakespeare's golden girls, warm-hearted, witty and brave. She is natural sister to Rosalind and Viola, and the catalyst by means of whom the other characters achieve redemption and self-knowledge.

For it seems to me that the play is, after all, a Morality Play, charting the progress of many diverse souls to a state of ultimate grace, with the exception of those who are too far gone to be saved – the Queen and Cloten.

'Whom best I love, I cross' says Jupiter, and it is the key to understanding.

Imogen and Posthumus will achieve a far greater joy than could have been theirs, had they not passed through the fire to emerge true gold, and the smelting process changes both of them. Imogen, who, in the first bitterness of soul at discovering that Posthumus has ordered her death, denounces all men for his sake and casts him from her heart, can forgive him in the last scene with no more reproach than:

Why did you throw your wedded lady from you?

and Posthumus, who at his discovery of Imogen's supposed adultery can break forth with the magnificent anti-woman speech beginning:

Is there no way for men to be, but women
Must be half-workers?

and ending

. . . I'll write against them,
Detest them, curse them: yet 'tis greater skill
In a true hate, to pray they have their will:
The very devils cannot plague them better,

has learnt from the true prompting of his own heart that love is more important than morality, and while still believing her guilty can say:

> *You married ones,*
> *If each of you would take this course, how many*
> *Must murder wives much better than themselves*
> *For wrying but a little ?*

This would have been quite surprising to an Elizabethan audience accustomed to plays where wronged husbands were considered within their rights to murder their wives, and adulteresses invariably got what was coming to them. Unconventional morality, then, with the guiding light of the love that alters not where it alteration finds, even if the alteration lead to murder or adultery.

Cymbeline himself, finding himself finally, through no merit of his own, the victor of the field, has the grace to submit honourably to the Romans, his pride seeming a small price to pay for 'such a peace'. Again, the true value, not the conventional one.

Iachimo, the casual villain, who sins more from boredom and amorality than from wickedness, is shamed by the appalling suffering his flippant bet and the subsequent fabrication of false evidence has produced for two people whom he realizes surpass him in greatness of soul as much as he surpasses the miserable Cloten in intellect. Perhaps for the first time in his worthless existence he is given to think seriously, and there is hope for him too, although what he finds in his own soul leads to a self-disgust for which he feels the only cure is death. It is fitting that the precise, unorthodox morality of the play denies it him.

Pisanio has discovered that simply to be a good servant is not enough. The commands of conscience are more binding than the commands of whoever one happens to be serving at the time, and even in bondage one is not freed from responsibility.

In form, the play is untidy, ambling from London to Rome, Rome to Milford Haven, in scenes of very unequal length, introducing characters and dropping them again as the exposition of the extremely complicated plot demands. The very first scene is such a one, with two gentlemen, who otherwise do not appear, quickly giving as much of the story-so-far as may be decently done within dramatic convention, but it seems to me a clumsy device, and it is a relief when the next scene starts with some of the main protagonists – the Queen, Posthumus and Imogen – and one can feel that the play has really started.

The Queen is a character of pure evil, and in the Snow-White tradition of wicked stepmothers, but although she is a two-dimensional character, her evil is so extreme – with the hints of her poisoning cats and dogs up in her room – that she produces an agreeable frisson at her every entrance. She is the woman you love to hate, and yet it is into her mouth that Shakespeare puts the only piece of high patriotic verse in the play.

> *. . . Remember, Sir, my liege,*
> *The kings your ancestors, together with*
> *The natural bravery of your isle, which stands*
> *As Neptune's park, ribbed and paled in*
> *With rocks unscaleable, and roaring waters . . .*

It is a fine speech, reminiscent of John of Gaunt's, and would well have suited any of Shakespeare's heroes; it is one of the pleasurable oddities of this play, that here it is in the mouth of the arch-villainess. This occurs in the scene of confrontation with the Roman ambassador, and the Queen is not the only one who appears here to be out of character. Cloten, who has been represented to us as an oaf:

> *That such a crafty devil as is his mother*
> *Should yield the world this ass ? A woman that*
> *Bears all down with her brain, and this her son*
> *Cannot take two from twenty, for his heart,*
> *And leave eighteen*

and a coward, can still come out with pithy patriotism to delight the groundlings.

> *If Caesar can hide the sun from us with a blanket, or put the moon in his pocket, we will pay him tribute for light; else, sir, no more tribute . . .*
> *. . . if you seek us afterwards in other terms, you shall find us in our salt-water girdle: if you beat us out of it, it is yours; if you fall in the adventure, our crows shall fare the better for you; and there's an end.*

Perhaps Shakespeare was going through a state of disillusionment with England, to have fathered such speeches on the evil and the foolish, and yet make the heroine say:

... I' the world's volume
Our Britain seems as of it, but not in't;
In a great pool, a swan's nest: prithee think
There's livers out of Britain.

Iachimo's villainy is of a different order to that of the Queen and Cloten. He is not dedicated to it as she is, and he is not stupid as Cloten undoubtedly is, in spite of the uncharacteristic lines quoted above. Iachimo is a dilettante, a thrill-seeker and, most important, a Roman. Britain was, after all, a colony, and I do not imagine that the average Roman's opinion of 'natives' and 'native women' was any higher than the average Englishman's some hundreds of decades later. And then, the natives get so excited, and make silly bets, and it really is good sport to make them see how foolish, contemptible and un-Roman they are. His villainy is born of thoughtlessness, and to do him credit, he has aesthetic sense enough genuinely to admire Imogen, and enough stirrings of conscience to know he is being a cad – I don't suppose, at that point, the feeling was much deeper than that – even at the moment he is engineering her ruin.

The crickets sing, and man's o'er-labour'd sense
Repairs itself by rest. Our Tarquin thus
Did softly press the rushes, ere he waken'd
The chastity he wounded. Cytherea,
How bravely thou becomest thy bed! fresh lily,
And whiter than the sheets!

He has the brains and the imagination to suffer for it later.

Cloten's brand of evil is the most dangerous of all, born as it is of an animal stupidity not accessible to reason or conscience. Lustful, quarrelsome, and only half comprehending, he may kiss or kill at whim, and barely remember it afterwards, while his Grand Guignol plot to murder Posthumus and rape Imogen while wearing her husband's clothes – 'his meanest garments!' – shows him to be more than half crazed.

It is interesting to note that physically Cloten is as well formed as Posthumus, indeed, interchangeable from the neck down, if we may believe Imogen when she praises – in specific terms – the lineaments of the dead body she believes to be her husband's. The psychology here is intriguing and would bear examination; it also illustrates another central theme of the play, that nothing is what it seems, and that the mind and the heart are what matter, and not the outside. Almost all the characters are mistaken in their judgements of other people, because they accept exterior evidence, before discovering that 'It is the mind that makes the body rich' – to quote from another play, and,

> *Thersites' body is as good as Ajax',*
> *When neither are alive.*

to quote from this.

Cymbeline says of his queen, when the full extent of her treachery has been discovered after her death:

> *... Mine eyes*
> *Were not in fault for she was beautiful,*
> *Mine ears that heard her flattery, nor my heart*
> *That thought her like her seeming; it had been vicious*
> *To have mistrusted her ...*

Posthumus, having found wisdom, takes up the theme and applies it to himself:

> *To shame the guise o' the world, I will begin*
> *The fashion, less without and more within.*

But if appearances deceive at court, once in the country we are on familiar Shakespearean ground. In a wilderness, where life is hard and a man can only live by constant hunting, foraging and simple husbandry, we are again in the forest of Arden, or Bohemia, and the country virtues are extolled in a voice we recognize. In the cave to which the desolate Imogen comes, worn out by her loving pilgrimage, we meet Belarius, the banished man, close kin to Prospero and the banished Duke, at least as far as his opinions on the relative values of court and country. Living simply, respecting nature, and full of abhorrence for the thoughtless pomp of cities where:

> *... the gates of monarchs*
> *Are arch'd so high that giants may jet through*
> *And keep their impious turbans on, without*
> *Good morrow to the sun.*

Here also we meet the boys, Arviragus and Guiderius, Imogen's undetected brothers, strong, free and untrammelled with the impedimenta of polite society. Their unabashed and, it must be confessed, rather flowery expressions of love to Imogen in her boy's disguise, may strike modern audiences as a little over-effusive, but it is in key with their innocence, and if we are embarrassed, it is because we are corrupt. In them it is natural. Guiderius cuts off Cloten's head with exactly the same kind of ingenuous abandon as that with which he has embraced Imogen. When she is supposedly dead, the simplicity and strength of their grief should wipe away any sniggers induced by the preceding scene. What could be a stronger image than that evoked by this healthy young animal, as he bears in her body?

> *... The bird is dead*
> *That we have made so much on. I had rather*
> *Have skipp'd from sixteen years of age to sixty,*
> *To have turn'd my leaping-time into a crutch,*
> *Than have seen this.*

The echoes of fairy-tale have crept in strongly now; in wild Wales, Imogen is Snow-White again, living with rough creatures in a cave and poisoned at long-distance by her stepmother. Guiderius is Jack the Giant-Killer. As they lay out the dead bodies – Imogen and Cloten – in preparation for burial, we are reminded fleetingly of the Babes in the Wood:

> *... The ruddock would*
> *With charitable bill ...*
> *... bring thee all this,*
> *Yea, and furr'd moss besides, when flowers are none,*
> *To winter-ground thy corse.*

The famous dirge, 'Fear no more the heat o' the sun' is too well known for me to comment on it here, save to say that it never fails to move me, partly because I have heard it read at more actors' memorial services than I care to remember – which is beside the point. It remains, on its own merits, one of the most beautiful prayers for the dead that has ever been devised.

Jumping from the sublime to what can all too easily be the ridiculous; the masque of Jupiter and the ghosts of Posthumus' relations would seem to have been inserted more as an excuse for showing off the stage machinery and creating a moment of spectacle, than for any necessity of plot or character, and some of the verse, especially that of the relations, is such execrable doggerel that I do hope that Shakespeare had no hand in it. However, if the *deus ex machina* is well managed, it can be theatrically effective, and a compensation for not actually having seen any of the battles which precede it. Battles are notoriously difficult to stage successfully, and Shakespeare, while showing us snatches of soldiery between battles, for the most part makes use of the device of the Classic Theatre of having someone come on and describe the action, which is, to my mind, infinitely preferable, particularly with his mastery of word-painting.

From Posthumus' haunted prison – complete with the obligatory humorous gaoler – we pass gladly to the explaining-everything-to-everybody scene, which is extraordinarily effective and moving, even though the audience is in possession of all the facts already, and the only real interest can be in how the various characters react to the revelations made, and how long it takes them to make discoveries for themselves. It could be risible, it could be trite, but as we are in the hands of a master it is masterly done, and ultimately enormously satisfying.

> *Hang there like fruit, my soul,*
> *Till the tree die !*

says Posthumus to Imogen as they come together, and it is a poor pair of actors and a flinty hearted audience who do not experience a communal lump in the throat.

The long uphill journey to happiness is over, and as the company exit to light their sacrificial fires in thanksgiving to the merciful Gods, all is joy and peace. Peace between husband and wife, father and children, victor and vanquished, and each enlarged soul with itself.

1976

The Winter's Tale

FLORA ROBSON

I first heard about the possibility of appearing in *The Winter's Tale* when I was acting in New York in 1950. I had lunch with John Gielgud, who was also in a play there, and he described to me some of the plans that were being hatched to celebrate the Festival of Britain by a really splendid year in the theatre. He told me that he was hoping to play Leontes in a production directed by Peter Brook. Not long afterwards I was asked if I would be interested in appearing as Paulina in the same production. I was immediately taken by the notion, as she is one of the few completely warm and sympathetic mature women characters in Shakespeare and I liked the idea of being able to play her as part of the general 1951 celebrations.

I had only once before acted in *The Winter's Tale*, back in 1922 at the Theatre Royal, Bristol, in one of Ben Greet's repertory seasons. At that time I played Emilia, a lady-in-waiting. It was only my second day with the company and I had hurriedly learned the part the night before. I am afraid that I 'dried' twice in just about as many lines. I had not had the chance to appear in the play since then and, indeed, it has never been a very popular play. Although it has a very attractive, fairy-tale quality about it, it has one serious defect from the point of view of leading actors and actresses. The really pithy parts, the ones that tend to attract 'star' players, are confined to the beginning and end of the play. All the centre scenes are given over to the young lovers, Florizel and Perdita, and to the comedians, none of whom are generally played by 'stars'. From time to time there have been attempts to bridge this gap – either by the actor playing Leontes also appearing as Autolycus, or (as with Mary Anderson in the last century or Brenda Bruce quite recently), having the actress playing Hermione also playing her daughter, Perdita. But the trouble with this kind of solution is that it attracts undue attention for its 'gimmick' quality and really does little to help the play.

However, none of these tricks were to be used in the 1951 *Winter's Tale*. It was to be dressed in near-Tudor costumes and staged in a series of very simple, but very attractive, settings that were loosely based by the designer, Sophie Fedorovitch, on the structure of the Elizabethan stage. Some modern effects were allowed, like the whirling snow through which Father Time materialized and into which he disappeared. I found the costumes for Paulina especially grateful to wear, elegant and flowing, but without the uncomfortable bulkiness and weight which make accurate Tudor clothes sometimes such a trial for an actor and in which I have really suffered, especially when filming.

The play is, of course, supposed to be set in the ancient world. But the only obvious element from antiquity, and one that is a great problem to deal with when the setting is not Greek, is the very important Delphic Oracle. But, this problem aside, the play is about as much a part of the ancient Greek world as is *A Midsummer Night's Dream* ... 'and that's not much!' *The Winter's Tale* is really set in that once-upon-a-time country where all the best stories happen. The play is in a very strict sense a fairy-tale, the kind of story that Perrault wrote so well. The words, *winter's tale*, mean an old wives' tale, the sort of story that you tell to children in the firelight just before packing them off to bed. It has all the trappings of Snow White or Sleeping Beauty and this was one of the points that Peter Brook brought out very strongly, early in our rehearsals.

The fairy-tale elements are quite simple. There is a jealous king who falsely suspects his virtuous queen. She is thought to have died but reappears sixteen years later, vindicated. Their daughter is left for dead as a baby, but lives to fall in love with a handsome young prince, disguised as a shepherd, who is the son of the estranged couple's oldest friend. The two families are reunited through the good offices of what, in any self-respecting fairy-tale, would be the Fairy Godmother.

But within this once-upon-a-time framework move some of the most solid, alive people Shakespeare ever created. There is Leontes, a loving husband and father, suddenly torn apart by a totally irrational, all-consuming sexual jealousy, suspecting that his wife is betraying him with his best friend, fearing that his children are not his. He emerges from his passion to find that his young son is dead, that the wife he dragged to trial seems also to have died, and that in his madness he sent his baby daughter to be brutally killed in a far-off land. Hermione, his queen, is drawn as a model of wifely devotion, subjected to intolerable strains, but capable of flashes of fiery, human reaction. The Fairy Godmother, Paulina, is an outspoken, down-to-earth, commonsensical woman, the sort of slightly common, feminine realist who can hold her own in any surroundings and yet with a heart immediately responsive to the cares of others. Polixenes, the falsely suspected adulterer, though not so strongly characterized as the others, is still a reliable, dependable man. These are the people who bring the first and last parts of the play to vibrant life.

As we began to rehearse, after spending a full week working over the text, an idea began to grow in my mind. We all discussed it and it became a feature of the production. I should begin by explaining that I have been associated on and off during most of my professional career with plays and films either based on the life of Queen Elizabeth I or dealing with some aspect of the Tudor period. I think my interest must have begun with my very first professional engagement, when I played in *Will Shakespeare* by Clemence Dane, in 1921. Over the years since then I have been increasingly fascinated by the personality of Elizabeth and this has led to my reading very widely about her. It is impossible to attempt to recreate such great characters from the past without becoming very familiar with the places and times in which they lived. It fell out quite naturally, then, as the rehearsals for *The Winter's Tale* proceeded, that I should see more and more affinities between the people in the play – Leontes, Hermione and Perdita – and those of Elizabeth's childhood: her towering, jealous, heir-hungry father; Anne Boleyn, the mother she never really knew but whose shadow haunted her whole life; and Elizabeth herself, the lass unparalleled. I will put forward here a few of the correspondences as I saw them, the Tudor echoes, and leave you to judge for yourselves how relevant they are as you read the play.

To begin with we must remember that Shakespeare was sharing in the writing of *Henry VIII* not long before he wrote *The Winter's Tale*; that is around the year 1611. How much of *Henry VIII* he actually wrote himself seems to be the same kind of problem as 'how long was Cleopatra's nose?' . . . but the old saying is that 'Shakespeare comes in and out with Katharine'. Having played that unhappy woman myself, I can vouch for the fact that the scenes in which she appears do seem to have the right ring about them. Especially her trial – of which more in a moment. I think, myself, that when Shakespeare was working on *The Winter's Tale*, he had his head full of the events of the reign of Henry VIII, with the wrongs of Anne Boleyn, the jealousy of Henry and the general air of suspicion that must have permeated his court. All these ideas overflowed to colour and transform a simple fairy-tale with the totally real passions of a remembered king, queen and princess.

It can surely have been no accident that Shakespeare, having already worked on the trial of Queen Katharine, should place another trial scene, so very similar, in *The Winter's Tale*. Odd as it may seem that Queen Katharine and Anne Boleyn should be yoked together to provide his inspiration, there *is* a strong mixture of both of them in Hermione's speeches after her indictment.

> *You, my lord, best know*
> *(Who least will seem to do so) my past life*
> *Hath been as continent, as chaste, as true,*
> *As I am now unhappy; which is more*
> *Than history can pattern, though devised*
> *And played to take spectators. For behold me,*
> *A fellow of the royal bed, which owe*
> *A moiety of the throne . . . a great king's daughter,*
> *The mother to a hopeful prince, here standing*
> *To prate and talk for life and honour, 'fore*
> *Who please to come and hear. For life, I prize it*
> *As I weigh grief (which I would spare): for honour*
> *'Tis a derivative from me to mine,*
> *And only that I stand for . . . I appeal*
> *To your own conscience, sir . . .*
>
> III. 2. 32–45

I was given a book of Henry VIII's love letters during the run of *The Winter's Tale*, and was fascinated to find a letter written by Anne Boleyn from prison, which echoed extremely closely many of Hermione's lines. Sentences like – 'Neither let that stain, that unworthy stain of a disloyal heart towards your good Grace, ever cast so foul a blot on your most dutiful wife and the infant Princess, your daughter.' Or – 'But if you have already determined of me, and that not only my death, but an infamous slander must bring you the joying of your desired happiness, then I desire of God, that he will pardon your great sin herein . . . and that he will not call you to a straight account for your unprincely and cruel usage of me, at his general judgement seat, where both you and myself must shortly appear, and in whose judgement, I doubt not, whatsoever the world may think of me, my innocence shall be openly known, and sufficiently cleared.' Or, as Hermione says – 'Apollo be my judge'. The letter may or may not be genuine, but if not, then it must have been written by someone who knew Anne's style well, and managed to echo her very thought. It is intriguing also to compare Hermione's speeches with those of Katharine in *Henry VIII*, II.4. They are full of close similarities.

Now to turn to Henry. It seems to be a widely accepted fact by historians that one of the driving forces behind Henry's appalling behaviour was an overwhelming desire for an heir. Indeed, Anne Boleyn's final, fatal fault was that in her last weeks she did produce a son, but that he was still-born. (Hermione, too, comes to her trial just before the birth of Perdita.) In imitation of Henry, Leontes makes his own need for a son and heir abundantly clear. Like Pharaoh, he denies his god and has his first-born struck dead for the sin. He makes his anxiety about having no successor clear when talking to Florizel –

> *You have a holy father,*
> *A graceful gentleman, against whose person*
> *(So sacred as it is) I have done sin,*
> *For which the heavens, taking angry note,*
> *Have left me issueless . . .*
> *. . . What might I have been,*
> *Might I a son and daughter now have looked on,*
> *Such goodly things as you ?*
>
> V. I. 170–178

Before I leave the Tudor echoes, here are two which concern Elizabeth herself. Firstly, about her bastardy. Her mother was executed in May 1536 and Elizabeth was proclaimed illegitimate the following July, when she was but two and a half years old. Leontes dismisses the baby that is to grow up as Perdita, with the words –

> *. . . carry*
> *This female bastard hence, and that thou bear it*
> *To some remote and desolate place, quite out*
> *Of our dominions . . .*
>
> II. 3. 174–177

Finally, the words that are used about Perdita when she reappears at Leontes' court as an unknown girl from a far country. They recall very strongly the kind of language that was used about Elizabeth when, a longed-for princess, she reappeared from exile and took her place in the hearts of her countrymen.

> GENTLEMAN *The most peerless piece of earth, I think*
> *That e'er the sun shone on.*
> *... This is a creature,*
> *Would she begin a sect, might quench the zeal*
> *Of all professors else; make proselytes*
> *Of who she but did follow.*
> PAULINA *How! not women?*
> GENTLEMAN *Women will love her, that she is a woman*
> *More worth than any man; men, that she is*
> *The rarest of all women.*
>
> V. I. 94–102

Paulina does not, as far as I can see, fit into any of these Tudor parallels, but she is none-the-less real for that. She is a very rewarding women to play, standing as she does like a monument to sanity and commonsense when all around her are tearing themselves to pieces like operatic tenors. This sharp contrast became abundantly clear as we rehearsed the scene in which Paulina brings the newly-born Perdita to Leontes in an attempt to persuade him to forgive Hermione. The scene is straight comedy, but it is extremely difficult for the actor playing Leontes to change gear and suddenly find that the emotion he has been building up for some scenes is being torn to ribbons by Paulina who administers adroit pinpricks at the critical moment to deflate his balloon of passion – to mix my metaphors! For example: she is pointing out to the whole court, and to the glowering Leontes, how closely the baby resembles him –

> *Behold, my lords,*
> *Although the print be little, the whole matter*
> *And copy of the father; eye, nose, lip,*
> *The trick of his frown. . . .*

I found, when I was delivering that speech, that I was concentrating completely on the baby, that I was drawn irresistibly to a warmth for the poor wee thing and to a burst of fury against the dolts around me who could behave so stupidly towards such a poor mite and its innocent mother. It was a feeling which Shakespeare quite clearly put there to act as a ray of sunshine and sanity in the dark atmosphere of the Sicilian court.

The juxtaposition of somebody who is being pompous against someone who could not care less for pomposity, is always funny. I remember the lawyer husband of my friend, Margaret Kennedy, author of *The Constant Nymph*, once telling me the story of a particularly difficult woman in a court-room who argued back at everything anyone said, getting the whole court rattled, and especially the judge. Finally she was asked if there was anything she wanted to say before sentence was passed on her. 'Yes,' she replied. 'The judge up there is like a chewed piece of string!' The judge's temper finally snapped and he pounded on his desk, shouting, 'I'm not! I'm not! I'm *nothing of the kind!*' Leontes is very like that judge.

> LEONTES *I'll ha' thee burnt.*
> PAULINA *I care not:*
>   *It is an heretic that makes the fire*
>   *Not she which burns in't. I'll not call you tyrant;*
>   *But this most cruel usage of your queen*
>   *(Not able to produce more accusation*
>   *Than your own weak-hinged fancy) something savours*
>   *Of tyranny, and will ignoble make you,*
>   *Yea, scandalous to the world.*
> LEONTES *On your allegiance,*
>   *Out of the chamber with her! Were I a tyrant,*
>   *Where were her life? she durst not call me so,*
>   *If she did know me one. Away with her!*
>   [They make to thrust her forth
> PAULINA *I pray you do not push me, I'll be gone.*

Which is the most wonderful way to reduce things to their proper perspective and, incidentally, to pave the way for the audience to realize that they should not take all the ravings and unhappiness too seriously, there is a happy ending in store.

I have said that the play falls into three sections. The first section is Leontes', a grown-up world of sexual passion and ugly jealousy, where even the little prince Mamillius (the first part that Ellen Terry ever played on stage) is given weighted lines. Why is it that all Shakespeare's children are such knowing little tykes?

Of the second part of the play I can say but little. Not just because I was enjoying a rest and *The Times* crossword on most evenings when we were performing! But because it speaks for itself. It is a series of scenes, flooded with sunlight, in contrast to the sombre, brooding atmosphere of the first part and the saddened, but slowly lightening mood of the third. It is a time of playful, happy love-making between Florizel and Perdita; a time for that rogue-to-end-all-rogues, Autolycus, to get up to his delightful tricks: a time for some very literate peasants to be busy buying, reading and singing ballads; a time for the story of the lost princess and the handsome prince in disguise to be worked out against a background of 'homely foolery'.

The third and last part of the play belongs to Paulina. She extracts a promise from the contrite Leontes that he will never marry without her consent – a promise he gives all the more readily since she hints that she will be able to produce a Hermione Mark II. She then stage-manages Hermione's return to life and organizes a mellow, happy ending to the fairy-tale. She is the Fairy Godmother incarnate.

The scene of Leontes' reunion with his long-dead wife is one of the most moving to act in all Shakespeare. I always found myself in tears when John Gielgud reached out and touched her hand and ex-claimed 'O, she's warm!' After that, when Paulina has seen everyone happy and she is making a rather delightful fuss about it all, she finds herself having the tables turned by a rejuvenated, newly-humorous Leontes, and is saddled with a husband in much the same way as Queen Katharine prayed that Henry would find husbands for her bereft ladies-in-waiting.

> PAULINA   *Go together,*
> *You precious winners all; your exultation*
> *Partake to every one: I (an old turtle)*
> *Will wing me to some withered bough, and there*
> *My mate (that's never to be found again)*
> *Lament, till I am lost.*
> LEONTES   *O peace, Paulina!*
> *Thou shouldst a husband take by my consent,*
> *As I by thine a wife: this is a match,*
> *And made between's by vows ... Come Camillo*
> *And take her by the hand ...*
>
> V. 3. 130–143

Like *Cymbeline* and *The Tempest, The Winter's Tale* has a sunset ending, an idyllic resolution to all the fairy-tale adventures and unhappinesses. It is a play rich in vivid and unusual characters and living verse. And, for me, it contains one of the most lovable and alive women an actress could ever want to meet.

1975

The Tempest

JOHN CLEMENTS

I think that, of all Shakespeare's plays, *The Tempest* is the most difficult to stage, because, to me at least, it is the most difficult to interpret.

Is it, as some have held, merely a fairy tale concocted for a wedding party? Or was it, consciously, his farewell play, a final masterpiece, setting within its fantasy world a last parable of good and evil?

The more deeply one considers the play, the more possible interpretations one can find. Is it a warning against the dangers of colonialism? Or a warning of the folly of dabbling with the powers of the supernatural? Is it a morality on the right of inheritance by descent and the inherent obligations contained in that right? Is it a study of the nature of innocence on the one hand and ignorance on the other and the dangers of contamination of both at the touch of civilization? Or is it a last sad sigh at the transitoriness of the human condition, a dying echo of 'Tomorrow and Tomorrow and Tomorrow'?

Is it any of these things, or a fusion of some of them, or none?

The task of selection, of coming down positively on the side of one theme or another, confronts those of us who set out to tackle the almost superhuman task of interpreting this wonderful dramatic poem in terms of physical presentation in a theatre.

As with any production, no matter what the play, one must decide on the priority, the overriding essential at which one is aiming and to which all other considerations are secondary.

Most of Shakespeare's plays, to a greater or lesser extent, present a similar variety of choices, and it is clearly impossible to incorporate all the possible interpretations of any single text within the bounds of one production. Even to attempt to do so would confuse an audience and drive a cast distracted. Therefore, when starting on a production, one has to choose an interpretation which seems to hold the greatest truth for that particular moment in time and for that particular group of artists setting out to work together.

Often, after having worked with the play for months, such a choice may seem to have been a limited, even a mistaken, one. The play itself may have revealed new aspects, the words developed new meanings, the characters come to vivid life, sometimes a life different from the one they seemed to have at the start. All the same, one has to begin somewhere, to read the text as it lies on the page and try to shape it into a visual reality which will not betray the play's inherent nature.

Usually the clue to this shaping evolves out of an understanding of the interaction of the characters and the plot, the feeling of a living world that grows from observing the people of the play in the grip of its story. In this respect *The Tempest* provides a problem not met with elsewhere in Shakespeare.

Most of his plays, for instance, although they present many possible themes, do each reveal one which a producer can latch on to as a framework.

In *King Lear* one could choose senility as the theme – conceiving an exterior world where human relationships, the structure of the state, the very fabric of the universe, slide into ruin even as the interior world of Lear himself gradually sinks into decay and madness – both worlds being redeemed for a brief radiant moment of sanity in the arms of his ill-treated daughter, Cordelia.

In *Antony and Cleopatra*, the progress of the lovers' sexual obsession is signposted by the steady collapse of their temporal power as they kiss away kingdoms and provinces until, stripped of earthly hope, they embrace a love-death.

In *Hamlet*, the twisting and turning of the plot accurately mirrors the indecision of the prince himself – his 'thinking too precisely on the event' – gathering slowly to a culmination when he finally summons up his determination to act.

These are plays which present fairly clearly defined choices, easily built into the fabric of a production. But *The Tempest* does not allow the same easy choice. Quite the reverse. In spite of all the possibilities I listed at the outset, there is no single one that goes more than part of the way towards providing a sufficiently basic motivation for a production, and none of them allows for a full realization of the splendour that lies locked away in the text.

In fact, the rather hotch-potch plot and the routine and sometimes self-contradictory characters are not the starting point for finding the clue at all, for they are subordinate to the all-enveloping magic of the play's verse. If it is not stretching the argument too far, one could say that the plot and characters of *The Tempest* are abstractions and it is the hypnotic power of the verse that is the reality.

For *The Tempest* is first and foremost a great piece of music, every note of which must be played with the feeling, tone, rhythm and accuracy which a conductor must draw from an orchestra playing a work of, say, Delius or Debussy. It is, indeed, very much like a massive tone poem – the fury of the storm, the majesty of Prospero's conjurations, the rumbustiousness of the comics, the tenderness of the love scenes fusing together on a verbal level, not on the level of character, each individual element contributing its own colouring to the whole work.

Music occurs in many of Shakespeare's plays, either talked about or actually performed, but *The Tempest* stands alone in his opus as a play which is from the first moment to the last suffused with the feeling of music. Or, as Professor Spurgeon has put it –

'The dominant image in *The Tempest* is, as I have said, something more subtle than we have yet encountered . . . It is the sense of *sound* which is thus emphasized, for the play is an absolute symphony of sound, and it is through sound that its contrasts and movement are expressed, from the clashing discords of the opening to the serene harmony of the close.'

The still sad music of humanity, the music of the spheres, the food of love, these form a ghostly counterpoint which underlies the play's poetry. *The Tempest* breathes music to the listening ear.

> *The isle is full of noises,*
> *Sounds and sweet airs, that give delight and hurt not.*

The secure foundation of Shakespeare's immortality is, of course, his transcendent skill with words. In *The Tempest* this skill reached a new level of accomplishment, transmuting the base metal by an alchemy which he employed only fitfully in his earlier pieces. True, in *Macbeth*, the murky evocations of night contribute so forcefully to the dark atmosphere, the wood near Athens in *A Midsummer Night's Dream* is word-spangled by the glimmer of cold moonlight on dewdrops, but these are irregular bursts. In *The Tempest*, the mind consistently finds itself groping through levels of verbal beauty to try to reach the meaning, only in the end to realize that the process has involved an attempt to comprehend something as incomprehensible as a melody by Mozart. It is the journey, not the arrival, that matters.

Here, then, is the theme which can provide that overriding essential for a production. The play must be considered as a single unified piece of music. But the problem with which a producer is now faced is how to translate this pervasive sense of music and poetry into visual terms for an audience.

The first thing to be tackled, from which all other solutions will follow, is to decide where it all takes place.

We are told it is on an island. Yes. But is it the bare desolate place that the civilized Prospero tells us it is? Or the realm of delight that the uncivilized Caliban sees and hears? Or, again, the potentially fruitful terrain about which the good old Gonzalo eulogizes?

It is a personal view, I know, but I feel that the production should suggest a strange but unspecified locale, a realm of light and shadow, of constantly but unobtrusively changing atmosphere, a place where magic seems, even to our jaded and disillusioned eyes, a natural consequence of its environment and where distant intangible music is as unsurprising as it is in dreams.

To achieve this evocative abstraction we have to prevent the play from becoming stagebound by painted canvas and realistic rocks. Luckily, building on the brilliant work of Adolphe Appia, Gordon Craig and Granville Barker, the modern theatre has adopted, over the last few decades, a much freer style of production and, indeed, constructed more adaptable stages, such as that of the Chichester Festival Theatre, in which to deploy this rejuvenated style. Productions of *The Tempest* of recent years have benefited from this revolution, several of them achieving a timeless unlocated effect which lets the music of the play sing through, without being trammelled by fussy physical details.

In this kind of staging, productions of Shakespeare have followed very much the same lines as have productions of Wagner's operas, the clutter of Victorian realism being swept away and its place taken by limited harmonic colour schemes, sculptural settings which remain in place for the whole action of the play, costumes not tied to a specific period, evocative lighting effects, simpler movements.

This housecleaning has enabled producers to concentrate on the value of the words, on the music inherent in the text. It is as if the modern theatre were finding its own way of recreating the simplicity of the staging which Shakespeare knew at the Globe; finding it, not in a return to an exact historical replication of an Elizabethan theatre, but by using the vast range of modern techniques to their fullest extent. Simplicity is the most difficult thing in the world to achieve and needs the most imaginative effort.

Perhaps it is impossible to translate this understanding of *The Tempest* as a great tone poem successfully to the stage. It may be that it is too ephemeral a concept to be expressed in the concrete terms that a stage presentation necessarily entails. Perhaps those who say that we should not attempt it, that it is to be read and imagined, not seen, are right. Or, perhaps, only by hearing the play on the radio or on a recording, with one's powers of imagination allowed full rein, can one win the most from it.

But Shakespeare wrote for the theatre. Recordings and radio are welcome fringe benefits, nothing more. Divorced from regular physical performance his plays would die – or at best be translated into something quite different from their basic nature. As long as there are actors and directors, who work with living stages for living audiences there will be, again and again, attempts to achieve the impossible.

It is the certainty of that above all which makes the theatre, to me, the exhilarating, heartbreaking, nerveracking and glorious place that it is.

1971

King Henry VIII

HERBERT BEERBOHM TREE

Sir Herbert Beerbohm Tree's productions of Henry VIII *in 1910, designed by Percy Macquoid, was almost the last of those sumptuous revivals which had been rolling on and off the British stage for decades. Tree once epitomized his own opulent approach to Shakespeare in some advice to a timid actor: 'When an actor in my beautiful theatre carries a candle on to the stage, I tell the electrician to turn on two limelights, two whole battens of lights and twenty lamps in the footlights, representing in all some six thousand candle power. In my beautiful theatre one candle is represented by six thousand. Remember that when you act here.'*

To accommodate his massively powered revivals, Tree had to cut his texts with an axe, a butchering which aroused the continued wrath of his critics, foremost amongst whom was George Bernard Shaw. 'Mr Tree is not papering a blank wall, but barbarously whitewashing a fresco . . . not helping a lame dog over a stile, but breaking the leg of a lion . . . His occasional crimes against literature are positively blasphemous.'

The booklet, Henry VIII and his Court, *from which these comments have been taken, was written in 1910 when Tree was on holiday at Marienbad and was intended partly to illustrate the breadth of his historical research and partly as an answer to his critics. The purely text-book, historical background to Henry's reign has been omitted in this Introduction to emphasize Tree's apologia for his style of production. His defence, however, should be read with a fair pinch of salt to hand, for, in spite of his vehement protestations, Tree did not really trust any dramatist to know his job, least of all Shakespeare. His claim that 'an attempt was made to confine the absolute spoken words as nearly as possible within the two hours prescribed in the prologue' sounds reasonable; but, in the event, the performances of* Henry VIII, *heavily cut as the text was, still lasted for four hours – a considerable portion of which was spent in trundling scenery about and in visual and musical embellishments which merely elaborated the obvious. Though it must be said for the popular appeal of those embellishments that some of the incidental music by Edward German is still enjoyed today, over sixty years later.*

A small sidelight on Tree's relaxed attitude to time comes from one of his own anecdotes. 'The scene of Wolsey's fall in Henry VIII *sometimes played 29 minutes, sometimes 39. It depended on whether the nervous B ... or the phlegmatic K ... was in the prompt corner.'*

Tree's heavy pruning had other effects than just making room for spectacle. By excising what he called the 'Reformation scenes', the character of Wolsey was brought into greater prominence. Wolsey became one of Tree's most successful roles.

In 1910 the movement for reform in Shakespearean production, for a return to fuller texts and simpler, swifter, more evocative staging, was well advanced, notably under the revolutionary leadership of William Poel. In March of that year, surprisingly, Tree invited Poel's Elizabethan Stage Society to appear in his annual Shakespeare Festival at His Majesty's. It was rather like the Czar inviting an anarchist with a smoking bomb into the Winter Palace. That 1910 Festival included eleven plays by Shakespeare, acted by five companies apart from Tree's own. No doubt most of the plays were somewhat mauled, but the sad truth is that the theatre-going public has rarely enjoyed that kind of Shakespearean feast since Poel's bomb went off.

Tree, however, was a Czar with a difference. He was a practical, sensitive man of the theatre who knew a sound idea when he saw it. Even though he was clashing regularly in public with Poel over the possible founding of a National Theatre and rejected the ideas which lay behind Poel's approach to the stage in general, he was still quite capable of borrowing for his production of Henry VIII, *later in 1910, the innovatory apron stage and front lighting that Poel had used for his contribution to the Festival.*

Towards the end of his life Tree began to acknowledge the virtues of theatrical simplicity. 'Simplicity is certainly an enviable state. In life – as in art – it is only arrived at after wandering through the maze of complexity. It is the slow process of elimination of unessentials.' Sadly, he had arrived too late.

The period of Henry VIII was characterized by great sumptuousness; indeed, the daily life of the Court was compact of revels, masques and displays of splendour. *Henry VIII* is largely a pageant play. As such it was conceived and written; as such did we endeavour to present it to the public. Indeed, it is obvious that it would be far better not to produce the play at all than to do so without those adjuncts, by which alone the action of the play can be illustrated. Of course, it is not possible to do more than indicate on the stage the sumptuousness of the period of history covered by the play; but it is hoped that an impression would be conveyed to our own time of Henry in his habit as he lived, of his people, of the architecture, and of the manners and customs of that great age.

In the days of Henry VIII, the ways of society differed from our own more in observance than in spirit. Though the gay world danced and gambled very late, it rose very early. Its conversation was coarse and lacked reserve. The ladies cursed freely. Outward show and ceremony were considered of the utmost importance. Hats were worn by the men in church and at meals, and only removed in the presence of King and Cardinal. Kissing was far more prevalent as a mode of salutation. The court society spent the greater part of its income on clothes. To those in the king's set, a thousand pounds was nothing out of the way to spend on a suit of clothes. The predominant colours at Court were crimson and green; the Tudor colours were green and white.

It was thought desirable to omit almost in their entirety those portions of the play which deal with the Reformation, being as they are practically devoid of dramatic interest and calculated, as they are, to weary an audience. In taking this course, I felt the less hesitation as there can be no doubt that all these passages were from the first omitted in Shakespeare's own representations of the play.

We have incontrovertible evidence that, in Shakespeare's time, *Henry VIII* was played in 'two short hours'.

> *... Those that come to see*
> *Only a show or two, and so agree*
> *The play may pass. If they be still and willing*
> *I'll undertake may see away their shilling*
> *Richly in two short hours.*

These words, addressed to the audience in the prologue, make it quite clear that a considerable portion of the play was considered by the author to be superfluous to the dramatic action – and so it is. Acted without any waits whatsoever, *Henry VIII*, as it is written, would take at least three and a half hours in the playing. Although we were not able to compass the performance within the prescribed 'two short hours', for we showed a greater respect for the preservation of the text than did Shakespeare himself, an attempt was made to confine the absolute spoken words as nearly as possible within the time prescribed in the prologue.

In the dramatic presentation of the play, there are many passages of intensely moving interest, the action and characters are drawn with a remarkable fidelity to the actualities. As has been suggested, however, the play depends more largely than do most of Shakespeare's works on those outward displays to realize which an attempt was made on the stage.

That Shakespeare, as a stage-manager, availed himself as far as possible of these adjuncts is only too evident from the fact that it was the firing of the cannon which caused a conflagration and the subsequent burning down of the Globe Theatre. The destruction of the manuscripts of Shakespeare's plays was probably due to this calamity. The incident shows a lamentable love of stage mounting for which some of the critics of the time no doubt took the poet severely to task. In connection with the love of pageantry which then prevailed, it is well known that Shakespeare and Ben Jonson were wont to arrange the masques so much in vogue in their time.

Here I am tempted to hark back to the modern manner of producing Shakespeare, and to say a few words in extenuation of those methods which have been assailed with almost equal brilliancy and vehemence.

We are told that there are two different kinds of plays, the realistic and the symbolic. There are, as a matter of fact, nine and ninety different kinds of plays; but let that pass. Grant only two. Shakespeare's plays, we are assured, belong to the symbolic category. 'The scenery,' it is insisted, 'not only may, but should be imperfect.' This seems an extraordinary doctrine, for if it be right that a play should be imperfectly mounted, it follows that it should be imperfectly acted, and further that it should be imperfectly written. The modern methods, we are assured, employed in the production of Shakespeare, do not properly illustrate the play, but are merely made for vulgar display, with the result of crushing the author and obscuring his meaning. In this assertion I venture to think that our critic is mistaken; I claim that not the least important mission of the modern theatre is to give the public representations of history which shall be at once an education and delight. To do this, the manager should avail himself of the best archaeological and artistic help his generation can afford him, while endeavouring to preserve what he believes to be the spirit and the intention of the author.

It is of course possible for the technically informed reader to imagine the wonderful and stirring scenes which form part of the play without visualizing them. It is, I contend, better to reserve Shakespeare for the study than to see him presented half-heartedly.

The merely archaic presentation of the play can be of interest only to those epicures who do not pay their shilling to enter the theatre. The contemporary theatre must make its appeal to the great public, and I hold that while one should respect every form of art, that art which appeals only to a coterie is on a lower plane than that which speaks to the world. Surely, it is not too much to claim that a truer and more vivid impression of a period of history can be given by its representation on the stage than by any other means of information. Though the archaeologist with symbolic leanings may cry out, the theatre is primarily for those who love the drama, who love the joy of life and the true representation of history. It is only secondarily for those who fulfil their souls in footnotes.

Personally, I have been a sentimental adherent of symbolism since my first Noah's Ark. Ever since I first beheld the generous curves of Mrs Noah, and first tasted the insidious carmine of her lips, have I regarded that lady as symbolical of the supreme type of womanhood. I have learnt that the most exclusive symbolists, when painting a meadow, regard purple as symbolical of bright green; but we live in a realistic age and have not yet overtaken the new art of the pale future. It is difficult to deal seriously with so much earnestness. I am forced into symbolic parable. Artemus Ward, when delivering a lecture on his great moral panorama, pointed with his wand to a blur on the horizon, and said, 'Ladies and gentlemen, that is a horse – the artist who painted that picture called on me yesterday with tears in his eyes, and said he would disguise that fact from me no longer!' He, too, was a symbolist.

I hold that whatever may tend to destroy the illusion and the people's understanding is to be condemned. Whatever may tend to heighten the illusion and to help the audience to a better understanding of the play and the author's meaning, is to be commended. Shakespeare and Burbage, Betterton, Colley Cibber, the Kembles, the Keans, Phelps, Calvert and Henry Irving, as artists, recognized that there is but one way to treat the play of *Henry VIII*. It is pleasant to sin in such company.

I contend that *Henry VIII* is essentially a realistic and not a symbolic play. Indeed, probably no English author is less 'symbolic' than Shakespeare. *Hamlet* is a play which, to my mind, does not suffer by the simplest setting; indeed a severe simplicity of treatment seems to me to assist rather than to detract from the imaginative development of that masterpiece. But I hold that, with the exception of certain scenes in *The Tempest*, no plays of Shakespeare are susceptible to what is called 'symbolic' treatment. To attempt to present *Henry VIII* in other than a realistic manner would be to ensure absolute failure. Let us take an instance from the text. By what symbolism can Shakespeare's stage directions in the Trial Scene be represented on the stage?

A Hall in Blackfriars. Enter two vergers with short silver wands; next them two scribes in the habit of doctors . . . Next them with some small distance, follows a gentleman bearing the purse with the great seal and a Cardinal's hat; then two priests bearing each a silver cross; then a gentleman usher bareheaded, accompanied by a sergeant-at-arms bearing a silver mace; then two gentlemen bearing silver pillars; after them, side by side, the two Cardinals, Wolsey and Campeius; two noblemen with sword and mace, etc.

I confess my symbolic imagination was completely gravelled, and in the absence of any symbolic substitute, I have been compelled to fall back on the stage directions.

Yet we are gravely told by the writer of an article that 'all Shakespeare's plays' lend themselves of course to such symbolic treatment. We hear, indeed, that the National Theatre is to be run on symbolic lines. If it be so, then God help the National Theatre – the symbolists will not. No 'ism' ever made a great cause. The National Theatre, to be the dignified memorial we all hope it may be, will owe its birth, its being and its preservation to the artists, who alone are the guardians of any art. It is the painter, not the frame-maker, who upholds the art of painting; it is the poet, not the book-binder, who carries the torch of poetry. It was the sculptor, not the owner of the quarry, who made the Venus de Milo. It is sometimes necessary to re-assert the obvious.

Now there are plays in which symbolism is appropriate – those of Maeterlinck, for instance. But if, as has been said, Maeterlinck resembles Shakespeare, Shakespeare does not resemble Maeterlinck. Let us remember that Shakespeare was a humanist, not a symbolist.

The end of the play of *Henry VIII* once more illustrates the pageantry of realism, as prescribed in the elaborate directions as to the christening of the new-born princess.

It is this incident of the christening of the future Queen Elizabeth that brings to an appropriate close the strange eventful history as depicted in the play of *Henry VIII*. And thus the injustice of the world is once more triumphantly vindicated; Wolsey, the devoted servant of the King, has crept into an ignominious sanctuary; Katharine has been driven to a martyr's doom; the adulterous union has been blessed by the Court of Bishops; minor poets have sung their blasphemous paeans in unison. The offspring of Anne Boleyn, over whose head the Shadow of the Axe is already hovering, has been christened amid the acclamations of the mob; the king paces forth to hold the child up to the gaze of a shouting populace, accompanied by the Court and the Clergy – trumpets blare, drums roll, the organ thunders, hymns are sung, the joy bells are pealing. A lonely figure in black enters weeping. It is the Fool!

[1974]